Roots:
Let the Old Testament Speak

This is vintage Motyer; it is affectionate–the writer's sheer delight in 'the law of the Lord' tends to ooze out from behind the print; it is **fresh**–he's familiar with the scholarly waterfront but Jacob-like has wrestled and stewed over these texts himself (and his struggle is our gain); it is **devious**, for Alec clearly wants to hook you on the Old Testament! Huge kudos to 'Focus' for this format.

Dale Ralph Davis
Minister in Residence, First Presbyterian Church,
Columbia, South Carolina

This is a masterful panorama of the Old Testament. Helpful thumbnails of each book, illuminating engagement with the text, perceptive connections with our own day and faith combine to make this a superb overview of the Old Testament. The arrangement of material along the timeline of history is immensely useful and at a stroke clarifies how the Old Testament flows toward the New; but the real genius of the book is that it begins with that destination: with Christ, whose Scripture it was. Seasoned preachers and inquiring beginners alike will gain from every page. Read it: it's brilliant!

Dominic Smart
Minister of Gilcomston South Church
Aberdeen, Scotland

Roots:
Let the Old Testament Speak

Alec Motyer

EDITED BY
John Stott

CHRISTIAN
FOCUS

Dr Alec Motyer is a well-known Bible expositor and from an early age has had a love for studying God's Word. He was formerly principal of Trinity College, Bristol. *Roots: Let the Old Testament Speak* benefits from his career of Old Testament study, his mastery of the Hebrew text and his knowledge of Old Testament background.

Copyright © Alec Motyer 2009

ISBN 978-1-84550-506-6

10 9 8 7 6 5 4 3 2 1

Published in 2009
Reprinted in 2014
by
Christian Focus Publications Ltd.,
Geanies House, Fearn, Ross-shire,
IV20 1TW, Scotland, Great Britain
www.christianfocus.com

Previously published in 2001 as *The Story of the Old Testament* by Candle Books.

Cover design by Paul Lewis
Printed by Bell and Bain, Glasgow

MIX
Paper from
responsible sources
FSC® C007785

Contents

DEDICATION

By the year 2000 Shirley Lewis and Bill Medcalf
will have been my friends of sixty years.
To dedicate this book to them is a
very small payment
for the debt I owe them.

PREFACE

D r Alec Motyer has had a lifelong warm-hearted attachment to the Old Testament. Not only has he studied it on his own, and expounded it from many pulpits, but for years he was Old Testament lecturer at Trinity College, Bristol, where something of his love for the Old Testament rubbed off on generations of his students.

There can be no doubt that this book benefits greatly from Alec Motyer's lifetime of Old Testament study. His mastery of the Hebrew text, his knowledge of the Old Testament background, and his conviction that Jesus Christ is the fulfilment of the law and prophets together give him a rare ability to paint the big picture and to tell the 'story within the story' of the Old Testament.

The theme of *Men with a Message* (OT), as of *Men with a Message* (NT), which indeed their titles indicate, is that the Holy Spirit chose, fashioned and equipped the biblical authors in such a way as to convey through each appropriate and distinctive truths. In other words, there is a significant correspondence between the men and their respective messages. It is an essential aspect of our belief about inspiration, that, far from smothering the personalities of the biblical authors, the Holy Spirit prepared and used them. So each author was free, under the superintendency of the Holy Spirit, to develop his own theological emphasis, historical enquiries and literary style. As Alec Motyer has put it, the biblical authors are 'colourful persons' who possess 'such individual distinctiveness that each prophet stands out unmistakeably from every other'.

I have valued Alec Motyer's friendship for many years. I also admire his scholarship, his fidelity to Scripture and his enthusiasm for the Old Testament. He and I have been co-operating in the 'Bible Speaks Today' series, published by IVP, since he is editor of the Old Testament expositions, and I of the New. In addition, it is a great pleasure that the authors of the two *Men with a Message* books are a father-and-son team, consisting of Alec Motyer (OT) and Steve Motyer (NT).

John Stott 2000

Author's Preface

Ⅰt has been a joy to write this book. For as far back as I can remember I have loved the Bible, and for only a slightly shorter period I have tried to get others to do the same. When I was privileged to enter full-time pastoral ministry in 1947, it soon became clear to me that, as far as I was concerned, teaching the Word of God and encouraging others into an informed engagement with the Word of God occupied the centre ground. To be invited then, when 'retirement' has run a good deal of its course, to take up this task in written form has been a privilege, delight and hard work all rolled into one.

This book first appeared in 2001 under the title *The Story of the Old Testament*. The project (like so much else) started with John Stott who, in the 1950s, wrote the first *Men with a Message*, dealing with a selection of New Testament authors. This book was a superb contribution to biblical understanding, and after many years of yeoman service, was given a second lease of life by my son Stephen in 1993. It is humbling and deeply gratifying that my parallel book will now, God willing, stand alongside his, however far short my actual accomplishment falls.

I am intensely grateful to Christian Focus Publications for their willingness to give my book a new lease of life, and for the much more accurate and attractive title they have chosen. I am favoured indeed to have fallen into such expert and helpful hands. Above all, however, I feel that whatever merits this book may possess in clarity arise from the eagle eyes and comprehensive knowledge of John Stott, who has read the book in three or four versions and who has never flagged in patience or allowed me to lose the vision towards which the book aspires. Happily, our friendship of so many years has also not only survived but thrived on this experience of working together.

May our gracious God who gave us the Bible now be pleased to make his word live for many, many readers!

Alec Motyer
Poynton, 2009

A Note to the Reader

One of the features the reader will immediately notice is that this book has an immense number of biblical references. I could see no other way of solving the problem that the Old Testament contains far too much material of consequence to be fitted into a book of moderate length. Others tell me that readers do not look up references, and if space allowed, I would happily write them all out. The same applies to the wonderful stories which abound in the Old Testament. Readers have pointed out that I may be assuming too much knowledge of the Bible by making unexplained allusions. The alternative would be to retell the stories, but my narrative skill would not come up to that of the inspired writers, nor would it be good use of such limited space; hence, again, references to try to fill the gap. Read this book slowly and take time to look up the references provided.

Where the Hebrew Bible has a different scheme of versification from the English Bible, I have not felt it right to take up space to note the differences.

Some of the material presented here has had a previous life. Chapter 3 has been round and about as a lecture and one form of it is now part of a chapter in the symposium, *Preaching the Living Word* (Christian Focus, 1999). Chapters 3, 5, 6, 8 and 10, though written for this book, appeared in a much-abbreviated form in *Covenanter Witness*, the magazine of the Reformed Presbyterian Churches of Scotland and Ireland. A slightly shorter form of chapter 17 can be found in my book *A Scenic Route through the Old Testament*, published by the InterVarsity Press, and used here by kind permission.

I would hope that readers will find that the book can be used with all Bible translations, but I have tended to provide my own translations of any passages quoted at length. Where I have not done so, I generally quote from the *New King James* version.

Alec Motyer

I

STARTING WITH JESUS

The Old Testament is a very wonderful book. Think of its people – Abraham and David, to look no further – larger than life yet intensely human, belonging to the distant past and yet portrayed with such vividness and relevance that it is as though we just missed meeting them. Or recall the height and depth of thought in the Psalms and prophets, not to mention the beautiful and subtle Hebrew in which they were first expressed.

For many of us, our earliest contact with the Old Testament came when we heard it read in church, and – though we could not have put it like this – even as children we were gripped by dramatic storylines, and by the interplay of character, as when, for example, the two great 'fixers' of the ancient world, Laban and Jacob, locked horns. We meet nonsense characters like Samson and tragic figures like Saul, and we find that all the problems of life have already been faced by our forebears in the faith. There is the unrelieved, profitless tragedy of war, the wonder of human love and endurance, the thrill of life and the darkness of death.

Overarching all, there is a compelling revelation of God in creation and redemption, in mercy and judgment, a God of wisdom, love and power, passionate in his concern for his people, faithful to his promises, inflexible and age-long in his purposes. Yes, indeed, the Old Testament is a magnificent and magnetic book.

DESERT SANDS

But not all can see it. In their most candid moments, many would confess that back beyond the title page that divides Matthew from Malachi they have a mental picture of desert. The Old Testament seems so large. Much of it, at first sight, makes for demanding reading (like the prophets); some of it (like Leviticus) seems to belong to another world; and when we think about the many stories which are both easy and entertaining, we tend not only to say, 'Yes, but why are they there?' but also, sometimes, to be alarmed or offended by the behaviour of even leading characters. Can this be the word of God? And, indeed, does it matter?

AN UNHELPFUL NAME

The title, Old Testament, creates difficulties of its own. If it is 'Old' and we are people of the 'New', surely we may properly let it fade away into history. Besides, it seems very unlike the New Testament, even contradictory: all those wars when Jesus is the Prince of peace; all those commandments to obey when we are not under law but under grace. And can the God of the Old Testament be a God of love like the Father, Son and Holy Spirit?

These are serious questions which we will try to face in the course of this book, but we must begin with a little general clearing of the ground. That is why this chapter is called 'Starting with Jesus'.

CHRISTLIKENESS

When God wants to give us his very best, he gives us whatever will make us like his Son. This is the ultimate blessedness he has for us

(1 John 3:2); it is also the explanation of the often strange, even unwelcome, twists and turns of life's pathway (2 Cor. 4:10-11).

The call to grow into the likeness of the Lord Jesus Christ challenges us comprehensively. It touches not only the way we live and the sort of character we seek to form (1 John 2:6; 3:3), but also our way of appraising life and making decisions (Phil. 2:5-8). It means following Christ's thoughts, his grasp and communication of truth (John 15:15; 1 Cor. 2:16). When, therefore, we seek some sure vantage point from which to look at the Old Testament, what better question can we ask than, 'How did Jesus see it?'

JESUS' TEACHING

The Lord's teaching in Matthew 5:17-20 makes five important assertions:

1. The Old Testament is 'the Law or the Prophets' (v. 17a).
2. Jesus is the fulfilment of the Old Testament (v. 17b).
3. The Old Testament has permanent validity for the earthly church (v. 18).
4. The Old Testament is to be obeyed by the children of the kingdom (v. 19).
5. It is crucial to assured citizenship (v. 20).

These five points will provide our framework for this chapter.

THE BIBLE AS JESUS KNEW IT
The 'map' of the Old Testament, as we have received it, can be easily drawn.

1. The Law
Genesis, Exodus, Leviticus, Numbers, Deuteronomy

2. The Prophets
   a. *The Former Prophets:* Joshua, Judges, Samuel, Kings
   b. *The Latter Prophets:* Isaiah, Jeremiah, Ezekiel, Hosea, Joel, Amos, Obadiah, Jonah, Micah, Nahum, Habakkuk, Zephaniah, Haggai, Zechariah, Malachi

3. The Writings
Psalms, Job, Proverbs, Ruth, Song of Songs, Ecclesiastes, Lamentations, Esther, Daniel, Ezra, Nehemiah, Chronicles

---

1. Jesus' Bible: The Law and the Prophets (v. 17a)

The Bible which the Lord Jesus Christ knew fell into the same three sections as the Hebrew Bible does to this day. He spoke of it as, 'Moses and the Prophets and the Psalms' (Luke 24:44 NKJV). 'Moses' covered the first five books of the Bible (Genesis to Deuteronomy); 'the Prophets' included the history books (Joshua, Judges, Samuel and Kings), the books of the 'major' prophets (Isaiah, Jeremiah, Ezekiel), and the twelve 'minor' prophets (Hosea to Malachi). 'The Psalms' was the first book of the third division of our Lord's Old Testament, more comprehensively called 'the Writings', which comprised Psalms, Job, Proverbs, Ruth, Song of Songs, Ecclesiastes, Lamentations, Esther, Daniel, and finally, Ezra, Nehemiah and Chronicles. Interestingly, then, when the Lord Jesus reviewed the legacy of sin inherited by the people of his generation (Matt. 23:35) he began with the murder of Abel in Genesis (4:8), the first book of the Bible, and ended with the murder of Zechariah in 2 Chronicles (24:21), the last book of his Bible.

In the narrow sense, then, 'Law' means the five books of Moses, and 'Prophets' is the title of the second division of the Old Testament. But there is a wider use of both words. In Matthew 11:13 NKJV, for example, Jesus says, 'the law prophesied until John', meaning that his whole Bible reached one of its culminating points in the ministry of the Baptist. Again, pointing a questioner to all the existing Scripture (Luke 10:26), he asked, 'What is written in the law?' Or again, he accused the Emmaus walkers of folly in their slowness to believe 'all that the prophets have spoken' and immediately explained his words by expounding 'in all the Scriptures the things concerning Himself' (Luke 24:25-27 NKJV).

The Old Testament as law and prophecy. In the broad description, 'the Law or the Prophets', then, we can discern two facets of the whole Old Testament. The word 'law' (torah) means 'teaching', the loving instruction of a caring parent

(Prov. 1:8; 4:1-2). As such, of course, it includes rules and regulations, but when we read the word our first thought should not be of legislation but of information – all the truth the Lord wishes his earthly people to have – about himself and about the world, as well as about ourselves and the way we should live.

Just as we can make the mistake of restricting 'law' to legislation, so we can restrict 'prophecy' to prediction. Now, plainly, the Old Testament is a predictive book. No sooner has sin entered the world than the defeat of the serpent is forecast (Gen. 3:15), and from then on the stream of prediction increases, whether it be the entrance of Abram's family into their promised possession (Gen. 15:16), or the glories of the royal Messiah (Isa. 9:1-7; 11:1-9), or the arrival of the Messianic forerunner (Mal. 4:5-6). In many ways nothing is as characteristic of the Old Testament as an intense air of expectation nourished by predictions.

Yet this is only one of the ways in which the prophets performed their God-given task. They were never 'fortune-tellers'. When they foretold, it was in order that those to whom they ministered might, firstly, know their God now in the light of what he would yet do, and, secondly, reform their lives now so as to be ready for his coming acts. John the Baptist put it in a nutshell: 'Repent, for the kingdom of heaven is at hand!' (Matt. 3:2). He offered a prediction ('at hand'), a present instruction in the light of this expectation ('Repent') and a theology: God is a King bringing in his kingdom, and a holy God demanding repentance as the way to prepare.

This sums up the whole prophetic ministry of the Old Testament: revealing the Lord, ministering to the present, declaring the future. If we ask, then, 'were the prophets foretellers or forthtellers?' they were both, but their foretelling was part of their forthtelling. They were inspired to proclaim the truth about God, recalling his past revelation of himself in word and deed, and appealing for a present obedience in the light of the predicted future.

2. Jesus and Fulfilment (v. 17b)

In the life of the Lord Jesus Christ we find two aspects or levels of fulfilment of the Old Testament.

a. Factual Fulfilment

At the simplest level, there is straightforward fulfilment of facts prophesied in the Old Testament. Micah specified Bethlehem as the birthplace of the royal Messiah, and so it was (Micah 5:2; Luke 2:1-7). In gardening terms, this is rather like planting an annual. All the promise for the future is there in the seed; the gardener plants the seeds once and what they 'predict' is fulfilled.

In the New Testament, factual fulfilment of the Old Testament comes about in two ways. Sometimes fulfilments (like the birth at Bethlehem, or the way the soldiers shared out the Lord's clothing, John 19:23-24) happened in the way events turned out, without any conscious cooperation by those involved. God was sovereignly at work bringing his word to pass. Whether in the decree of Caesar Augustus in the high reaches of imperial policy (Luke 2:1) or in the self-serving acts of the Roman executioners, God rules the world to achieve his promises and purposes. 'Has He said, and will He not do *it*?' (Num. 23:19). This is the dignity of the Old Testament as the word of God.

But sometimes fulfilment came through knowing obedience, as when Jesus said, 'I thirst', so 'that the Scripture might be fulfilled' (John 19:28). Another and even more telling example of this obedience-fulfilment is Matthew 26:53-54. Jesus' uniqueness as the Son gave him immediate access to the Father, the right to ask and receive legions of angels. But it was more important to him that 'the Scriptures be fulfilled'. This is what he meant when he said that he always did what pleased his Father (John 8:29 NKJV). The Old Testament was the book of God in which he found the will of God, and, through his obedience, this book masterminded his perfect life.

b. Realisation

A deeper level of fulfilment is best thought of as 'realisation'. To return to the gardening metaphor, it is like a perennial. The first year's flowering begins to show what is there, but years of maturing bring the flower to perfection far greater than the first year's almost tentative display. Yet it is nothing new; it is what was always there.

Carpenters might like a different illustration: the surface grain of a fine piece of timber displays its beauty and quality; the end-grain shows the depth and fullness that has always been there. Jesus is the 'end-grain' of the prophetic Scriptures. He is what was there and intended from the start.

It will be one of the most fascinating aspects of our study of the Old Testament to see this probing and deepening at work, always moving forward to the climactic flowering in Jesus.

3. The Old Testament: The Imperishable Word (v. 18)

It would not have surprised his disciples that our Lord affirmed the enduring validity of the Old Testament (Matt. 5:18). They would have taken it for granted that God's word is imperishable. It is we who must face candidly the Lord's estimate of the Bible as he knew it and, out of reverence for him, adjust our misunderstandings until we see the beautiful wholeness of the word of God, the Old and New Testaments as one divine revelation.

This wholeness has been expressed in many ways, but one of the most helpful is John Bright's suggestion of a two-act play. If we only had Act Two, we would have to ask, 'But where has it come from? Who are these people? What is the clue to understanding their relationships and conduct? Why does it reach this denouement?' And if we only had Act One, we would say, 'Yes, but where is it going? How will it develop? Will the hinted climax come and in what form?'

Without the New Testament, the Old is going nowhere, it is only a might-have-been, an unsubstantiated longing. And without the Old, the New lacks explanation. Its very words require Old Testament definition, and its central event, the cross, is inexplicable without the Old Testament's teaching, in Leviticus and elsewhere, about its sacrifices.

Jots and tittles. When we see the Old Testament and the New related like this, it comes as no surprise that Jesus should affirm that as long as 'heaven and earth' continue the Old Testament stands – and does so in its written form (Matt. 5:18). The 'jot' of which he spoke is the Hebrew letter 'y', the smallest letter in the Hebrew alphabet, no bigger than an inverted comma; a 'tittle' is a small pen-mark which distinguishes one Hebrew letter from another. Down to the smallest letter, the least stroke of the pen, says the Lord Jesus Christ, this is the imperishable word of God.

4. A Word to Obey (v. 19) and 5.   A Life to Live (v. 20)

The fourth and fifth of our Lord's affirmations about his Bible are linked. Matthew 5:20, with its opening, 'For', explains verse 19, and together verses 19 and 20 draw a conclusion ('therefore' v. 19) from verse 18. The word of God is permanent (v. 18), and 'therefore' (v. 19) its commandments are crucial to our status within God's kingdom, because (v. 20) kingdom members are required to exhibit a superior righteousness, reaching beyond the external conformity of the Pharisees into an inner righteousness of the heart.

A *Superior Righteousness.*

There is a basic principle here which is easy to state but not always simple to apply to the detail of the Old Testament. The principle (v. 20) is the superior righteousness required of kingdom members. Through the Bible 'righteousness' has a single meaning: that which is right with God.

In Matthew 5:19-20 the requirement of righteousness looks in two directions:

- In verse 19 it is righteousness of life exhibited in obeying the Bible's commands, a righteousness which an observer can see, and which consists of conduct obedient to the norms laid down by God.

- Towards the end of verse 20, there is a deeper righteousness, outclassing that of those experts in righteousness, the Pharisees, a righteousness which permits entrance to the kingdom – a righteousness of the character and person.

Jesus spells out his understanding of this righteousness in the 'contrast-sayings' in verses 21-48. He meant a righteousness of transformed emotions (vv. 22, 28), a righteousness of fidelity to our pledged word (vv. 31, 37), a righteousness of generosity of spirit (vv. 38-42) and a righteousness of godlikeness (vv. 43-48). It was a righteousness, therefore, of inner transformation displayed in outward relationships and actions.

The Old Testament foresaw the advent of this righteousness (Jer. 31:31-34; Ezek. 36:27). It also foresaw the fundamental gift of divine righteousness (Isa. 53:11; 54:17) from which all this transformation arises. But it is the saving work of the Lord Jesus Christ (Phil. 3:8-12) and the persistent, transforming work of God (Phil. 2:13) which brings about the 'new person', the image of God (Eph. 4:22-24). On our side, our obedience is the key factor and it is this that our Lord is emphasising. There are commands to be obeyed if the new life is to be lived.

Seriousness Not Superficiality
According to our Lord's teaching in Matthew 5:19, the commandments of his Bible are to be treated with the utmost seriousness: it is this that determines promotion and demotion in the kingdom. Yet it is all too easy even for deeply earnest Christians to marginalise the Old Testament – and, after all, does not Paul teach that all commandments, even the Ten Commandments, have been overtaken by the single command to love one another (Rom. 13:8-10)?

A moment's thought exposes the superficiality of such thinking: Provided I love my neighbour am I now free to commit adultery with his wife, steal his silver and denigrate his good name? No, indeed: rather, the law of love in Christ compels me to keep these laws. Because I love my neighbour, I must all the more zealously safeguard the purity of his marriage, his right to personal possessions and the integrity of his reputation. To be 'under law to Christ' (1 Cor. 9:21) enforces upon me whatever God commands in his word.

That is all very well, someone may say, but what about the Old Testament's seemingly offbeat regulations? Does Exodus 23:19 still apply, with its prohibition of seething a kid in its mother's milk? Well, no, because the Lord Jesus abrogated all food laws (Mark 7:19): they had served their purpose and their day was done. But at the same time it would be a superficial approach to the Old Testament simply to discard them. It is now understood that the broth produced by seething a kid in its mother's milk was considered to have magical properties for fertility. Even if the 'food' aspect of the prohibition is gone, the integrity of our walk with God, our trust in him alone to provide our needs and bless our enterprises, must still be preserved from anything questionable, anything that savours of the world's ways of securing profit, prosperity, security or fertility. The regulation is gone but the principle remains.

Probably the sacrifices detailed in Leviticus seem as distant from us as any part of the Old Testament. We do well to recall, then, that it was because he understood the sacrificial system so deeply and truly that Isaiah was able to depict the wonder of the coming Servant and his great substitutionary bearing of sin (Isa. 53), and that the author of Hebrews (chs. 9–10) was able to continue the same theme in his matchless and crowning exposition of the death of Jesus.

Any sort of cavalier attitude to writings which the Lord Jesus reverenced as his Bible and as the word of God should be anathema to the Christian. As we shall see, however, not all the problems that arise as we apply the Old to the New are easily solved. The Old Testament commands the death penalty for offences against the Ten Commandments. Does the New Testament perpetuate or terminate this law? The Old Testament requires the observance of one day in seven as a holy day. Does the New Testament which, though it quotes the other nine, fails to quote the fourth commandment, reimpose or lift this obligation?

No, not all problems of aligning the Testaments are subject to obvious answers. But whether we consider ourselves bound to the letter of a law or to the principle that first animated it, we must not on any account seek to evade or diminish Christ's requirement of obedience.

Further reading

Useful books on the Old Testament

R.B. Dillard, T. Longman, *An Introduction to the Old Testament* (Apollos, 1995)
W.S. LaSor, D.A. Hubbard, F.W. Bush, *Old Testament Survey* (Eerdmans, 1982)
J.A. Motyer, *A Scenic Route through the Old Testament* (IVP, 1994)
C. Wright, *Knowing Jesus through the Old Testament* (Marshall Pickering, 1992)
T.D. Alexander, *The Servant King* (IVP, 1998)
B. Cotton, *Journey Through the Old Testament* (Christian Focus, 1995)
A. Harman, *Learning About the Old Testament* (Christian Focus, 2003)
E. Clowney, *The Unfolding Mystery* (Presbyterian and Reformed, 1998)
J. Barton, *Reading the Old Testament* (Darton, Longman & Todd, 1984)
Throughout the Old Testament, *The New Bible Commentary*, 21st Century Edition (IVP, 1994) should be consulted

Chapter 1
J. Bright, *The Authority of the Old Testament* (SCM, 1967)
J.R.W. Stott, *The Sermon on the Mount, The Bible Speaks Today* (IVP, 1978)
J.W. Wenham, *Christ and the Bible* (IVP, 1973)

THE BIBLE AND ITS CULTURAL CONTEXT

According to then current law, the childless Sarah was permitted to suggest a secondary wife for her husband, claiming for herself any children of the union (Gen. 16); the same laws allowed her to disinherit such children if she herself subsequently gave birth (Gen. 21).

WHAT IS THE PRESENT-DAY RELEVANCE OF BIBLE LAWS?

Possibly in the case of Sarah it is not particularly difficult to decide whether these stories constitute an example or a warning, a permission or a prohibition, but over the whole field of the Old Testament these questions prove far from easy.

THE THEONOMIC VIEW

This view holds that Old Testament laws continue in force unless rescinded or modified by further revelation. As Poythress observes, 'at the heart of theonomy is the conviction that God's Word is the only proper standard for evaluating all human action', personal, social, judicial, governmental, and 'this deserves the support of all Christians'. This sounds perfectly acceptable until we seek to apply it to detailed cases. Must we avoid seething a kid in its mother's milk? It is a clear commandment (Exod. 23:19; Deut. 14:21); it is not rescinded in the New Testament (unlike the food laws, Mark 7:19), nor has later revelation explicitly modified it. In its own day it was a necessary prohibition, for the broth resulting from the process was important in the fertility magic Israel was forbidden to practise. Thus the Bible speaks out of and into its own culture. What, then, are we to make of it?

THE CULTURAL ARGUMENT

A common use of the cultural argument relativises this (and much more of the Old Testament). Such laws belonged to their own day and not to ours. They may interest the antiquarian; they say nothing to the theologian or ethicist. Does this apply also to the Old Testament view of homosexual practice, to the death penalty and to the civil laws appropriate to a church-state as Moses envisaged it but not to the 'separation of powers' widespread today?

A modified form of the argument is more honouring to the Old Testament as part of the imperishable word of God: that the practice of a law may be culturally restricted but its principle is abiding. To continue with the example of 'seething kids', the principle is that the people of God must not seek prosperity by occult means, or by giving first place to other powers (market forces / astrology), or by glorifying the gods of fortune (lotteries).

Certainly any simplistic or bland appeal to 'culture' to sidestep or to eviscerate biblical law is out of the question. Within the New Testament, the cultural argument against the head-covering (1 Cor. 11:1-16 NKJV) exposes the absurdity of using culture as a bludgeon: Do we actually know what 'head-covering' meant? Can it (surely not!) be equivalent to wearing a hat? What does Paul mean when he says – 'we have no such custom' (v. 16)? – that it is not worth making a fuss over, or that it is impermissible to argue with an apostle? But, especially, what about the angels? It is certain that angels are not culturally restricted, and 'because of the angels' must mean that there are issues involved that transcend contemporary culture and reach to the present day.

PRINCIPLE EXPRESSED IN PRACTICE

Like theonomy in its most rigid form, the cultural argument has a nice simplicity. But in practice both prove workable only with adjustments which their pure theory ought to resist. There may, however, be a workable approach. The principle involved in the distinction between clean and unclean foods was the distinctiveness of the people of God, expressed by their distinct dietary habits. In this case, the practice belonged in one sphere (diet) and the principle it embodied belonged in another (spiritual status). The principle remains, the practice does not. But in the case, for example, of homosexual practice (Lev. 18), practice and principle coincide. There is no other way in which it could be said that the practice is now abrogated but the principle remains, or that the principle can be expressed along other lines.

Where the practice and the principle have only an ancient cultural or a biblically imposed link, the practice has lapsed but the principle it once expressed remains: where practice and principle are, in the nature of the case, inseparable, both remain.

Further reading
V.S. Poythress, *The Shadow of Christ in the Law of Moses*, Appendix B, a searching evaluation of theonomy (Presbyterian and Reformed Publishing, 1991)
D.J. Hesselgrave and E. Rommen, *Contextualisation* (Apollos, 1989)
D.A. Carson & J.D. Woodbridge (Ed.), *Scripture and Truth* (Baker, 1992)
R. Dorothy, *Finding Christ in the Old Testament* (Christian Focus, 2003)

2

THE MESSAGE AND ITS MEN

In the first chapter we looked back at the Old Testament through the eyes of our Lord Jesus Christ. Now we need to stand inside the Old Testament and listen to what it has to say about itself.

OUR INHERITANCE
In the Hebrew canon, the books are not in the same order as in our English Bibles. Our order follows that of the Greek translation of the Old Testament called the Septuagint and usually denoted by the Roman numerals LXX. Begun in Alexandria about 250 BC, the standard of translation varies a great deal, but, as the work proceeded, the individual books were, it seems, grouped according to logic – the histories together, poetical books together, the prophets together. It is not known why the English translators chose to follow this rather than (as they should have done) to reproduce the Hebrew canon.

THE THREEFOLD BOOK: THE GATHERING LIBRARY
The threefold arrangement of Law, Prophets and Psalms (the Writings) is very ancient. As we saw, it is reflected in

our Lord's words in Luke 24:27 and 44. Much earlier, in the prologue to the apocryphal book of Eccliasticus, the author notes that his grandfather studied 'the law and the prophets and the other books'. This would bring the threefold group-ing back to before 200 BC.

We owe a debt of gratitude to the dedicated, painstaking hands that gathered and preserved the Old Testament. The text of Isaiah is a case in point. Until the discovery of the Isaiah Scroll among the Dead Sea Scrolls (1947 onwards), the oldest Hebrew text of Isaiah available to us dated from the tenth century AD. The Isaiah Scroll, however, is earlier by over a thousand years and the overwhelming similarity of these two texts is a breathtaking testimony to devoted and accurate copyists and conservators.

Lost Books
Occasional references (Num. 21:14; Josh. 10:13; 2 Kings 1:18; etc.) indicate the existence of other books, now 'lost', which did not excite the same conserving reverence. Two questions arise:
- Why did they 'get lost'?
- Why was the present Old Testament canon preserved?

The Old Testament Canon
The most important answer to these questions is that the books in the Hebrew canon are the ones which imposed their authority on the Old Testament church. They were not selected; rather, they selected themselves. We do know that in the centuries immediately before the birth of Christ, the rabbis held discussions about included and excluded books but, as R.T. Beckwith says, 'By the beginning of the Christian era the identity of all the canonical books was well known and generally accepted.' After the destruction of Jerusalem in AD 70, Jamnia (in NE Judea, Jabneel in Josh. 15:11) became the headquarters of the Sanhedrin and the centre of rabbinic studies. It was at the Council of

Jamnia (AD 100) that the Old Testament canon as we know it was finally acknowledged.

An illustration (as applicable to the New Testament canon as to the Old) may help: suppose a doctor is treating a patient for a dietary problem. He might say, 'I can't honestly tell you in advance what foods will suit you, but here is a likely list for you to try.' Some weeks later the patient returns with a short list of foods found agreeable. It is only in a very secondary sense that the patient can be said to have chosen the items on the list; in the first instance, they chose him.

In this sort of way the authority inherent in the biblical books imposed itself on the church, and the task of the church was to recognise and accept. This was done piecemeal, so that, at the end, such debates as took place were largely a matter of form and touched on whether, for example, the Song of Songs should continue to be recognised: it was already 'in' and the question raised was whether it should hold the position it had already established for itself.

Canon and Chronology

It is very likely that the order of books in the canon broadly reflects the order in time in which they came individually to be recognised as authoritative.

a. The Law. Verses like Genesis 36:31 and Deuteronomy 34:5 and 10 indicate that the books of Moses did not reach their present form until after Moses' time. But by the time of Ezra (458 BC, compare 7:6, 10, 12, 14, 21) there was a publicly recognised Law of Moses.

b. The Prophets. 2 Kings 25:27-30 also puts the completion of the histories in the post-exilic period. Specialist opinion differs as to the date at which the books of the pre-exilic prophets reached their present form – though convincing proof is yet to be produced that they were not complete within the lifetime of their stated authors.

In any case, exilic and post-exilic prophets would have been added to the canon over the years.

c. The Psalms. Very probably the building of the Second Temple (516 BC) provided the motivation to gather all the authorised songs of Israel into the book of Psalms.

In this way, the canon 'accumulated' as the canonical books imposed themselves as the proper spiritual diet for the people of God.

THE OLD TESTAMENT SEQUENCE		
Detailed dates can readily be found in the excellent article 'Chronology, OT' in the *New Bible Dictionary* (IVP, 1996). The following offers a general outline.		

DATE BC	EVENTS	BOOK
2000–1650	The Patriarchs: Abraham to Joseph	Genesis
1500–1200	Israel in Egypt: Moses, Joshua	Exodus-Joshua
1200–1050	Judges	Judges, Ruth
1050–930	The united monarchy: Saul, David, Solomon	1 and 2 Samuel, 1 Kings 1-11
930–722	The divided monarchy: Judah and Israel	1 Kings 12 – 2 Kings 17
930–722	The kings of Israel. The Prophets	
930–586	The house of David	
870–820	Elijah, Elisha in the north	
760–722		Amos, Hosea, Jonah in the north
740–680	The Prophets	Isaiah, Micah
660–580		Jeremiah, Nahum, Zephaniah, Habakkuk

586–539	The Babylonian Exile	Obadiah, Ezekiel
539 520	The returned community The Second Temple	Haggai, Zechariah
460–439		Ezra, Nehemiah, Malachi, (?) Joel

REVELATION AND INSPIRATION

As we step further inside the Old Testament to listen to what it is saying, two further questions arise:

- How does the Old Testament explain itself?
- What is the authority which these books possess?

The answer lies in the words 'revelation' (God revealed himself) and 'inspiration' (God equipped chosen human agents to receive and transmit what he wished to reveal).

God's Word

In Genesis 1 the Creator gave the command to be fruitful, to the beasts by fiat (Gen. 1:22), but to the human pair by personal address (Gen. 1:28). The distinction between the beast and the human creation is seen in the difference between 'saying' (v. 22) and 'said to them' (v. 28). Humankind is distinctive in hearing the word of God through the speech of God.

- The man and woman in the Garden are pre-eminently people under the word of God (Gen. 2:16-17).
- In due course, Abram is marked out from the teeming populations of Mesopotamia and Canaan because he hears God's word: 'the LORD said' (Gen. 12:1; 17:1; etc. NKJV).
- Later still, Moses defines Israel as special because they are the one people who have heard the voice of God (Deut. 4:33).
- Leaping far ahead, when Amos reviews the surrounding pagan world he accuses them of crimes against humanity (Amos 1:3, 6, 9, 11, 13; 2:1), of flouting

the common voice of conscience. Judah, however, is charged with rejecting the law of the Lord (2:4): the Lord's people are guilty because they possessed the Lord's word – and scorned it.

REVELATION, INSPIRATION, INTERPRETATION

REVELATION

Revelation is God displaying his nature – as when he told Moses the meaning of his eternal name (Exod. 3:13-15).

INSPIRATION

Inspiration is God's gracious preparation and enabling of human minds to receive this revelation of himself. As 'natural' creatures, unillumined by the Spirit of God, we cannot receive revealed truth (1 Cor. 2:14). While some still speak of the Bible as 'the church's book' – recognised and authorised by ecclesiastical decision for transmission to the world – the fact is that chosen individuals were enabled by God to receive his revealed truth in order to bring it to the church. As Amos (9:7) notes, the Exodus, as an event in history, is not different from all other national migrations. The sovereign God 'stage-manages' all. Yet the Exodus was different because the Lord linked it with the interpretative ministry of Moses.

PROPOSITIONAL REVELATION

At what point was Moses 'inspired'? Some would still say that it was in the historical event of the Exodus that God was revealed as 'the God who acts' and that Moses was the first to struggle to interpret what God's act might possibly mean.

But this is not what the Bible teaches. Moses was made wise before the event by the word God spoke to him (Exod. 3 and 4). This is called 'propositional revelation' – God speaking: the God of truth articulating the truth of God.

Because of this revelation of truth, Moses knew beforehand what the coming acts of God would mean. The act, when it came, confirmed the word which had preceded it.

The same is true even of the cross of the Lord Jesus Christ. There is nothing in the sight of three crosses that would make an observer single out the centre cross, but behind the event lies the whole flow of predictive and interpretative Scripture, the teaching of Jesus himself – not understood at the time but brought to mind after by the ministry of the Holy Spirit (John 14:26; 16:12-15) – and the propositional revelation granted to the apostles (1 Cor. 2:7-16).

In this way, inspired people have safeguarded for us what God revealed, and the Holy Scriptures are the deposit of revealed truth. Far from the Bible being the 'church's book', the church is 'the Bible's people'.

ARE SOME PARTS OF THE BIBLE 'MORE INSPIRED' THAN OTHERS?
* *To say this would be to confuse 'inspired' with 'inspiring'.*
Genealogies spring to mind, or the minutiae of the sacrifices in Leviticus, or the obscurities of Ezekiel's visionary temple (Ezek. 40–48). From time to time different parts of the Bible come home to us with different degrees of application. But every part of the Bible is there by divine intent, backed by the same divine work of revelation and inspiration, each with its own 'time of testimony' (1 Tim. 2:6).

* *Revelation and inspiration even govern the error the Bible contains.*
In Job, the slurs of Satan (1:9-11; 2:4-5) and the untruths of the friends (42:8) are recorded with the same care as the profoundest theology – for, regarding Satan, it is important for us to know his ways and lies; and as regards the friends, there are many cases where truth is best learned and safeguarded by the exposure of relevant falsity.

* *What about supposed errors of fact?*
Is it possible to extend this notion of error in the Bible to cover cases where it is said that scientific or historical enquiry casts doubt on the biblical record? Some people say that the Bible is inerrant in what it teaches but not necessarily in what it touches. Thus, Scripture 'touches' on many matters marginal to its salvation-history, its central theological interest, and may, in these instances, reflect contemporary thought rather than eternal truth.

There are some very questionable assumptions behind this position:

1. That human wisdom is sufficient to know what is important and what can be marginalised or discounted. This was the position of Marcion, who ended by creating his own canon of Scripture, excluding what he found unacceptable.

2. That there are matters biblical, historical or scientific which are so established as to be non-negotiable – whereas these disciplines abound in once 'assured' positions now long since abandoned.

3. That at points where the Bible and (for example) history or science now lie in conflict, we have rightly understood what the Bible is affirming.

INTERPRETATION

The doctrines of revelation and inspiration, and belief in scriptural in-errancy make the Bible no plainer to the reader. The same Scriptures lie alike before those who affirm and those who resist inerrancy – with this difference only, that while the concept of inerrant, divinely and verbally inspired Scripture of itself solves no problems, it makes all problems infinitely worth solving.

The true attitude to a Bible held to be revealed by God, transmitted through agents inspired by God and couched in the words of God, must be worded thus: 'What the Bible is found to teach, I hold myself bound to believe.'

The crucial activity in relation to the Bible is the use of every aid and the dedication of every ability to discovering what the Bible means by what it says. One of the tragedies of church history is that interpretations have been accorded an infallibility due only to the Scriptures themselves, with consequent divisions, excommunications, separations and denominations. Only the Scriptures are infallible.

Further reading
G.E. Wright, *The God who Acts* (SCM, 1952)
J.A. Motyer, *Look to the Rock* (IVP, 1996)
L. Gaussen, *The Divine Inspiration of Scripture* (Christian Focus, 2007)

Revelation: How Did the Word of God 'come'?

Of this, we are told little or nothing. The words, 'the LORD ... said' (e.g. 17:1 NKJV) resound through Genesis. The phrase, 'The LORD said to Moses' is the foundation of Exodus to Deuteronomy. 'This is what the Lord says/has said' is either stated or implied for every word spoken by the prophets.

Isaiah twice testifies to a voice 'In my ears' (5:9; 22:14), that is, there was an objective communication of an intelligible word.

Jeremiah, hesitant and insecure (1:9), needed a more direct reassurance, and he tells us that the Lord understandingly 'put out His hand and touched my mouth, ... and said ... "Look, I have put My words in your mouth"', implanting the word by direct divine ministry.

Ezekiel, with his rich and restless imagination, was given a fuller (but still only illustrative) understanding (2:7–3:4). Like Jeremiah, his claim was not just to possess the word of the Lord – as it were, the gist of the Lord's message – but 'the words of the Lord'. He was sent to 'speak my words to them' (2:7; 3:4) and, in order to make possible this identity of human voice and divine words, he was given all that he needed (2:8–3:3).

PROGRESSIVE REVELATION

Hebrews 1:1 offers a concise statement of God's revelation-plan.

a.   He did not reveal all his truth at once but spoke *polumeros*, 'in many portions', spread (as we see in Scripture) over a two-thousand-year time span.

b.   He also spoke *polutropos*, 'in many ways' – in the recorded lives of individuals, and in Israel's history, through the spoken word, and the voice of song.

All this is included under the single heading of 'prophecy', God's message: 'God spoke.'

GOD'S TRUTH

Since God is the 'God, who cannot lie' (Titus 1:2 NKJV), this whole accumulative process, from beginning to end, is truth. God's revelation-plan was not evolutionary, in the sense that early and primitive ideas are found to be erroneous, and are superseded by later and more developed understandings. Rather, the truth which 'God spoke' to start with provides a foundation for what 'God spoke' next, and so on to the climactic word which 'God spoke ... in a Son', his final word couched in a unique Person.

This view of Scripture is usually called 'progressive revelation', though 'cumulative revelation' might be a more exact description.

Inspiration: Ezekiel's Affirming Word

The terms used by Ezekiel explain what he (and all the prophets) meant by the words, 'Thus says the Lord', or, 'This is what the Lord has said.'

- The word of God came to Ezekiel from outside himself: 'a hand was stretched out' (2:9).
- Ezekiel did not compose the word: he 'found it' (3:1, NIV 'what is before you').
- This word was given in a complete form, not admitting human additions: the scroll is written 'on both sides', literally 'inside and outside'.

- It was imparted to Ezekiel, made part of his being, by divine agency: 3:2, literally, 'He caused me to eat the scroll.'

The Whole Person

Ezekiel's experience was that becoming the vehicle of the words of God did not mean that he became a tape recorder or a keyboard. He was a full, true, human person, required to respond with his whole personality.

Morally and *volitionally*, he contrasted with the rebellious people to whom he was sent by being the first to obey the word he had been given (2:8).

Intellectually, the scroll was spread out before him (2:10) until he had read it and registered its contents: 'lament ... mourning ... woe'.

Emotionally, 'it was in my mouth as honey for sweetness' (3:3).

The whole word of God engaged the whole person.

Enhanced Personalities

We need to remember that the inspiration extended to Ezekiel and those like him was a unique divine act. We have no comparable experience to help us to understand it, and, as is the case with all such uniquenesses, our logic only misleads. Logic would suggest that if a person is to receive and then speak the actual words of God, personality and thought processes must be suspended. But it was not so. Indeed, quite the contrary. The prophets were not depersonalised.

The books of the prophets display their sharply distinct personalities, their individual literary styles and mannerisms, their word-preferences and emphases. Amos' knowledge of world history and politics (1:3–2:3) came from study and research; the articulate, reasoned and often highly poetical nature of the prophets' messages cannot have been attained without labour. It is plain that, whatever processes were involved in the marvel of inspiration, far from being bypassed or violated, the personalities and abilities of the prophets were used, preserved, and, indeed, enhanced. The prophets – the very people who explicitly claimed that their words were the Lord's words and the Lord's words their words (Amos 1:1, 3) –come before us as colourful persons, even larger than life, with such individual distinctiveness that each prophet stands out, unmistakably, from every other.

Inspiration: Jeremiah, the Authentic Word

Jeremiah takes us an essential stage further in our enquiry. He was perturbed by the existence of contemporary prophets preaching messages which contradicted his. This would not have troubled Isaiah, but Jeremiah's insecurities and nervousness forced the issue. He would have appreciated the question raised by the (false) prophet, Zedekiah in 1 Kings 22:24, 'Where-ever did the Spirit of the LORD go on from being with me to speak to you?' – in other words, 'Can you demonstrate the reality of your inspiration as against mine?' Jeremiah would have said, 'That's my problem in a nutshell.'

Testing the Word

As Jeremiah wrestled with this (23:9-40), he concluded that a prophet must be judged by

- his personal life (v. 14);
- the moral rigour of his ministry and message (v. 14);
- the secret reality of his relationship with the Lord (vv. 18, 22).

The false prophets had no divine commission (v. 21), because they had not 'stood in My [the Lord's] counsel' (v. 22), and therefore the word they spoke was their own and not the Lord's (v. 26), lies and not truth (v. 25), straw and not wheat (v. 28).

Receiving the word. The word 'counsel' (sod) lies at the heart of Jeremiah's case. It means:

a. *secret*, in the sense of being let into a secret (Job 15:8);
b. *counsel*, the gathering of those belonging to a decision-making group (Jer. 6:11; Ps. 89:7), the 'fellowship' of close friends (Ps. 55:14 NIV);

c. counsel, the decision reached or the advice given (Prov. 15:22).

The true prophet, urges Jeremiah, has been granted a place in the sod of the Lord (Jer. 23:18, 22). The Lord is pictured with a heavenly 'counsel' with whom he consults before taking action (1 Kings 22:19-22), and the prophet is a co-opted member. In this way he enters into 'sweet fellowship' with the Lord himself, is 'let into his secrets', and then becomes the earthly messenger of its counsels.

Amos can say that this is the invariable experience of the prophet: 'The Lord God will do nothing without opening his counsel/sharing his fellowship/revealing his secret [literally, uncovering his sod] to his servants the prophets' (3:7).

It was in this context that the word of the Lord 'came' (literally, 'was', 'became a present living reality') to the prophet. We are told nothing about the mechanism or psychology of inspiration, only the reality of it expressed in ways that we can understand.

Inspiration and Holiness

Since true human nature is in the image of God, the nearer people approximate to that image the more truly human they become. Our problem with the prophets' claim to verbal inspiration arises from the fact that we put their experience in the wrong category, the category of the intellect. As we see it, it is only by being marginalised or overridden that the human mind can conceive and utter the very words of God.

Both the Old and New Testaments, however, link inspiration with sanctification, the image of God (Eph. 4:24). If a person is brought into such a close relationship and conformity to God and to the mind of God that the thoughts he thinks and the words he speaks are the thoughts and words of God, it is not that he becomes diminished in his humanity but enlarged. He is at that point more fully and completely human than ever before. So it was for the inspired authors of the Old Testament.

Was not the towering, majestic personality of our Lord Jesus Christ a by-product of the fact that 'whoever has seen me has seen the Father'? He was truly human because he was fully divine.

Bible writers were brought into such a fellowship with God that they were raised to this unique extent, that what they said was the word of God.

Prepared Agents

Illustrations are slippery customers. What preacher has not used an illustration only to find that a hearer has drawn a conclusion other than that intended? But think of a stained-glass window. It would be true to say that on the inside of the window the pure sunlight has been destroyed. It has been given shapes and colourations alien to its nature.

In the same way, it might be argued, the word of God exits from heaven in its perfection but passes through the filter of sinful personalities, and so is inevitably diminished, changed and damaged. Misunderstanding and error unavoidably creep in: sinners are like that. But, leaving aside the fact that even sinners often get things right, and that error is not inevitable in human thought and speech, think of a piece of stained glass: every colour and every shape is there by deliberate design, conceived and executed by the will of a master craftsman. The light cast by the window is not a mistake or a deterioration or a distortion: it is what the designer intended.

The Lord's Masterpieces

The inspired speakers and writers were the Lord's deliberate masterpieces of stained glass. The word of God passing through the filter of each carefully designed, patiently created personality (Jer. 1:5) did not receive alien colourations; it did not convey a mutilated message, but only that which the Designer intended, namely the pure, earthly realisation of the pure, heavenly word.

THE HEBREW TEXT

Writing is one of the oldest human skills and can be traced back, according to present knowledge, into the fourth millennium BC. Professor D. J. Wiseman, in an unpublished lecture, affirmed that if Moses did not keep a daily record, he is the only known leader of antiquity who failed to do so.

Written Records

When Genesis 5:1 mentions 'the book of the ongoing story of Adam' there is no reason why it should not be taken seriously, with the implication of written records preserved and handed down within the family.

Equally, it is as much against reason as against evidence to suggest that the prophets did not leave written records of their ministry, even editing them with their own hands. It is difficult indeed to imagine that a prophet should be aware that the words he was speaking were the very words of God and then leave them to the changes and chances of that game of Chinese whispers called oral transmission!

The books of the prophets fall, for the most part, into bite-sized pieces – not at all, therefore, word-by-word transcripts of preached sermons. Preaching has to be a much more elongated, leisurely exercise, with repetitions, elaborations and other tricks of the trade by which the preacher gives the hearers time to dwell on what is being said. In contrast, the books of the prophets look like carefully crafted summations, the distilled essence of the proclamation. What we have, therefore, are either notes from which the prophets preached or succinct statements of their preaching designed to be preserved. The individual units may even have been designed to be written up in public, like a wall-newspaper (compare Isa. 30:8).

Providence and Preservation

But the question must be faced that if the Lord went to the trouble of creating and shaping his messengers, inspiring

them and overseeing their expression of his word, why did
he not make that extra little effort to safeguard the precious
text through its years of transmission, so that it reached us in
pristine condition? Two things can be said in reply.

1. *The amount of damage to the Hebrew text is minimal.*

The evidence referred to earlier regarding Isaiah suggests no
small miracle of preservation. Earlier in the twentieth century
it was almost a matter of pride among Old Testament specialists
to find the text in 'disorder' and to rewrite it. Someone has
even said that 'emendation was the occupational hazard of
the Old Testament commentator'. But P.A. Verhoef, in his
introduction to *The Books of Haggai and Malachi* (Eerdmans,
1987, p. 18) remarks, 'My fifteen year experience in Bible
translation has strengthened the conviction that the majority
of proposed alterations to the text ... are really unnecessary ...
In most cases the meaning of the text is clear.' The suggestion
of a gross lapse of divine providence is unwarranted. The Old
Testament text is in a remarkable state of purity for such an
ancient document.

But we may say, 'Even "a remarkable state of purity" is not
total purity! If the Lord kept his written word so pure that
Jesus was able to assert its validity down to the "jot and tittle",
why is it not completely pure?' This leads to the second point.

2. *The answer lies in the general principle of the providence of God.*

Why did God not preserve humankind without sin? Why did/
does he not guard his earthly creation from environmental
pollution? Why has he not kept his church free from error?

In all these areas, as well as in the biblical text, the same
features appear. On the one hand there is a truly remarkable
degree of preservation – with abundant surviving evidences
of the image of God in fallen humanity, the surpassing beauty
of wonder of creation and the continuance of essential gospel truth amid much church apostasy. On the other hand,
we find a 'standard' divine procedure whereby that which is
committed to us becomes our responsibility to preserve.

Yet in fact, notwithstanding our inadequate stewardship, there is really no place where the meaning of the word of God is so lost that truth itself is imperilled or we are left uncertain where the truth lies.

The Fun of Having a Bible

Sometimes we who affirm a verbally inspired Bible have been teased for needing to retreat into a spurious security, and mocked for unwillingness (if not pathetic inability) to face the scary freedom and risky open-endedness of unfettered enquiry. Not so! Verbal inspiration solves no problems of interpretation and offers no prepackaged answers. To say that the Bible is the word of God does not make its meaning any clearer or solve any of its problems; it simply guarantees that the meaning is worth every effort to find and that every problem is supremely worth solving.

Further reading
R.T. Beckwith, 'The Canon of the Old Testament', in *New Bible Dictionary* (IVP, 1996)

AUTHORSHIP OF THE PENTATEUCH
From the earliest days the first five books of the Bible have been assigned to Moses. This assignation has always included Genesis even though Genesis itself registers no authorship claim.

THE THEORY OF THE FOUR DOCUMENTS
Particularly since the days of Astruc (1753) and Eichhorn (1780), and then gathering momentum and reaching its classical formulation in the work of Graf (1866) and Wellhausen (1876), it became commonplace to see Moses as hardly more than a cipher figure, imparting pseudo-antiquity and authority to a compilation of four separate 'documents' (see chart below):

1. A document, noted as 'J' because it used the divine name *Yahweh* (or *Jahweh*), dated 950 BC;

2. A document called 'E' because it used the noun 'God', *Elohim*, dated 850;

3. The book of Deuteronomy, designated as 'D', the 'book of the law' discovered during Josiah's reformation (2 Kings 22 and 23), 639 BC;

4. 'P', a post-exilic Priestly document which codified Israel's religious and other laws.

REASONS FOR THE THEORY

Behind this process of fragmentation lay a number of suppositions:

1. It was said that Exodus 6:2-3 pointed to a pre-Mosaic time when the divine name, Yahweh, was not known. If this is so, then Genesis passages using Yahweh must be post-Mosaic.

2. Passages which, to the average reader, seemed to relate similar incidents in the lives of different patriarchs (for instance Abraham's and Isaac's deceptions about their wives, Gen. 12:10-20; 26:1-11) were interpreted as parallel accounts of the same event, but appearing in different 'documents'.

3. Genesis 37 links the enslavement of Joseph to both Ishmaelites and Midianites and was understood to be a 'conflation' from various sources.

4. Plainly non-Mosaic material (Gen. 36:31; Deut. 34) speaks against Mosaic authorship, and points to later authors and editors.

Helped by the then fashionable concept of the evolution of religion, Wellhausen decided that the highly developed ceremonies of the Priestly document pointed to its late (post-exilic) origin, and with this clue, he spread the Pentateuchal material out along a timeline – see below.

MODIFYING THE THEORY

The Wellhausen construction continues to pervade Pentateuchal studies even though modern specialists who hold to it tend to think in terms of four 'streams of tradition' first running in parallel and then combining, much at the dates Wellhausen proposed. Behind this moderate revision lies the abandonment of the concept of evolution in religion, and the recognition that much that Wellhausen considered late existed in Israel from earlier times, even from the beginning.

OPPOSING THE THEORY

Against this consensus, there have always been those who refused Wellhausen's schema. The Scandinavian school of Old Testament specialists has spoken out against the validity of the Divine Name as a criterion for isolating different documents. Their position can be put bluntly like this: the documentary theory works, except where it doesn't work, at which point its devotees emend the text to make it work (see Nielsen).

Older conservative writers have long recognised this (see Orr, Finn). But with evolution gone, with the recognition that all Pentateuchal 'streams' go back to the remote past, and with the crucial factor of the Divine Name challenged, the way was beginning to open for a reassessment of the five books.

1. Archaeology has revealed the 'antiquity of higher culture' (see Albright), and has added its weight to the recognition of the accuracy of the patriarchial records within the time and culture they claim for themselves (see Kitchen).

2. Exodus 6:2-3 is more properly understood as meaning that Moses received a revelation of the significance of the name, Yahweh, not a (mere) revelation of the name as such (see Motyer). This well accords with Genesis where, not Yahweh, but 'God Almighty' (El Shaddai) is the main component in the revelation of God (for instance Gen.17:1-2).

3. The use of the name, Yahweh, and the nouns for 'God' throughout the Pentateuch can better be understood either as a matter of literary variety, or theologically, as expressing some particular aspect of the divine nature appropriate to each context (see Cassuto).

4. As distinct from the enthusiasm for fragmentation evident from Wellhausen onwards, there is a more recent emphasis on cohesion, unity and carefully worked out literary patterns. This applies to the whole of Old Testament study (see Childs), and not least to the Pentateuch. See, for example, Wenham, Matthews and especially Garrett. Within the Pentateuch, there is evidence (as is proper) of post-Mosaic editing (see Manley), and of pre-Mosaic written records (see Garrett), but there is no substantial or unanswerable difficulty in the way of seeing Moses as foundational to the Pentateuchal record, just as he is central to its post-Genesis history.

Further reading

W.F. Albright, *From Stone Age to Christianity* (Doubleday, 1957)
U. Cassuto, *From Adam to Noah* (Magnes, 1961)
_____ *From Noah to Abraham* (Magnes, 1964)
B.S. Childs, *Introduction to the Old Testament as Scripture* (SCM, 1979)

A.H. Finn, *The Unity of the Pentateuch* (Marshall, no date, but after 1891)
D.A. Garrett, *Rethinking Genesis* (Christian Focus, 2000)
D.A. Hubbard, 'The Pentateuch' in *New Bible Dictionary* (IVP, 1996)
K.A. Kitchen, *Ancient Orient and Old Testament* (Tyndale, 1966)
G.T. Manley, *The Book of the Law* (Tyndale, 1957)
K.A. Matthews, *Genesis* (2 vols) (Broadman, 1996)
J.A. Motyer, *The Revelation of the Divine Name* (Tyndale, 1959)
E. Nielsen, *Oral Tradition* (SCM, 1954)
J. Orr, *The Problem of the Old Testament* (Nisbet, 1908)
G.J. Wenham, *Genesis* (2 vols) (Word Books, 1987)
J.W. Wenham, 'Moses and the Pentateuch', in *New Bible Commentary Revised* (IVP, 1970)

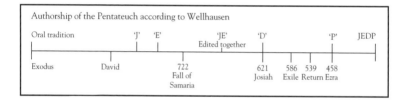

Authorship of the Pentateuch according to Wellhausen

Oral tradition		'J'	'E'	'JE' Edited together	'D'			'P'	JEDP
Exodus	David			722 Fall of Samaria	621 Josiah	586 Exile	539 Return	458 Ezra	

3

MOSES:

PENTATEUCH PANORAMA

B ut what is the Old Testament about? We have listened to the Lord Jesus telling us how unique his Bible is, and how important. We have also listened to the Old Testament talking about itself, telling us that its men were brought into God's close fellowship, lifted up to become more really themselves than ever before, and given God's very words to speak. If these two things do not excite us to come to grips with the Old Testament, whatever will?

So, what is it all about? Can we sum up the contents of this long and varied book?

THE INCOMPARABLE MOSES

The task is not as daunting as it might at first seem. Notwithstanding that the Old Testament is so big, that it has such a long list of authors, that it contains a wide variety of literature (prose and poetry, history, parable), and that it varies in its interests and emphases, yet everything in one way or another goes back to Moses. He is the great spring from which all the rivers flow and divide.

Moses was special, indeed unique:

1. The prophet

'[T]here has not arisen as yet a prophet in Israel like Moses whom the LORD knew face to face, (or) in respect of all the signs and wonders which the LORD sent him to do in the land of Egypt' (Deut. 34:10f.). Moses became the test by which every subsequent prophet was judged. Time had elapsed since he had died but, though prophets had come and gone, he was still incomparable.

- He had a special relationship with the Lord ('face to face').
- His ministry was validated in marked ways ('all the signs and wonders').
- He was central to the great Exodus-redemption event (Exod. 6:6-7).

2. The Mediator

'A prophet from among you, from your brothers, one like me, the Lord your God will raise up. To him you must listen, just like all you asked of the Lord your God in Horeb in the day of the assembly' (Deut. 18:15f.). Moses was the model to which even 'the Prophet' (compare John 1:21, 25) would conform.

When the Lord appeared on Mount Sinai (Exod. 19:18-20), the people felt overwhelmed by such divine majesty and begged Moses to mediate (Exod. 20:18-21). It was, indeed, the Lord's purpose that he should do so (Exod. 19:9). He intended to give Moses a unique place in this foundational revelation of the God of redemption (Exod. 6:6-7) and law (Exod. 20:2ff.). The Lord spoke to him, and he spoke the Lord's words to the people (compare Exod. 6:29–7:23; Deut. 4:1-2).

3. The one close to God

'Moses is trustworthy in all my house. Mouth to mouth I will speak with him, visibly, not in riddles' (Num. 12:7f.). Moses was granted a special clarity of revelation and intimacy of fellowship with the Lord. The rare expression, 'mouth to mouth', reappears in Jeremiah 34:3 (literally, 'your eyes will see the eyes of the king of Babylon and his mouth will speak with your mouth'). Just as, in the Old Testament, 'seeing eye to eye' is to see plainly and unmistakably (Isa. 52:8), so to speak 'mouth to mouth' is to communicate with total clarity. It is worth comparing this with Baruch's experience when he took down Jeremiah's dictation: 'He wrote from the mouth of Jeremiah all the words of the Lord' (36:4); 'He pronounced all these words to me with his mouth, and I wrote them with ink in the book' (36:18). Of course, as we have seen, this could be said of any of the prophets, but in Moses' case the intimacy was lifted to a new level: 'the form of the Lord he will behold' (Num. 12:8). He saw the Lord's 'shape', some outward and visible expression of the Lord's invisible person, the experience David anticipated in glory (Ps. 17:15).

Exodus 33:11 puts this special intimacy beautifully: 'And the Lord used to speak to Moses face to face like a man speaks to his friend.'

THE MOSAIC DEPOSIT

An age-long tradition reaching back to the Lord Jesus and beyond has seen the first five books of the Old Testament as 'the books of Moses' and, apart from Genesis, which registers no claim as to its authorship, this tradition arises from the insistent testimony of Exodus to Deuteronomy. It is, incidentally, particularly the case with the two books, Leviticus and Deuteronomy, which so much modern teaching most confidently denies to Moses. It is simplest, as well as most honouring to the Bible, to accept its own testimony and to use the name of Moses to cover this huge foundational deposit of biblical truth, called the Pentateuch, or 'fivefold' book.

Two unequal parts

Within the glorious sweep of the Pentateuch, Genesis 12 (or more accurately, 11:10) marks a new beginning. Up to that point the record has dealt with universals – creation (Gen. 1, 2), the entry of sin, infecting the whole of both the human race and the environment (Gen. 3–5), the flood (Gen. 6–9), and the scattering of the people at Babel (Gen. 10–11). But from Genesis 12 onwards all becomes particular. The genealogy in Genesis 11:10-26 leads into the story of one man, Abram/ Abraham, and so exclusive does the focus on him and his descendants become that, though occasionally he interacts with others, he seems on the whole to walk through an empty landscape. At that time Canaan was thickly populated, but of this Genesis tells us nothing. Its concern is with one man and his family, and though the family grows in size, the exclusive interest remains till the end of Deuteronomy.

INSIDE INFORMATION

Bible history, however, is never a mere recital of facts. There is always the story-within-the-story, the inside information. In Bible history-writing there are always:

1.   The facts, 'what happened'. For example a migration of Hebrews out of Egypt.
2.   What God was doing. The Hebrews involved in this migration understood it in a particular light: that their God, who had brought their father Abraham out of Ur (Gen. 15:7) and their father Jacob down to Egypt (Gen. 46:3-4), was again at work as the Lord of history bringing them out (Exod. 3:7-8). The fact of migration was an act of God.
3.   The meaning. This act of God went beyond political deliverance. It was a redemptive act whereby, through the sacrifice of the Passover, the Lord brought people who would otherwise have fallen under his judgment into his salvation.

Three Levels

German terminology distinguishes these three levels of understanding as Historie, Geschichte and Heilsgeschichte: the story itself, the inner significance of the story as a work of God, and the story told as the history of God's saving enterprise.

In Bible history, the 'real story' is that God set up a relationship between himself and the one man Abram/Abraham and with his family after him. This relationship is called 'the covenant', a unilateral, free undertaking by the Lord that 'you will be my people and I will be your God' (Gen. 17:7; Exod. 6:7; compare Deut. 4:20; 7:6; 14:2).

THE BEGINNING

We have noted the universal viewpoint of Genesis 1–11. But there is more than that, for the theme of these chapters is not just 'the world'; it is the sovereignty of God over the world.

THE PENTATEUCH	
GENESIS 1–11	GENESIS 12–DEUTERONOMY 34
UNIVERSAL Creation Fall Flood Scattering	PARTICULAR Abraham and his expanding family

THE COVENANT IN THE GARDEN OF EDEN

One great storyline holds the Pentateuch together: the covenant. Some find the thought of covenant in God's dealings with Adam, and there is much to be said for this, because the main biblical ideas of covenanting are indeed found in Genesis 1 and 2:

- The initiative of the Lord God in benevolence (Gen. 2:1-15, 18-23);
- The giving of the law of the Garden (Gen. 2:16-17) and of marriage (Gen. 2:24-25).

The first couple receive a free bounty from God which they enjoy through a responsive life of obedience. Adam and Eve live in the Garden by divine appointment, and as long as they obey, the richness of the Garden is theirs. The man and the woman are the royal family of Eden.

- He is sovereign as Creator (1:1–2:3). His word of command is the sole and sufficient cause of all things.

- He is sovereign in benevolence (2:4-17). He makes his caring arrangements and provisions for Adam without consultation or hindrance.

- He is sovereign in a world of sinners (3:1–6:4): the great rebellion makes no difference. Humankind may think to overthrow the rule of God, but the rule remains: he still orders things without consultation or hindrance.

- He is sovereign in judgment and grace (6:4–9:28). The whole of humankind merits destruction, and the sovereign God plans to bring in that destruction (6:5–9:28). But in the case of one man, a death-deserving sinner like all the rest, there was a sovereign interposition of grace issuing in salvation: 'Noah found grace' (6:8 NKJV). Here, as always in the Bible, grace is unmerited, undeserved favour. The expression 'so-and-so found grace/favour' never means that the person sought favour, worked for it and found it by personal endeavour (e.g. Ruth 2:20), or deserved it – how could it, for 'grace' is undeserved favour? The translation (rightly) is, 'Noah found grace', but the meaning is 'grace found Noah'.

- He is sovereign in world rule (11:1-9). Humankind plans to use technology (the discovery of bricks and mortar) to make itself safe, by creating a secure society behind high walls. But the Lord will never permit humans to be the authors of their own salvation. They build up to heaven, but he has to come down to see what they are doing! All they purposed bows to his sovereign will.

This is a marvellous theology, exalting God, humbling human pride, exciting submissive faith. It does, however, raise a problem. When Genesis 12 abandons the universal standpoint of chapters 1–11 for a particularised focus on one man and one nation, does this mean that the all-sovereign God has admitted to defeat? Does it mean that, with the world in rebellion, he must now content himself with lesser objectives? How absurd! This sovereign God cannot be thwarted.

Covenant Beginnings

a. Noah

From the very beginning we see that whenever God narrowed his purpose down to the particular, it was in order that he might bring his grace to the universal. The Lord's dealings with Noah were covenantal. We have already seen that the idea of covenant was implicit in Genesis 1 and 2. Here it is explicit (see boxed feature, p. 56). When 'grace' interposed to save Noah (Gen. 6:8) and to change him (Gen. 6:9), the Lord described this by saying 'I will implement my covenant' (Gen. 6:17-18). This covenant, however, which began with the one man Noah, came to be expressed, after the Flood, in worldwide terms (Gen. 9:12-13; 15:18) and to be symbolised by the world-embracing rainbow (chs. 13–16). The Lord purposed grace for his whole creation.

b. Abram

Abram is introduced by one of those features of the Old Testament which can easily be overlooked – or dismissed as boring – a genealogy. Following the confusion and scattering at Babel (Gen. 11:1-9) Genesis backtracks to Shem, son of Noah. 'God is working his purpose out as year succeeds to year.' We know nothing of most of the names on this list, but they all had their place in God's unforgotten purpose. What he began in Noah, he pursued, generation after generation, until at the appointed time the appointed man was born, to whom he said, 'in you shall all the families of the earth be blessed' (Gen. 12:3).

FROM ONE MAN TO A NATION

Genesis 12 to Deuteronomy 34 traces the story of Abraham and his family:

* Abram's entry into Canaan (Gen. 12:1-5) and the promise that the land would come to his future descendants after a period of suffering (Gen. 15:13-16);

- The descent of Jacob, Abraham's grandson, and his family into Egypt (Gen. 48), and their subsequent enslavement (Exod. 1);
- The Exodus (Exod. 2–12): deliverance and redemption (Exod. 6:6-7);
- The journey under divine guidance (Exod. 13:21-22) to Sinai (Exod. 14–19) and their long stay there; the giving of God's law (Exod. 20–24) and the institution of sacrifice (Exod. 25–Lev.);
- The forty-year wilderness experience before they reached the borders of Canaan (Num.) and Moses' final addresses to his people prior to his death and their entrance to the promised land (Deut.).

THE SIGNS OF THE COVENANT

Circumcision, like the 'bow in the clouds' (Gen. 9:12-17 NKJV), is called a 'sign of the covenant'. The two signs make a vivid contrast: the former enormous, public and universal, the latter tiny, hidden and individual.

THE PURPOSE OF THE SIGNS
The bow in the clouds signifies the promise of God: when the bow appears God remembers his promise, and Noah (and every informed observer) is alerted to what God has promised.

In the same way, the imposition of the covenant sign of circumcision on Abraham's body makes him the recipient and bearer of the divine promise. Just as Noah would see the bow and say, 'God has promised,' so Abraham would see his own marked body and say, 'God has promised.'

CONTRASTING SIGNS
God himself set his bow in the clouds (Gen. 9:13) but Abraham is required to set the covenant sign on himself and his infants. If he is to keep the Lord's covenant he must immediately become the obedient man by obeying the command to circumcise.

DIVINE PROMISE
But circumcision does not symbolise Abraham's response or his obedience. This is why Paul (Rom. 4:11 NKJV) calls circumcision not 'a seal of faith' but a 'seal of the righteousness of faith'. It speaks not of human response but of divine promise. Circumcision marks the first occasion on which the covenant man shows the reality of his covenant status by obeying a divine command.

GENESIS 12–DEUTERONOMY 34: GOD'S COVENANT

This long section of the Pentateuch begins with the solemn inauguration of this covenant (Gen. 15; 18), moves on to its formal ratification (Exod. 24:4-8) and continues with a series of elaborations, which we will presently discover.

If we place ourselves with Abraham in Genesis 12 and look ahead over the years to the death of Moses at the end of Deuteronomy, we see four great events, standing out like mountain peaks, two close at hand, two farther away:

- Covenant inauguration (Gen. 15);
- Covenant obligation (Gen. 17);
- Covenant sacrifice, the Passover (Exod. 12);
- Covenant lifestyle (Exod. 19–Deut. 34).

1.Covenant Inauguration (Gen. 15)

Here we see a true revelation of the God of the Bible who loves to make and keep promises.

Your 'shield'

Abram has just put himself at risk of reprisal by defeating the kings of the east in battle (Gen. 14), and the Lord meets him at this point of nervousness by promising 'I *am* your shield' (15:1 NKJV).

Your 'great reward'

But Abram has also thrown away the chance of becoming enormously wealthy by refusing to take any of the spoils of battle (14:22-23). The Lord again intervenes by proposing himself as Abram's 'great reward'.

A Son

This raises a severe problem: what is the point of 'reward' if there is no heir to inherit it (15:2-3)? A third divine promise fills this void (15:4-5).

Land

But there is still more, for the Lord's promises always exceed our known needs. The fourth divine pledge recalls the existing promise of a gift of land (12:7; 15:7).

The Covenant

All this, however, suddenly becomes too much for Abram: his faith, great though it is (15:6), needs a prop, and the Lord provides this in the ceremony of covenant inauguration.

The Lord requires Abram (Gen. 15:9f.) to take specified animals and, having divided each carcase, to make a path between the severed halves. This (to us) strange ceremony is explained in Jeremiah 34:18-21. It is a form of solemn oath-taking in which the covenant-maker invokes upon himself, should he break his oath, the fate that had befallen the animals between which he was passing (Jer. 34:18, 20). It is as if he said, 'So may it be done to me and mine.'

In Genesis 15:12-17 we see three important facts:

- Abraham is immobilised by a divinely induced 'sleep' which leaves him as an observer but denies him any participation in the oath-taking.

- The Lord appears in a symbol which looks forward to Moses and the Exodus: literally, it is 'an oven (with) smoke and flame of fire'. Soon the Lord will be present among his people, not as a nomad's portable oven belching smoke and flame, but in the towering reality of the pillar of cloud and fire (Exod. 13:21-22; 14:19), the fire of divine holiness, graciously shrouded by the cloud which marks the presence of God (Exod. 19:18).

- The Lord alone goes on oath, for he alone makes the great covenant undertakings. The promise is solely his to make, and he alone accepts the responsibility of keeping it. What Genesis does not say but we know by hindsight is that the day will come when the Lord will take upon himself the penalty of our broken promise.

Genesis 15:18 is exact: 'on that day' – the day the promise was made and sealed in the appropriate ceremony – the Lord 'inaugurated a covenant with Abram'.

2. *Covenant Obligation (Gen. 17)*

The people who are brought into covenant relationship with the Lord – the recipients of freely given divine promises which God alone underwrites – must demonstrate their privileged status by responding with a distinct manner of life.

In Genesis 17:2 the Lord confirms (literally, 'sets') his covenant between himself and Abram. The covenant is not simply a promise inaugurated in the past, it is also the unchanging mode of relationship between the covenant Maker and the covenant recipient.

Promise
Genesis 17 reiterates the element of promise in the covenant:

* *Personally (17:4-5)*
Abram becomes Abraham, the 'new man' with new potentialities and powers: the childless man becomes the father of multitudes;

* *Domestically (17:6)*
Abraham will be the progenitor of a family of kings and nations;

* *Spiritually (17:7)*
The Lord makes a commitment that he will be God to Abraham's 'seed';

* *Territorially (17:8)*
Abraham, and his descendants will possess the promised land.

Law
Alongside the promise, Genesis 17 lays down the law of covenant living (17:1):
* A life in fellowship (walk before me);
* A life of perfection ('be perfect').

Within the covenant, blessing is enjoyed along the pathway of obedience. Obedience is not the condition of entrance into the covenant, but the mode of life proper to those within it.

3. Covenant Sacrifice, the Passover (Exod. 12)

We saw in the case of Abram (Gen. 15:18) that sacrifice and covenant inauguration belong together. Genesis offered no explanation of this, but Exodus shows exactly how sacrifice lies at the basis of the covenant.

Slaves in Egypt

At the divide between Genesis and Exodus, Jacob's family are resident aliens in Egypt, and their great patron, Joseph, is dead (Gen. 50:26). As a growing immigrant population, they soon come under suspicion and then persecution (Exod. 1). The remedy for their plight starts when 'God remembered His covenant' (Exod. 2:24 NKJV). The rest of the story – their deliverance, journeyings and final entrance to Canaan – tells how the Lord faithfully stands by his covenant promise, fulfilling what he has undertaken by means of divine covenant-keeping acts.

The Lord has a double purpose for his enslaved people:

1. He determines to deliver them from Egypt, breaking Egypt's power by the hammer blows of his plagues (Exod. 7:14–11:1).
2. He wills to bring his people to himself by redemption, and he does this through the blood of the Passover lamb.

This double divine purpose is stated in Exodus 6:6-7:

> I *am* the LORD.
> I will bring you out from under the burdens of Egypt;
> I will deliver you from their servitude;
> I will redeem you with outstretched arm and with great judgments;
> I will take you as my people, and I will be your God.

God's Protection

Up to the moment of the Passover, the danger to Israel had been human, the genocidal policy of Egypt. On Passover night, however, the threat becomes divine, for the

Lord himself enters Egypt in judgment (Exod. 12:12). But the blood of the lamb becomes the people's protective covering. The Lord who came in judgment 'passed over' in peace when he 'saw the blood' (Exod. 12:13). This blood, therefore, fulfils a propitiatory role, satisfying the justice of God in relation to those who claim its protection (Exod. 12:22).

Substitution and Propitiation
The blood of the lamb is propitiatory because it is substitutionary. This is a truth intrinsic to the way the story is told. In every Egyptian house one lies dead (Exod. 12:30), the token but terrible judgment of God. In every Israelite house, likewise, one lies dead, the slaughtered lamb (Exod. 12:8-10). The technical word which we must happily come to terms with here is substitution: the judgment of God has fallen upon a substitute. It is to make this point that Exodus 12:3-4 insists so strongly on the careful choice of the lamb in order to secure an exact equivalence between the number and the needs of the people and the choice of the lamb under whose death they take shelter (v. 4). Just as Pharaoh had one firstborn son upon whom the judgment fell, so the whole person whom the Lord would save – Israel – is God's 'firstborn' (Exod. 4:22), and the lamb is their substitutionary equivalent.

PHARAOH'S HEART

Exodus speaks of 'Pharaoh's heart' in three ways:

1. The Lord hardened Pharaoh's heart (4:21; 7:3; 9:12; 10:1, 20, 27; 11:10; 14:4, 9);
2. Pharaoh hardened his heart (8:15, 32; 9:34);
3. Pharaoh's heart became hard (Exod. 7:13, 33; 8:19; 9:7, 35).

All three statements are true and must be held together: every disobedience is a deliberate hardening of the heart, results in the heart becoming hard, and does so under the moral, providential ordering of God.

God alone foresees and determines the point at which human disobedience with its consequent heart-hardening merits divine judicial action whereby the heart is declared irretrievably hardened. At the time of Moses, Pharaoh had reached this point of no return.

(See further on Isa. 6:9-13, pp. 195-6.)

---

4. Covenant Lifestyle (Exod. 19–Deut. 34)

Israel have come out of Egypt as the Lord's redeemed. They have sheltered under the blood of the lamb (Exod. 12:21-23). Their promised destination is Canaan (Exod. 3:7-8), but as they follow the guiding pillar (Exod. 13:21-22) it is not to the promised land that they come but to Sinai, the mountain of covenant law (Exod. 19).

The theological truth here is that those who have been redeemed by the blood of the lamb must come to the place where they hear the law of the Lord: his law is not a system of merit whereby people, by good works, seek divine favour; but a divinely revealed way of life whereby those who have already been brought into his favour by redemption can live according to his will: it is a lifestyle of responsive obedience for the redeemed.

PATTERNS IN REVELATION

There is no more important – or exciting – exercise in Bible study than analysis. Nothing more fully opens the door of biblical truth than to discover the patterns in divine revelation. Genesis opens a covenant sequence, and Exodus reinforces it.

- Genesis 15 and 17 establish the ideas of covenant sacrifice followed by covenant law;
- Exodus 12 explains the meaning of sacrifice (propitiation);
- Exodus 19 begins an elaborated statement of law.

The principle is fundamentally important in the Bible: those redeemed by the blood of the lamb have been brought out of bondage into the freedom of obeying the law of the Lord (Exod. 20:1-2).

Covenant solemnisation

If the whole Egypt-to-Sinai story is a display of this truth on the grand scale, Moses' ceremony of covenant-solemnisation at Sinai (Exod. 24:4-8) encapsulates the same truth in miniature.

- The altar with its twelve pillars (24:4) represents the situation achieved by the Exodus: the Lord has brought his people – the twelve tribes – to himself (Exod. 6:7), and they are now permanently secure in his presence as if set in stone.

- The blood of the sacrificed beasts is divided into two and, as at the Passover (Exod. 12:13), the first 'movement' of the blood is godward – it is sprinkled on the altar (24:6). This is the blood of propitiation and reconciliation.

- The law of God is read to the people of God and they respond by committing themselves to obedience (24:7).

- The remaining blood is sprinkled on the people (24:8). This means that their sins continue to be forgiven as they seek to live obediently (compare 1 John 1:7).

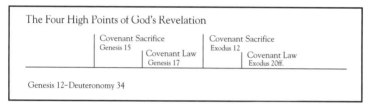

The Four High Points of God's Revelation

	Covenant Sacrifice Genesis 15		Covenant Sacrifice Exodus 12	
		Covenant Law Genesis 17		Covenant Law Exodus 20ff.

Genesis 12–Deuteronomy 34

Just as redeeming grace brought the people to the place where they could hear the law, so redeeming grace accompanies them as they set out on the life of law-keeping. The blood of sacrifice caters for their lapses from the life of obedience. This is the heart of the meaning of the Mosaic sacrificial system.

Covenant Elaboration – Sacrifices

Exodus 25 to Leviticus 27 are in the main taken up with the sacrificial and priestly system God revealed to his people through Moses. The Tabernacle (Exod. 25–40, see especially 29:43-46) is the Lord's tent where he intends to live at the heart of his tent-dwelling people. But since he is the holy God, special arrangements are needed both to guard his holiness and to make it possible for sinners to dwell where he dwells. The sacrifices are the provision he makes for this

(Lev. 17:11). Exodus 25 to Leviticus 27 spell out the place, meaning and requirements of sacrifice in the ongoing life of the Lord's redeemed, covenant people.

Covenant Elaboration – Law
In Deuteronomy a sustained attempt is made to apply the law of the Lord to the life of the people of the Lord. In this way, on the very borders of Canaan (Deut. 1:1-5), Moses prepares his people to live in the promised land in ways that befit those whom the Lord redeemed and for whom he has kept his promises.

The Twofold Law of Moses
The 'law of Moses' is more than 'the law of commandments *contained* in ordinances' (Eph. 2:15 NKJV), the moral law before which we stand condemned. It is also the law of the sacrifices, the shedding of blood, speaking godward, of propitiation, relationally of reconciliation, and experimentally of forgiveness. It is both the law of divine requirement, looking for obedience, and the law of grace, sheltering, providing for our inevitable lapses from obedience, our 'falling short of the glory of God' (Rom. 3:23).

And in the Mosaic system we see a truth proclaimed by the whole Old Testament, and consummated in Christ: that law, in the sense of requirement, the law as lifestyle, is always 'sandwiched' in grace. The foundational act of redeeming grace (Passover, Calvary) leads into a life of responsive obedience. The life of obedience is lived under the shelter of, and accompanied by, the ever-available effectiveness of that same saving grace.

NUMBERS AND ALL THAT
There is still Genesis 12–14; 18–40; Exodus 1–2; 13–19; and Numbers. Of course, in one way these chapters are simply the essential historical framework, the *Historie* within which God's covenant work was the *Geschichte* and *Heilsgeschichte*, the 'inside story'. But closer examination shows that all these passages have a common theme.

Start with Numbers, a strange 'history book' if ever there was one. It is the story of forty years, and yet it records only three main stories – three events in forty years! They are:

- The mission of the spies (Num. 13–14)
- The rebellion of Korah (Num. 16–17)
- The threat of Balaam (Num. 22–25)

These are all marvellous stories, marvellously told, but they are also much more. They are telling illustrations of the persevering love and care of the Lord for his people, his determination that, contrary to their deservings (spies), intentions (Korah) and abilities (Balaam), they will inherit his promises.

The Spies
In Numbers 13–14 we read of the mission of the spies to prospect the land of Canaan. Of the twelve men sent, ten bring back a negative report of Israel's prospects of ever conquering the inhabitants. Two, Joshua and Caleb, return a minority verdict, summoning their people to advance as an act of obedient faith. But Israel refuses to enter the land and, in return, suffers divine chastisement. The nation is consigned to a forty-year wilderness experience (Num. 14:28-35) until all those who have refused to enter have died out (Deut. 2:14-16). Yet – and here is the wonderful thing – the Lord's purposes themselves do not alter or falter. Numbers 15:1 says, 'After you enter the land ...' The people are rebellious, unworthy, and under chastisement, but neither the Lord nor his purposes change.

Insurrection
Numbers 16–18 tells of a populist attempt under Korah (16:1-3) to wrest leadership from Moses and Aaron, to increase the power of the Levites (16:9-10), and to impugn what Moses has achieved (16:13-14). But, once more, the

Lord is not deflected from his purposes, nor from his chosen agents. In Numbers 17–18 the Lord reaffirms the Aaronic priesthood. People may reject what he provides but he does not change.

Balaam

In Numbers 22–24 we meet with Balaam, a man with supernatural or occult powers. He is hired by Balak, king of Moab, to impose a curse on Israel, for it was an accepted fact that 'he whom you bless *is* blessed, and he whom you curse is cursed' (Num. 22:6 NKJV). The wording here recalls the Lord's word to Abram (Gen. 12:3) and must surely be deliberate. The Balaam story becomes a contest to see whose word will prevail, Balaam's or the Lord's, and who has the right, Balaam or Israel, to be the key to the blessedness of others. But Israel knows nothing of the presence of this dire threat aimed against them – not until it was long past, and Balaam has been captured in the course of the Midianite war (Num. 31:1, 8). Then it all comes out. While they were, all unknowingly, under threat, the Lord was secretly at work (compare Exod. 1:8-21), cancelling the deadly threat (compare 1 Cor. 10:13), turning the curse into a blessing (23:11; etc.).

Divine Persistence

This is the clue to all the passages in Genesis, Exodus and Numbers which both link and divide the great covenantal statements of sacrifice and law: the Lord's persistence with an undeserving, recalcitrant people, his determination to keep his promises, and his providential care and protection in spite of the people's unworthiness and weakness.

What a study this is, if only space allowed us to pursue it! The great Abram lapsed in faith (Gen. 12:10-20; 20:1-17) but the Lord remained faithful (12:17; 20:6). Even the subdued Isaac (and who wouldn't be subdued who lay bound on an altar and saw a knife descending? [Gen. 22:9]) fell into the same error (Gen. 26:1-11) but proved the faithfulness of the same Lord (26:1, 12). And what of Rebekah, who substituted trickery for reliance on the promise of God (Gen. 27; compare 25:23)? Or Jacob, who replaced faith with the 'I-can-handle-it' syndrome? Or the ceaselessly grumbling Hebrews of Exodus 15–17?

Here is all the sadness and culpability of human self-regard and unbelief, and all the wonder of divine, loving perseverance. A summons indeed to 'wonder, love and praise'!

THE PENTATEUCH

This, then, has been the great Mosaic panorama – what the Pentateuch is all about – and the heart that does not leap in excitement and adoration is dead indeed! The Pentateuch is much more one book than it is five, and in its deep unity it sums up what the Old Testament is all about – and, beyond the Old Testament, the whole Bible.

Further reading

J.A. Motyer, *The Message of Exodus* (IVP, 2005)
J. L MacKay, *Exodus* (Christian Focus, 2001)
A. Harman, *Deuteronomy* (Christian Focus, 2007)
J. Currid, *Exodus*, Vol. 1 Chapters 1–18 (Evangelical Press, 2000)
—*Exodus*, Vol. 2 Chapters 19–40 (Evangelical Press, 2002)
V. Poythress, *The Shadow of Christ in the Law of Moses* (Presbyterian & Reformed, 1991)
C. Wright, *Walking in the Ways of the Lord* (Apollos, 1995)
— *Living as the People of God* (IVP, 1983)
G.J. Wenham, Ed., *He Swore an Oath* (Paternoster, 1994)
D.J. Wiseman, Ed., *Essays on the Patriarchal Narratives* (IVP, 1980)

On the covenant
T. McComisky, *The Covenants of Promise* (Baker, 1985)
W.J. Dumbrell, *Covenant and Creation* (Paternoster, 1984)
J. Bright, *Covenant and Promise* (SCM, 1977)

4

Moses:
Foundational Principles

W hen the people moved on from Sinai they took the values of Sinai with them.

The Indwelling God

The Lord who came to the people at Sinai (Exod. 19:18) continued to live among them (Exod. 29:42-46). The Tabernacle – its plan (Exod. 25–31) and its manufacture (Exod. 35–40) – does not make for fascinating reading, but it expresses one of the Bible's greatest truths, the reality of the indwelling God.

Numbers 2 provides a plan of the camp of Israel in the wilderness days, and it is simplest to think of a cruciform pattern with the Judah-tribes, in a line to the east (vv. 3-9), the Reuben-tribes southward (vv. 10-16), Ephraim with Manasseh and Benjamin stretching out to the west (vv. 18-24), and the line of the northern tribes under the leadership of Dan (vv. 25-31).

At the crossing, the very heart of the camp, is God's tent (v. 17). The picture is beautiful; the reality is daunting, for if 'the LORD your God is walking about within your camp' then 'your camp must be holy' and 'he must not see in you anything to offend' (Deut. 23:14). The historical event of Sinai would recede back into history but the reality of the Sinai experience remained with them.

THE HOLY GOD

God's revelation of himself at Sinai is of a holy God. Probably the basic idea of 'holiness' is separation, but since this prompts the question, 'Separate from what?' – making holiness a rather negative idea – it is better to think of radical distinctiveness. Not only the Lord but the 'gods' all claimed this radical distinctiveness: distinctiveness of sphere, of character, of requirements.

One of the few places where holiness is referred to is Genesis 38:21 in the brilliantly told story of Judah's moral collapse. Not knowing that the girl who caught his eye was his daughter-in-law, Judah thought he would indulge himself with a prostitute (v. 15, Hebrew *zonah*, the ordinary word for prostitute). When, however, his friend went on Judah's behalf to pay the girl and could not find her, he asked, 'Where is the holy girl?' (v. 21; Hebrew *qedeshah*). Then, as now, there were 'gods' approving of and requiring worship through sexual rites, and the men and women who gave their services to their gods in this way belonged to the divine sphere; they were 'holy'. For, basically, holiness simply means apartness, separateness, distinctiveness, belonging to the divine sphere of reality.

To the Lord, however, worship through 'holy girls' or 'holy men' (Deut. 23:17) was unthinkable. Rather, they were 'an abomination' (Deut. 23:18), for his was a different sort of holiness, the sort which, as soon as it was encountered, provoked a sense of sin, unworthiness and death (Isa. 6:3-5), in a word, ethical holiness.

The Sinai revelation of God's holiness had two focal points: sacrifices and law.

1. Sacrifices

The sacrificial system was a consequence of God's holiness. This alone enabled sinners to approach a holy God in safety.

Two passages in particular help us to enter into the conceptual world of the sacrifices.

a. Exodus 40:34–Leviticus 1:2

Moses had just completed the building of the Tabernacle, only to discover that when the Lord's glory came to occupy the tent (Exod. 40:35) not even he could enter. The Lord was dwelling at the centre of his people's camp but his 'glory', the manifestation of his holiness, excluded them from his presence. The divine nature itself seemed to nullify the whole purpose of the Tabernacle. Immediately, however, the Lord called from inside the tent (Lev. 1:1-2) to say (literally) 'when any one of you brings near what brings near to the Lord ...' The sacrifices were the Lord's provision by which those whom his holiness distanced from him could nevertheless 'draw near' to his presence.

b. Leviticus 17:11

The sacrifices are detailed fully in Leviticus 1:1–7:27 and their purposes are given: to 'make atonement' (Lev. 4:20, 26; 5:6, 10; etc.), to bring forgiveness (Lev. 4:20, 26, 31; 5:11, 13, 16; etc.), but Leviticus 17:11 offers a single comprehensive statement of their origin, purpose and efficacy. In a literal translation it reads as follows:

> For the life of the flesh is in the blood
> And I have myself given it to you, on the altar,
> To make atonement for your lives
> For it is the blood that makes atonement
> At the cost of the life / in the place of the life.

- 'Life' (lines 1, 3 and 5) translates nephesh, an individual centre or principle of life in animals or humans, often translated 'soul'. It is the union of 'flesh' and 'blood' (line one) and it is this union which constitutes a living creature so that when the union is sundered, death follows. 'Blood' separated from 'flesh' means death. The reference to the altar (line 2), the place of death, establishes that meaning here.

- The institution of sacrifice is a gift of God – not something we do to secure his favour, but a provision he makes for our need.

- The central purpose of the sacrifices is 'to make atonement' (line 3). The verb used here is a developed form of kaphar, 'to cover' (as in Gen. 6:14, where Noah 'covers' the ark with pitch). Arising from this verb, the noun kopher (as in Gen. 6:14 where it is translated as 'pitch') is 'that which covers'. But the noun extended its meaning to express the 'covering price' (Exod. 21:30; 30:12; Num. 35:31-32; Ps. 49:7), the price which, by 'covering' (providing an exact equivalent), meets and cancels a debt. Next, this extended meaning is expressed by kipper, the form of the verb in Leviticus 17:11. This means 'to make a kopher', 'to provide or pay the covering price'.

- The relation between that covering price and the sinner's need is expressed by the alternative translations in line 5. In the Hebrew the preposition 'be' can be used to express the price paid, 'at the expense of / at the cost of' (Num. 16:38; Josh. 6:26); but it can also express 'in the place of / in exchange for', as, for example, in the expression 'an eye for an eye' (Deut. 19:21). These two meanings, of course, lie very close together and both are applicable in Leviticus 17:11. Atonement – the payment of the price which covers the debt – is both 'at the expense of' the life of the sacrificial beast and 'in place of' the life of the sinner which, without such a substitutionary payment, would itself be forfeited.

THE DIVINE NAME

In the Old Testament God has many titles but only one name. In biblical thinking, a 'name' is often a summary statement of a person's character (for instance 1 Sam. 25:25!), and this is always true of the Divine Name, Yahweh. Once its significance was revealed (Exod. 3:13-15), it became a shorthand term for all that the Lord had made known about himself.

1. IN GENESIS

From Genesis 4:26 onwards the Divine Name appears in Genesis 116 times. The patriarchs knew the name and used it (for instance Gen. 14:22; 15:2). Yet study of Genesis shows that though they used the name, it was not yet the vehicle of divine revelation; for example, in Genesis 17:1 we read, 'Yahweh appeared to Abram and said to him, "I am El Shaddai".' They could call their God 'Yahweh' but they knew him as El Shaddai (Gen. 17:1; 28:3; 35:11; 43:4). Indeed, the knowledge of God in Genesis is always couched in terms of El (God):

- El Elyon, 'God Most High' (14:18-22);
- El Bethel (31:13);
- El Roi, 'God of Seeing' (16:13);
- El Olam, 'God of Eternity' (21:33)
- El Elohe Israel, 'God, the God of Israel' (33:20).

THE ALMIGHTY GOD

The meaning of Shaddai as a word remains uncertain, but a study of the occasions on which it occurs reveals its meaning when applied to God. The basic idea is clearly almightiness, but it is almightiness related specifically to human incapacity, transforming helpless humans, and standing by divine promises. El Shaddai is the God who is powerful where and when humans are at their weakest.

2. FOR MOSES

At the end of forty years in Midian, Moses found himself confronted by God (Exod. 3:1). He was to return to Egypt as Israel's liberator. Seeking to excuse himself from such a daunting task, Moses pleaded in turn:

- Inability (3:11-12);
- Ignorance (3:13-17);
- Ineffectiveness (4:1-9);
- Hesitancy of speech (4:10-12);
- A longing that anyone else at all should go rather than he (4:13).

Moses posed a strange problem: when he went to the people in the name of the 'God of their fathers' – the revelation of God in Genesis – they would ask him, 'What is his name?' Of course, we do not know why he thought they would do this, and can only surmise. Was the name 'Yahweh' a secret kept in Israel, which even Moses did not know, and which, therefore, they could use to test the genuineness of any claimant to a revelation? Or were they using 'name' just as a convenient way of asking, 'What revelation of God do you bring?' In any case, the meaning of the name was first revealed to Moses. This is the intention of Exodus 6:2-3, literally, 'By my name, Yahweh, *I did not make myself known to them.*' Yahweh was previously known only as a title but not as a name, encapsulating a revelation of God.

3. 'I AM WHO I AM'

With the form of this enigmatic revelation, compare Exodus 33:19, 'I will be gracious to whom I will be gracious, and compassionate to whom I am compassionate.' The additional relative clause is intended to emphasise the absolute freedom of the Lord in selecting the objects of his grace. It is equivalent to saying, 'I will be gracious, totally and absolutely, at my own discretion.'

In Exodus 3:14-15 the verb is the Hebrew verb 'to be', which, while it affirms existence, much more means 'active presence'. Hence, 'I am the actively present One, as, when and how I choose to be.' In Exodus 3:14-15 the first person singular of the verb 'I am' (*'ehyeh*) modulates into the third person singular, 'He is' (*Yahweh*). The Lord can say, 'I', but his people will say, 'He'. The Divine Name, then, affirms presence and action, but raises the question: What sort of action?

4. THE LORD REVEALED

The coming acts in which the Lord will reveal his presence and action are specified as those of the Exodus:

- Deliverance (3:16-17a);
- Inheritance (3:17b);
- Judgmental overthrow (3:19-20).

Note that the meaning of the name is revealed before any revelatory acts take place. Israel is not expected to look for actions, hope they identify them correctly and then try to deduce a theology from them.

Rather, their task is first to grasp in the mind what has been verbally revealed, and then watch it working out in action. What the Lord does confirms what he has already said.

The revelation of the Divine Name in Exodus 3 as the God who delivers his people, keeps his promises and overthrows his enemies is amplified in Exodus 6:1-8 by the added thought of redemption and reconciliation to God (vv. 6-7).

5. YHWH

The post-Old Testament Jewish scruple about saying the Divine Name out loud is reflected in most English Bibles. Among the Jews the four consonants of the divine nature YHWH were customarily provided with the vowels of the Hebrew word for 'Lord' or 'Sovereign', *'adonay*. This led to the meaningless hybrid formation 'Jehovah' – a non-existent word or name. The scruple has been maintained: wherever the Hebrew uses Yahweh, the translators use capital letters, LORD; and wherever lower case letters are used, 'Lord', the Hebrew had *adonay*. Where the Hebrew has *adonay Yahweh*, 'the sovereign Yahweh', the translators put 'Lord GOD'. What complications arise when we foolishly refuse the high privilege he extends to us, to address our God by his name as he desires to be known (Exod. 3:15)!

Further reading

J.A. Motyer, *The Revelation of the Divine Name* (Tyndale, 1959)
U.E. Simon, *A Theology of Salvation*, p. 89 (SPCK, 1953)

The Laying on of Hands

This concept of substitution – one taking the place of another – is fundamental to the Mosaic sacrifices, as is seen by the fact that one of the constants of the ritual was the laying of the offerer's hand on the head of the animal to be offered (Lev. 1:4; 3:2, 8, 13; 4:4, 15, 24, 29, 33). As so often happens in biblical symbolism, the act is not only required but also explained.

The Day of Atonement. One day in the year was set apart as the Day of Atonement, an annual 'wiping of the slate clean'. Two goats were brought and one, selected by lot (Lev. 16:7-8), was killed. Its blood – the blood of price-paying – was then brought into the Holy of Holies and sprinkled on the 'atonement cover' (kapporeth) of the Ark (Lev. 16:15). As at Passover (Exod. 12:13) and in the covenant-solemnisation ceremony (Exod. 24:6), this godward application of the blood was a propitiation, satisfaction and reconciliation, meeting the requirements of the holiness of God by a covering payment.

But in Leviticus 16 the sprinkling of the blood on the atonement-cover was unseen by those on whose behalf atonement was being made. The merciful God therefore appointed a visible ceremony whereby the watching people might know what had taken place secretly. The second goat was brought forward and Aaron laid his hands on its head (Lev. 15:21), confessing all Israel's sins and 'putting them on the head of the goat' which thus became 'sin-bearing' (16:22). The goat then carried their sins off into the desert, and was never seen again.

The laying on of hands was thus an act of appointing, acknowledging and creating a substitute, and of transferring sin and guilt. The principle of substitution is the living heart of the whole sacrificial system: the innocent in the place of the guilty.

THE SACRIFICES

BURNT-OFFERING

The burnt-offering is fundamental among the offerings commanded by the Lord, as is seen by the fact that it appears as a component of the peace-offering (Lev. 3:3), the sin-offering (for example, Lev. 4:8-10) and the satisfaction-offering (Lev. 7:3-5). In itself the burnt-offering brings three leading ideas together:

- Atonement (Lev. 1:4);
- Acceptance by God (Lev. 1:4);
- Consecration.

Consecration is the inherent idea, seen spectacularly in Genesis 22:13, 16. The burnt-offering expresses holding nothing back from the Lord: hence in Hebrew, 'olah', the 'going up', so called because the sacrificial beast in its entirety was consumed on the altar and ascended in the smoke. Noah's burnt-offering was a 'sweet smell' to the Lord (Gen. 8:20-21; Lev. 1:13), an idea continued in the affirmation that the burnt-offering is 'with a view to his acceptance (with favour) before the LORD' (Lev. 1:3).

PEACE-OFFERING OR FELLOWSHIP-OFFERING (Lev. 3)

This focuses on the enjoyment of peace with God and with other people. Unlike the other offerings, apart from the token burnt-offering, the meat of the sacrifice was for the fellowship meal (compare Deut. 12:7).

It is in connection with fellowship-offerings that Leviticus first dares to use the anthromorphism, 'the bread of the offering ... unto the LORD' (Lev. 3:11), metaphorically expressing the idea that the Lord was bidden to the feast, just as the offerer was obliged to include a wide range of others.

SIN-OFFERING

The sin-offering provided for forgiveness: specific offences (for example, Lev. 4:23) were brought to the Lord and forgiveness resulted (Lev. 4:20, 26, 31, 35). We need to remind ourselves that the Old Testament believer did not use the sacrifices as symbols, nor as an interim provision awaiting a perfect sacrifice, nor as foreshadowings of that sacrifice. The sin-offering was a divine provision (Lev. 17:11) to which was attached a divine promise (of forgiveness); in making his offering the believer rested in faith on that promise.

It took the genius of Isaiah to see that ultimately only a Person could substitute for persons in the matter of sin: hence Hebrews 10:1-18. Old Testament believers rested in faith on what God promised, exactly as we rest in faith on the promises he has centralised at Calvary.

THE SATISFACTION-OFFERING (LEV. 5:14–6:7)

The central meaning here is exemplified in the fact that there were situations in which the sacrifice godward needed to be accompanied by reparation manward (6:4-6). Hence the central thrust of this sacrifice was the total satisfaction of every claim that sin might exercise upon the sinner: every offence to God and to people was covered.

THEIR ORDER

It is interesting to note the order in which the offerings are mentioned:

- In Exodus 29:14, 18, 28 and Leviticus 9:8, 11, 18, it is sin-offering, burnt-offering and peace-offering. This is the order of human need: from our point of view we are ever aware of sin, and only when sin has been dealt with can we then consecrate ourselves to God and enter into peaceful fellowship.
- In Leviticus 6:9, 24; 7:11, it is burnt-offering, sin-offering and peace-offering. This is the order of priestly duty: twice daily, burnt-offerings must be offered on the Lord's altar where a perpetual fire must be maintained. Constantly sinners needed the priestly ministry of the sin-offering, leading them into peace with God.
- In Leviticus 1:3; 3:1; 4:3 it is burnt-offering, peace-offering, sin-offering. This is the order of divine desire: the Lord looks for a people wholly yielded to him, and enjoying fellowship with him

and with each other. In mercy, he provides a sin-offering to cater for their lapses from that holy obedience which is their great priority.

Further reading
R. Vasholz, *Leviticus* (Christian Focus, 2007)
P. Wells, *Cross Words* (Christian Focus, 2006)
G.J. Wenham, *Leviticus* (Eerdmans, 1979)
F.D. Kidner, *Sacrifice in the Old Testament* (Tyndale, 1952)

2. Law
The law also was a consequence of God's holiness.

Law and Freedom
We have already noted that the giving of the law followed the work of redemption. It cannot be said too often that in the Old Testament (as in the New) the law is not a ladder of merit whereby we try to climb into God's good books; it is a way of life revealed for those who by his saving grace are already accepted by him.

Exodus 20:2 expresses this in terms of liberation: the law is not a bondage imposed, but a sign that bondage is at an end. When the Lord has brought his people 'out of the house of bondage', he reveals his law. As we have seen, the Garden of Eden is the perfect illustration of this principle: as long as Man and Wife obeyed the law of the garden (Gen. 2:16f.), they enjoyed the liberty of the garden. Liberty is not found in freedom from law but comes through the 'law of liberty' (James 1:25; 2:12), the law that liberates (compare Ps. 119:45).

Law and Likeness
This nexus of law and liberty finds its explanation in the nature of the law which the Lord gives his people. Leviticus 19 is the key. It is a strange chapter, a mixum-gatherum of all life. Without apparent concern for logical order, it covers family life (v. 3), religion (vv. 4-8), charity (v. 9f.), theft, oath-taking (vv. 11-12), finance (v. 13), care in society (v. 14), the courts (v. 15), gossip and testimony (v. 16), hatred in the heart, vengefulness (vv. 17-18), cattle-breeding, agriculture, clothing (v. 19), sexual misdemeanour (vv. 20-22), arboriculture

(vv. 23-25) – and, with the same apparent whimsicality of selection, continues through to commercial honesty in verses 35f. Yet there is a point to the muddle – life itself is like that, and any day, resisting neat programming, will present us with just such mixed experiences and responsibilities.

Who God Is

The heaped-up regulations have, however, one thing in common: the recurring reminder, 'I *am* the LORD' / 'I *am* the LORD your God' (vv. 3, 10, 12, 14, 16, 18, 24, 25, 28, 30-32, 34-37 NKJV). Our immediate thought is to see this as a statement of authority: I am the Lord: it is for me to dictate and for you to obey (compare Deut. 6:1-2), but that is not the point here. 'LORD', with four upper-case letters, is the conventional representation of the Divine Name, Yahweh, with its stated 'explanation' (Exod. 3:14 NKJV) 'I AM WHO / [what] I AM.' The sanction behind the various laws in Leviticus 19 is not divine power or status but divine character: this is what you must be because I am what I am. Every law in the glorious profusion of Leviticus 19 in one way or another derives from and expresses the nature of the divine Lawgiver. They are not arbitrary regulations snatched out of the air but are part of what we may call the 'preceptual image of God', the nature of God revealed in the commands of God.

Take an unlikely example, the seventh commandment. The Bible is clear that sexuality is not part of the divine nature, so how does a prohibition of adultery reflect the Lawgiver? In this way: that marriage is a covenant (e.g. Mal. 2:14); and adultery is covenant-breaking, a violation of the character of the God who cannot break his word (Num. 23:19). So the seventh commandment arises from and expresses the inflexible fidelity of the Lord.

The law, then, is a particular statement of what God is like. It is the image of God spelt out in the commands of God. Consequently, it is the perfect law for human beings who were 'made in the image of God'.

Obedience

It is the bringing together of the two images of God and man; it is the pattern of the true human life because it is the pattern (in principle) of the divine nature. The 'text' of which Leviticus 19 is the 'sermon' is God's words in verse 2: 'You must be holy because I the LORD your God *am* holy.' Obedience is the way in which we match our lives to his; obedience conforms us to the 'preceptual image of God', and therefore 'triggers' in us the created image of God which is our true nature.

The Law of Liberty

In obeying his law, we become what we truly are. This is, of course, what James meant when he wrote of Christians 'looking into the law of liberty' (1:25), and of living as those who will be judged by 'a law of liberty' (2:12 NKJV). The essence of freedom is to 'be yourself'. The validity of this principle, however, depends on first reaching a correct definition of what 'yourself' means. The definition of our true nature is the biblical revelation of human-kind 'in the image of God'. Therefore the 'law that liberates' is the law that matches and derives from the divine nature itself.

This needs a little further exploration, and we will give ourselves the excitement of pursuing it.

DEUTERONOMY

AUTHORSHIP
Deuteronomy makes a strong and all-pervasive claim to be the words of Moses but no book has been more confidently denied to Moses by the majority of modern specialists.

CONTENT
The book is continuous with Genesis to Numbers. Israel is poised to enter the Promised Land, and Moses, himself forbidden to enter, offers his final instructions for life in the land. This homiletical, oratorical setting of Deuteronomy accounts for the way it adapts and develops (though without contradicting) preceding legislation. The Decalogue (Deut. 5) is a case in point.

EDITORIAL COMMENTS
As a book, there are clear signs of editing (1:1; 4:44; 29:1; 31:30; 33:1). Moses could, of course, himself have provided these editorial divisions,

but it is more sensible to see a later editor at work, accounting also for the narrative of Moses' death, along with other concluding comments (34:1).

DEUTERONOMY AND KING JOSIAH

Noting the discovery of the Book of the Law in Josiah's day (621 BC, 2 Kings 22:8, compare Deut. 28:61) specialists have thought it right to date Deuteronomy, also called 'the book of the law', in some proximity to that discovery. But this is not a foregone conclusion:

- There is a moral problem in setting a late date, that is not answered by the confident assertion that to ascribe a later book to Moses would have been a recognised device to claim authority for it. So much material in Deuteronomy is irrelevant to the time of Josiah (for example, the commands to exterminate the Canaanites and their religion) that this could only have been included as a deliberate fraud. The same applies to all the material in Deuteronomy now acknowledged to be ancient: Why would an author from Josiah's time dredge it up for the occasion if not to provide deceptive verisimilitude for his book?

- The factors involved in Josiah's reformation could equally well have been met by, say, the 'discovery' of Leviticus. The link with Deuteronomy is not obvious or inevitable. To claim, however, that substantially the whole Pentateuch was unearthed in the course of Temple renovation overlooks the fact that the book discovered there was then read before the king. We are clearly dealing with a volume of manageable length, but the identification with Deuteronomy and the conclusion that therefore Deuteronomy was a seventh-century production are not proven.

DEUTERONOMY AND HITTITE TREATIES

In the second millennium BC, Hittite kings were accustomed to impose treaties on their vassals. Generally they included:

1. A preamble, the parties to the treaty (compare Deut. 1:1-5);
2. A historical review, the relationship between the parties (Deut. 1:6–4:49);
3. General stipulations, the principles on which the continuing relationship would rest (Deut. 5–11);
4. Detailed stipulations (Deut. 12–26);
5. The gods called as witnesses to the treaty (compare Deut. 32:1);
6. Blessings following obedience and curses upon disobedience (Deut. 27:9–28:68).

7. The comparison with Deuteronomy, though not absolute, is striking, but the more significant point is that the Hittite treaties belong in the Mosaic period, and are a considerable make-weight in ascribing Deuteronomy fundamentally to Moses.

Further reading
A. **Harman**, *Deuteronomy* (Christian Focus, 2007)
G.T. **Manley**, *The Book of the Law* (Tyndale, 1957)
J.G. **McConville**, 'Deuteronomy', *New Bible Commentary* (IVP, 1994)
— *Grace in the End* (Paternoster, 1993)
J.A. **Thompson**, *Deuteronomy*, Tyndale Old Testament Commentary (IVP, 1974)
P.C. **Craigie**, *The Book of Deuteronomy* (Hodder, 1976)

CREATION AND ITS CROWN

In Mosaic thought, then, there is the grace of God which redeemed (at the Passover), and shelters (in the life of obedience), and there is the donation of law to furnish the pattern for the redeemed life. The essence of covenant-living is the reflection in our lives of the likeness of the Lord who redeemed us and brought us within the circle of covenant grace. The foundation of all this lies in the narrative of creation where we see Mosaic revelation of 'the image of God' as the true definition of humanity.

One Only God

Genesis 1:1–2:3 would require a library of books to itself. Mystery unfolds upon mystery from the start, when God created both space ('heaven and earth') and time (the sequence of darkness and light), enabling the narrator to speak of even-ing yielding to morning on the first day, even before time and light were 'organised' into their normative form by the ordinance of sun and moon (vv. 14-18).

The Creator is the source of the purposeful development of the creation. The initial material substrate which he created was tohu and bohu, defined in Jeremiah 4:23-26 as dark (v. 23), unstable (v. 24), without human, animal or vegetable life (vv. 25-26). Out of this apparent meaninglessness, step by step, the Creator made an ordered, meaningful world in which everything is both where and what it is by his expressed will ('God said', vv. 3, 6, 9, 11, 14, 20, 24, 26 NKJV; 'God called', vv. 8, 10, compare Ps. 33:6, 9; 148:5-6 NKJV).

Furthermore, God so organised the initial creation that its developing life still remains within the parameters of his original design. His vegetable creation contains its own seed, and is restricted within its own kind.

These three insistences – the creation of the whole, the dominance of the Creator's expressed will and the provision within the initial creation for the ongoing life of creation – are, of course, fundamental to its monotheistic testimony. Marduk, the Babylonian creator-god, was obliged to clear the field of opposing 'divine' forces before he could begin to create. Genesis knows nothing of any power outside the will of the sole Creator God. Nor are other spiritual entities responsible, as in polytheism, for differing items or aspects of the created order. The astral deities of paganism are fancies derived from the awesome magnificence of the Lord's created heavens. The fertility gods of Canaan are ruled out by the in-built factor of fertility in the initial creative act of the one God. It is out of this contrast between the nonentities and the only God that Psalm 96:5 can say, 'The gods of the peoples are imitation-gods' – not elohim but elilim! – bogus pretenders with hollow claims; but, 'THE LORD made the heavens!!' (emphatic in Hebrew)

Design and Purpose

With careful, purposeful balance the work of creation moves forward: the light and darkness of day one (vv. 3-5) are brought within the formal organisation of sun and moon on day four (vv. 14-19); the distinct spatial realities of sky and water (day 2, vv. 6-8) become the habitat of birds and fish (day 5, vv. 20-23); the establishment of the firm earth (day 3, vv. 9-13) with its crucial capacity for fertility becomes the home of land animals and the stage for human life (day 6, vv. 24-30). In this way the great account of creation reaches its intended climax: a creature bearing the divine 'image' (vv. 26-27).

The Image of God

This 'image' is not something humankind possesses, but is what humankind is. It is not this or that part or capacity, but the whole.

Outward Shape.

It starts outwardly with appearance and shape as the words 'image and likeness' uniformly demand. This is not, of course, to say that God exists in an outward form, or that visibility is part of the divine essence. God is Spirit (Isa. 31:3; John 4:24). But, throughout the Old Testament, the Lord from time to time clothes himself with visibility, and wherever he does so the form is human. When Manoah's wife says that 'a man' came to her, the 'man' is discovered to be the 'Angel of the LORD' and Manoah is overcome by having 'seen God' (Judg. 13:22 NKJV).

But this is not a divine condescension – God taking human form to 'accommodate' himself to humankind. It is a revelation that there is a visible form that uniquely matches the invisible divine glory, and that humankind was created in that image and likeness. This is the dignity of the body in biblical thinking: the body in its outwardness is as much the 'person' as are the inward and intangible constituents of personhood.

Man and woman

Genesis 1:26, 28 links the image of God with the 'dominion' given to the human pair. The 'male and female' of verse 27 are addressed together in the plural imperatives of verse 28, so that 'dominion' belongs to the man and woman together. This concurs with the testimony of Genesis 5:1-2 that the matrimonial couple are in a special sense 'man' (Adam), and in their togetherness (as well as in their individuality) possess and display the image, blending and binding diversity in unity.

The human couple are personally addressed by the Creator ('said to them' 1:28, contrast v. 22 'and said'). Furthermore, in Genesis 2:16-17 the human pair alone in all creation live consciously under obligation to the law of God and the man begins to exercise dominion by distinguishing and categorising the animal creation with significant names (Gen. 2:19-20). The image of God, therefore, includes:

- The spiritual capacity to be addressed by God;
- The moral capacity to live under his law;
- The rational capacity to study and order the world around.

GENESIS 1 AND 2

It is commonplace to speak of Genesis 1 and 2 as 'two accounts of creation' and then to show ways in which they are contradictory.

SUPPOSED CONTRADICTIONS

1. The literary style of 1:1–2:4a is measured prose-poetry; Genesis 2:4b-25 is annalistic;

2. The first 'account' has a majestic, transcendent view of the Creator, contrasting sharply with the homely, companionable God of the second;

3. In the first account the creation of humankind comes last; in the second, the man is already present at the beginning.

The conclusion is therefore drawn that the two accounts belonged originally to two disparate and contradictory sources.

A HARMONIOUS RELATIONSHIP

The observations made about the two chapters are plainly correct, but the conclusion drawn is erroneous.

1. The meaning of Genesis 2:4a. Traditionally translated, 'These are the generations of', as a formula it recurs in Genesis 5:1; 6:9; 10:1, 32; 11:10, 27; 25:12, 19; 36:1, 9; 37:2. In all of these places it is best understood as introducing what follows.

2. The meaning of the word toledoth ('generations'). Arising from the verb yalad, 'to bring forth, give birth to', the form of the noun obliges it to mean 'what emerges', and hence, not simply 'story' or 'history' but 'subsequent story', 'emergent history', or, simply, 'what happened next'.

CONCLUSION

Genesis 2:4-25 is the story emerging from Genesis 1:1–2:3. We 'emerge' from the formal, God-centred, statement of the work of creation into the reality of the inhabited earth. The work of creation is God-centred and the Creator is transcendent in relation to his created universe. What emerged was a world centred on human activity, in which the Creator condescends to come down and walk alongside. Logically, humankind is the climax of the creative enterprise. Far from contradicting each other, Genesis 1:1–2:3 and 2:4-25 belong together in an ordered, balanced presentation.

Why the Fall Was Serious

The silence of Genesis 1 as to why God created heaven and earth in the first place is matched by the silence of Genesis 3 as to why he permitted the tempter to tempt and the first couple to fall. The Bible rarely tells us all we would like to know; it always tells us what we need to know. In this case, we learn that there was a tempter and a temptation, and that by falling into sin the first couple involved the whole of their posterity, generation after generation to come.

How could such a simple, single act of taking forbidden fruit bring such dire consequences? Was this a case of divine overreaction? No. Two facts must be recognised.

a.   The law of the forbidden tree was the sole law of the Garden: there was no other.
Outside this single prohibition lay that whole world of liberty and liberality.

b.   The woman began by acquiescing in the serpent's slur on the character of God (Gen. 3:5).
Adam and his wife had not yet been recipients of a fully orbed revelation of God, but one thing they did know: God is good. They had experienced the sheer benevolence of God in providing the woman for the man and the Garden for them both. But when the serpent maligned the Lord God by insinuating that his benevolence was but a veneer behind which, fearful for his own position, he was holding humankind back from its proper dignity of godlikeness (3:4-5), the woman proffered no denial. Then the temptation itself came (3:6):

- Human emotions were drawn to what was forbidden ('Good for food ... pleasing to the eye');
- The human mind contradicted the divine mind by logically concluding that a tree of knowledge must 'make one wise', whereas the divine logic had said that it would bring death (2:17);
- The human will surrendered and took the fruit.

In this way the whole law of God was broken, and the divine character as known was contradicted by the whole human personality, emotions, mind and will.

Dreadful results followed:

- Openness (2:25) became secretiveness (3:7);
- A good conscience before God was lost (3:8-10);
- Childbirth became agony (3:16);
- Ecstatic delight (2:23) became sullen resentment (3:12);
- The proper balance of creation (3:15) and of marriage (3:18) was destroyed;
- The economic basis of life was ruined (3:17-19);
- The Garden was exchanged for the outside world (3:24);
- Humankind is discovered to be sinful by birth (4:5-8);
- Sin now arises in the heart without any external tempter (4:8);
- Marriage is corrupted by polygamy (4:19);
- Death prevails even over the utmost longevity (5:5; etc.);
- Sinfulness goes beyond earthly bounds and becomes cosmic (6:1-4);
- All humankind is wicked to the heart (6:5), a grief to the Lord (6:6) and justly under judgment of death (6:7).

THE TALKING SERPENT

Genesis describes vividly how the woman was addressed and tempted by a talking serpent. What are we to make of this? When Genesis 3:15 speaks of the 'crushing of the serpent's head' it is speaking metaphorically of the final defeat of 'that ancient serpent, the devil, or Satan', by whatever means his usurpation will be terminated. Is the whole of Genesis 3, then, metaphorical?

In reply to the question, 'Did a serpent really talk to her?' the answer is that something or somebody must have done. In that original, innocent, 'good' and 'very good' couple there was no internal voice of temptation. They were not yet what we, by inheritance and entail from them, have become. Were Satan, then, to have manifested himself in his own person (if he can do such a thing), he would have inevitably lost the contest before it had started. He had to conceal his evil nature and evil intent behind some innocuous reality. A voice apparently coming out of the goodness and beauty of the created order offered his best hope of success.

It is simplest, and fairest to the Genesis history, to accept the talking serpent. The Bible is very sparing in its accounts of the miraculous, and, compared with other ancient literatures, virtually free of mythical 'wonders'. We should come, therefore, to the serpent in Genesis 3 and to Balaam's ass (Num. 22:30), with neither credulity nor incredulity, but with sober acceptance in the light of the Bible's serious record.

Further reading

J.A. Motyer, *Look to the Rock* (IVP, 1996)

G.J. Wenham, *Genesis* (Word Books, 1987)

The Unchanged God

We noted in chapter 3 that the onset of rebellion and sin made no difference to divine sovereignty. But neither did it make any difference to divine goodness. At the very moment when the edict of death (2:16-17) should have been enforced (3:15), the Lord chose to speak of ongoing life and of the coming deathblow to the usurping serpent. Likewise, when the whole human race is diagnosed, wept over and condemned (6:5-7), divine grace singles out Noah and his family for salvation (6:8) within a covenant that embraces 'all flesh' (9:17), and, even though sinful self-sufficiency has taken control of human thinking (11:1-9), a divine purpose is unobtrusively (11:10-26) moving forward to the man, Abram, in whom all peoples will come into blessing (12:3).

Moses

Surely it is impossible to review the Pentateuch as we have done, to discover its internal cohesion, to feel something of the depth and breadth of its concerns and concepts, without also sensing behind it a single personality of unique stature and an intellect matching the architectural dimensions of this mighty literature. Someone rightly said that if Moses himself had not been mentioned we would have to invent him. To this man we owe not only the foundational principles of biblical theology, and the unchanged, even if expanding, river of revelation, but the programme in embryo of which the whole Bible is itself expanded text.

Further reading

The Holy God
J.R.W. Stott, *The Cross of Christ* (IVP, 1987)
L. Morris, *The Apostolic Preaching of the Cross* (Tyndale, 1955)
G.J. Wenham, *The Book of Leviticus* (Eerdmans, 1979)
P. Jensen, *Graded Holiness* (Sheffield, 1992)

Creation and its Crown
F.D. Kidner, *Genesis*, Tyndale Old Testament Commentary (IVP, 1967)
G.J. Wenham, *Genesis* (Word, 2 vols, 1987, 1994)
K. Matthews, *Genesis 1–11*, New American Commentary (Broadman, 1996)
J.A. Motyer, *Look to the Rock* (IVP, 1996)
W. Eichrodt, *Man in the Old Testament* (SCM, 1951)

5

History Is His Story

World War II is a matter of fact; telling the story of World War II is a matter of selection; understanding World War II – why it happened, who 'won' it – is a matter of interpretation. Whenever anyone undertakes to write narrative history these three things are involved.

Facts

First, the historian must assemble his facts and try to establish what actually happened, for, as the German historian Otto Ranke insists, the historian's overriding concern is 'how it really was'. If we may use the word 'sacred' of the work of the historian, the facts are sacred or, as David Bebbington puts it, the evidence must 'discipline' the writing.

Selection

'Selection is the essence of writing history' (Tuchman). This has to be so because it would be impossible to set down the totality of all that happened in a single day, never mind a year or an age. But there is more to it than that.

Every historian, faced with the huge array of facts that make up any period of time, has to decide what is the 'essential story', and therefore what is central and what is peripheral. At this point the skill and the integrity of the historian become crucial: the skill to separate wheat from chaff, significant from insignificant, and the integrity to keep prejudice at bay, to acknowledge the inevitability of bias and yet to avoid the tendentiousness which manipulates the facts in order to grind a personal axe.

One has only to read diaries edited for publication by their authors, or memoirs published by central characters in great events, to see what a narrow line divides 'what happened' from 'what I would like to have happened', or 'how others will remember me' from 'how I would like to be remembered'.

What a delicate and difficult matter it is, then, to write history!

INTERPRETATION

The presentation of narrative history involves the same story-telling art as that of a novelist, for narrative history is the art of telling a story but, unlike fiction, the facts pre-date the telling, and their relative importance, their inter-connections, and, up to a point, their chronology must control the art of the narrator. Chronology is possibly the main area where the given facts and the artistry of the historian most often come into tension for, to quote Tuchman again, while 'events do not happen in categories; they happen in sequence', yet, 'sometimes, to create a proper emphasis, the crucial event and the causative circumstance have to be reversed ... One must juggle with time.'

KEY DATES

According to the usually accepted dates:

BC	
1300	Moses
1150	Joshua
	Judges

1045	Saul
1000	David
960	Solomon
930	The divided kingdom
	Israel:
722	The fall of Samaria to Assyria
586	The fall of Jerusalem to Babylon
539	The return from Exile

Further reading
See the excellent chronological chart in *New Bible Dictionary* (IVP, 1996)
The adjusted chronology of Roth, *A Test of Time* (Century, 1995) should at least be noted here and throughout the Key Dates in the coming chapters.

HISTORY AND BIBLE HISTORY

Since the great corpus of the Bible from Joshua to 2 Kings is an exercise in narrative history, it has been necessary to try to see it like this against the background of what today's narrative historians think about their chosen field.

Like all history, Bible history is also selective. At no point are we told all there is to know or all we might like to know. The highly selective and sometimes almost alarmingly brief accounts of the kings (e.g. 2 Kings 21:1-18) come from a much more extensive archive available to the historian (e.g. 1 Kings 11:41; 2 Kings 21:17), but, as we shall see, Joshua, Judges and Samuel-Kings exemplify respectively three typical approaches to narrative history:

- Does history have a 'message' (Joshua)?
- Does history expose a need for which a solution can be suggested (Judges)?
- What answer does history give to a key question (Samuel-Kings)?

THE LORD OF HISTORY

Before we allow the books to answer these questions, however, we must note two principles which the Old Testament affirms about the flow of history. We have already seen that the great attempt to throw off divine Lordship and to become autonomous (Gen. 3) made no difference to the sovereign rule of the Lord God. He who had been sovereign in benevolence, bestowing his bounty with an imperious love (Gen. 2), is now sovereign in reordering a world of sinners. If he did not consult Adam regarding his vocation to be a gardener or his need of a 'help meet for him', neither does he take note of the sinful couple's assumption that the Garden will afford them shelter (Gen. 3:8). He imposes on them the spiritual, economic and domestic consequences of what they have done, and blending sovereign justice with an equally sovereign mercy addresses those who merit death (2:17) in terms of life (3:15). The once so voluble serpent has nothing now to say.

Genesis 2 and 3 thus hold together the moral responsibility of humans and the unfettered sovereign rule of God. It fell to Isaiah (10:5-15) to give this view of history its classical expression.

1. God's Sovereignty

The bracketing verses (5, 15) assert total divine executive direction even of earth's superpowers, in this case, Assyria. So total is the Lord's sovereignty that only inanimate models will suffice: the king of Assyria, for all his imperial power, is but a stick, an axe and a saw in the hands of God. There is only one Lord of history, however the flux and mix of events and personalities might suggest otherwise.

2. God's Righteousness

The power that thus 'wields' Assyria is moral in intent. The rod is a rod of anger (v. 5), and the object of the anger is guilty Jerusalem (v. 6).

3. Conflict with Evil Powers

Though the Assyrian is the Lord's rod, axe and saw, there is yet a conflict of wills to be taken into account. The Lord's will is to use history as the arena of moral providence, punishing the guilty and using the forces within history to that end. The will of the king of Assyria, however (vv. 7-11), is to use history as an arena of self-aggrandisement and proud imperialism. In coming against Jerusalem he is not bowing to the will of God but rising in self-importance to fulfil his own sense of destiny, his self-assumed right to be the world-ruler. Therefore, the Assyrian will find that for him, too, history is the arena of divine moral providence in which his guilty pride will meet its reward (vv. 12-14).

In Isaiah 37:29b, dealing with this same incident, Isaiah hints at the illustration of horse and rider. These two distinct centres of energy and determination are so identified that in today's show-jumping ring the commentators can award the clear round either to the horse or to the rider. Yet, at the same time, the two are totally distinct, with all the energy and drive in the one and all the direction and control in the other. Thus the Lord 'rides' earth's grandees, giving to their individual and responsible powers the direction that makes them accord with his sovereign and moral purposes.

THE CREATOR AND HIS WORLD

The view that history is the arena of divine moral providence is basic to the Old Testament. Both in Moses' historical review in Deuteronomy 1–11, and in the definitive statement in Deuteronomy 27:1–30:15, the link is made between obedience and blessing, disobedience and cursing. It is subsequently restated, for example in Judges 2:11-23 and 2 Kings 17, as well as being exemplified in the details of the whole narrative of Joshua to 2 Kings. We live in God's world, where his moral rule prevails: virtue is rewarded and sin is punished.

Deuteronomic History

It is because they so clearly and frequently state the link, given in Deuteronomy, between obedience and blessing that the books of Joshua to Kings are often described by commentators as 'Deuteronomic history'. For the same reason, they are correctly called 'the Former Prophets', because they exist so to tell the story of Israel's history as to reveal the moral rule of the Lord over his people and his world. The description 'Deuteronomic' is not, however, wholly accurate, for this view of history is not at all exclusive to Deuteronomy; it runs throughout the Bible (e.g. Lev. 26) and is, indeed, the only view of 'how history works' that accords with the biblical doctrine of creation.

Why Is Suffering a Problem?

Based on Genesis 1–3, the rest of the Bible insists that we live in the world of a good and holy God, and this finds its echo in our own intuition. We feel it to be, not just a fact, but a problem when things are not 'fair'. We automatically want to know, 'What have I done to deserve this?' We face evil, wrong and suffering and ask, 'Where is God?' These instinctive reactions show that we have an innate awareness that God exists, that he rules and that he is good. It is this which gives rise to our sense of unease and questioning in the face of life's adversities.

It is this understanding of the world that allowed a poet to write Psalm 1 with its almost bland correlation of goodness and prospering (vv. 1-3), wickedness and perishing (vv. 4-6). This is certainly not intended to be a description of how things are or ever were, nor is it correct to understand it as a summary of how things ought to be: it is a statement of faith, a creedal statement of the same quality as the affirmation, 'I believe in God the Father Almighty', in a world – and often in personal experience – which suggests that he is anything but. It is the only fundamental view of the world and of history the Bible allows.

The Mercy of God – the Third Ingredient

Barry Webb, in his masterly study of the book of Judges, takes issue with a too-simple definition of the Deuteronomic view of history. There is more to it than a view of the Lord dispensing rewards and punishments with an even hand. History cannot be reduced to an equation (after the manner of Job's friends) whereby we can always forge the link between sin and suffering, goodness and prosperity. There is always a third factor alongside virtue or sin on the one hand, and due reward on the other. There is, marvellously, a ceaseless tension within the heart of God. The book of Judges, says Webb, 'is far from evincing a simple moralism ... a mechanical theory of history ... Yahweh *is* angry at Israel's apostasy but *cares too much for it* to let it disintegrate ... In the face of apostasy Yahweh does not so much dispense rewards and punishments as oscillate between punishment and mercy' (my italics).

Webb saw God's mercy and punishment in Judges, but it is as wide as the Bible: as we have seen, the edict of death (Gen. 2:16-17) was blended into the ongoing saga of life with the promise of the Conqueror (Gen. 3:15). The final triumph of that Conqueror is 'held back' by the dominance of divine mercy to a fallen race (2 Pet. 3:8-9).

JOSHUA: HAS HISTORY A MESSAGE?

Historically and thematically, the book of Joshua is continuous with Deuteronomy. Joshua 1:1 picks up the narrative of the death of Moses (Deut. 34), the Lord's promises to Joshua – concerning the land (1:2-4) and concerning Joshua himself (1:5-6) – look back to Moses, and the place given to the 'book of the law' (1:7-8), and echo the Mosaic-Deuteronomic recipe for good success (e.g. Deut. 30:15-16). In a formal sense, then, Joshua tells 'what happened next'.

Fact and Interpretation

Narrative history, however, as we have seen, is essentially a blend of selection and interpretation. The historian cannot determine what facts are significant until he decides on a principle of selection. In the case of the book of Joshua, the anonymous historian found that the story he had to tell dictated the way the story should be told.

The Facts of the Conquest

Joshua records the history of the conquest of Canaan. It was mounted from a base camp at Gilgal by Jericho (1:1–5:12) in a three-pronged campaign against the centre (5:13–8:35), the south (9:1–10:43) and the north (11:1–23). The selection of facts is subject to this plan. Therefore, for example, the book concentrates on conquest (e.g. 12:1-24), but only hints at the quite separate and much more sporadic work of occupation (e.g. 13:1-6; 18:3).

The Meaning of Conquest

Of much more concern to the biblical historian is the interpretation of the facts he has selected – the story within the story. His narrative begins with a divine word to Joshua: the death of Moses makes no difference to the declared intention of God (1:2).

1. The promises made to Moses, going back to Abraham (Gen. 15:18), Isaac (Gen. 26:4) and Jacob (Gen. 28:13), still stand and, indeed, determine the way in which coming events will be shaped (1:3).

2. The presence of the Lord with his people guarantees the power inherent in the promises (1:5-6).

3. Joshua's fidelity to the word of God brings that same power into his own timorous experience (1:7-9).

We see this assurance worked out in the following chapters:

- The invincibility of the promises of God is Joshua's theme to the Reubenites (1:13-15);

- The same truth penetrated into Jericho (2:9-11). Rahab's reiterated 'we heard' (2:10-11) puts the power where it belongs. Well before the armies of Israel arrived, the word of God had already guaranteed victory.

- Before Jordan was crossed, Joshua pledged divine wonders (3:5) and affirmed that the divine promises would be kept (3:10). He heralded the event itself with the dramatic cry, 'Look! The ark of the covenant! The Sovereign of all the earth is crossing over before you into the Jordan!' (a literal translation of 3:11).

- The word which broke the spirit of Jericho continued its work in the kings of central Canaan (5:1). Contrary to the practice of any ordinary earthly commander, Joshua disabled his fighting men by circumcision (5:8), for their victory did not depend on human prowess but on their fidelity to the law of God and their inheritance of his promises.

- Jericho was conquered because by obedience (5:13–6:15) they received the divine gift (6:16).

- When obedience lapsed, defeat ensued (7:1-21). When disobedience had been dealt with (7:22-26), the sequence of obedience – gift (8:1) resumed.

- This committed obedience, which was the key to receiving the gift of God (8:7), was visibly enshrined in the very fabric of the land. Mounts Gerazim and Ebal respectively were identified with the blessing that follows obeying God's law and the curse upon disobedience (8:30-35). The historian labours to stress Israel's obligation to the whole word of God (8:34-35).

- The defeat of the southern (10:1-15) and northern (11:1-14) coalitions follows, and the completed conquest is explained by the fact that the Lord commanded Moses, Moses commanded Joshua, and Joshua left no command unobeyed (11:15-16, 23).

- The giving of Hebron to Caleb (14:6-15) brings the obedience-principle to bear on the individual. The Lord's promises are a secure basis for personal as well

as for national life. Incomplete obedience meant incomplete inheritance (16:10). But with resolute obedience no power could prevent the promised inheritance (17:14-18), because nothing could possibly fail
of anything the Lord had spoken (21:43-45). It is to
this awareness and to the matching life of obedience
that Joshua's final addresses summoned his people
(23:14). His 'great stone' once again centralised the
law of the Lord among the Lord's people (24:26-28).

JOSHUA AND THE CANAANITES

If the frightful slaughter inflicted by Joshua's armies on the inhabitants
of Canaan were recorded simply as a fact, we would still be appalled
but we would put it sadly down to 'man's inhumanity to man'. That
Joshua was obeying a command of God (Deut. 20:16-18; Josh. 10:40;
11:20) makes the event one of the major moral problems of the Old
Testament.

THREE COMMENTS

1. The slaughter of the Canaanites must be seen in the context of
    the Old Testament's worldview. In Genesis 15, when the Lord
    was promising the land of Canaan to Abram, he indicated that
    much must happen before the promise could be kept. There were
    experiences which, in divine providence, Abram's descendants
    had to pass through (15:13-14), but, even more to our point, there
    was the principle of the divine moral government of the world to
    be safeguarded: the centuries-long wait for the fulfilment of the
    promise was necessary because 'the iniquity of the Amorites has
    not yet reached its fullness' (15:16).

    The land of Canaan, in which Abram was a resident alien but
    which would one day be his, was at that point legally possessed
    by the Amorites. Were the Lord to implement his promise there
    and then, he would be an accessory before the fact of unlawful
    eviction and appropriation of another's property. In his long for-
    bearance, the Lord gave the Amorites centuries of probation and
    waited until their dispossession was a punishment justly due to
    their deeds.

2. The slaughter of the Canaanites belongs, therefore, to the revealed
    truth of divine moral government of the world. Before the Flood
    there was a clear moral assessment of the situation (Gen. 6:5-7);

> before the overthrow of Sodom, the Lord instituted a commission of enquiry (Gen. 18:20-21); the judgment which Amos foresaw on nations who had violated the laws of conscience and committed crimes against humanity was accompanied by itemised charges which they had to answer (Amos 1:2–2:3).
>
> 3. These are features of the Old Testament revelation which we must accept in a spirit of faith:
>
>   • We live in God's world;
>   • God is a holy God;
>   • No sin passes unrecorded;
>   • The history of the world is a divinely supervised arena of moral providence.
>
> **Further Reading**
> **D.R. Davis,** *Joshua* (Christian Focus, 2008)

The Facts Reveal the Message

Did the Joshua-historian, then, discover his message within the facts or did he manipulate the facts to produce the message?

Anyone who adopted the latter view would indeed be hard to please. Bible history is, of course, theological history: that is to say, it takes the presence of God in world affairs seriously and there can be no doubt about the historian's purpose. The book of Joshua was written to show that:

• The 'mainspring' of history is the purposeful rule of God;

• The course of history is determined by the fact that the Lord makes and keeps his promises;

• The first priority of the people of God is to align themselves obediently with his word.

JUDGES: HISTORY EXPOSES A NEED

The book of Judges is, of course, continuous with Joshua (Judg. 1:1), and its opening chapter deals selectively with a theme already announced in Joshua (16:10; 18:3), namely, the partial occupation and settlement of the totally conquered land. But it would be far from true to say that Judges was written simply to fill a gap that would otherwise exist in the historical record. In its own right the book is a unified work of the historian's art.

Failure and Mercy

From its earliest days in Canaan, Israel lapsed from obedience (1:1-36), and needed to be called to repentance (2:1-5). This turned out to be the pattern of their life in the promised land (2:1-23). There was constant rebellion but an equally constant mercy of God for his fragile people shown in his sending judge-saviours to deliver them. The central section of the book (3:1–16:31) offers a review of the work of these judges and in 17:1–21:25 the historian returns to his opening theme of Israel's failure, offering selected episodes to illustrate specific areas of disobedience.

Life at the Top: the Judges

The book of Judges is best remembered for the great stories of the named Judges and their deeds of derring-do, but the book does not hide the fact that, striking as were their achievements, they were essentially failures.

The attractive *Othniel* gave the land forty years' respite (3:11), as did *Deborah* and *Barak* (5:31), and *Gideon* (8:28). The dour *Jephthah* only managed six years (12:7), and the buffoon *Samson* twenty years (16:31). The promise was that Samson would 'begin to save Israel' (13:5) and that is all he did. Indeed this is a fitting epitaph for all the Judges.

The Verdict on the Judges

The work of the Judges was episodic, their results limited, their effect temporary, and their lives and characters showed the prevalence of sin and error alongside that element of faith which is all that Hebrews 11 commends. Great stories, great leaders, great failures!

Meanwhile, at the Grass Roots …

The move from the end of chapter 16 into chapters 17–21 is comparable to stepping out of strong sunlight into a dark, dank cellar, from fresh air into the smell of decay. This would seem to be the author's intention. What was going on at ground level while the charismatic judges were reaching for their glittering prizes?

- 17:1-13. It was a time of religious declension and apostasy, with illicit shrines served by renegade Levites.

- 18:1-31. It was a time of social unrest and violence in which the theological basis of land tenure was forgotten (Lev. 25:23). What the discontented wanted, they grabbed.

- 19:1-30. It was a time of moral collapse. As the story of the Levite develops it goes beyond sexual misconduct (19:1-2) to sexual depravity (19:22) and unspeakable grossness (19:25).

- 20:1–21:25. It was a time of national division, arbitration by the sword, solutions fudged and problems left unsolved.

The verdict on the people
The disobedience of the people to the Lord's command to occupy (Judg. 1–2) masked deeper disobediences (Judg. 17–21), issuing in all-embracing declension and corruption.

The Need and the Solution
As the Judges-author sees it, then, history exposes a need covering religion, society, morality and nationhood. History also indicated, he noted, that the answer does not lie in episodic leadership, however God-given, talented and momentarily successful.

What then? The author proposes his solution. As he traces the fourfold collapse of the Lord's people in chapters 17–21, he inserts in each section a telling comment:

- 17:6. In those days there was no king in Israel: every man did what was right in his own eyes.

- 18:1. In those days there was no king in Israel.
- 19:1. In those days ... there was no king in Israel.
- 21:25. In those days there was no king in Israel: every man did what was right in his own eyes.

The form of these comments, with the first and the fourth and the second and third matching, indicates that the author understands himself to be offering a balanced solution to the ills history has exposed. If only we had a king!

SAMUEL TO KINGS: THE SEARCH FOR A KING
The book of Judges must surely be a very early piece of writing. It could well have preceded the institution of monarchy in Israel as part of a national groundswell of longing, reflected in 1 Samuel 2:10 and finally given expression in 1 Samuel 8:5. This is the setting in which the book would be most comfortable.

Alternatively, Judges might belong to the honeymoon period of the reigns of Saul, David or Solomon. But the later years of these kings indicate failure at one or other of the points of need exemplified in Judges 17–21.

- Saul succeeded religiously (1 Sam. 28:3) but failed nationally.
- David unified the nation round himself and Jerusalem, but failed morally (2 Sam. 11–12).
- Solomon, after a brilliant start, failed religiously (1 Kings 11:1-8).
- The egregious Rehoboam (1 Kings 12) brought about the sundering of the kingdom.

After that, who could plead monarchy as the solution to anything?

The Search for the Ideal King
Nevertheless the solution proposed by Judges would not go away, and it determined how the historian presented the books of Samuel and Kings.

THE BOOK OF RUTH

Ruth is placed in the third section of the Hebrew canon, but the attempt by the Greek translators of the Septuagint to be more logical in the order of the books succeeded in this case. Ruth forms a perfect bridge from Judges to Samuel for its narrative begins (1:1 NKJV), 'in the days when the judges ruled', and it ends (4:22) by emphasising Ruth's own position as David's great-grandmother.

The history of Ruth is told in a way that brings out certain important emphases.

- There is another side to the picture of corruption painted in Judges 17–21. There were still individual people whose devotion to Yahweh was fresh and pure – the sort of faith Ruth learnt from her husband and in-laws (1:16-17; 2:12). There were still communities where greeting in the name of Yahweh was naturally given and sincerely reciprocated (2:4), and where the provisions of his law were observed (3:12; 4:1-6). Even in those days of spiritual decline and apostasy, the Lord had not left himself without witness.

- The genealogy in 4:18-22 sums up another part of the book's purpose. Reaching back to the story of Judah's shame and the birth of Perez (v. 18, Gen. 38), it moves on through the unknowns, Hezron to Nashshon, alludes to Salmon who married Rahab, the erstwhile prostitute from Jericho (Matt. 1:5), and, recording four more generations, concludes with the birth of David.

How strangely and yet infallibly the Lord works out his purposes! Judah's thoughtless immorality; the people of whom we know nothing; the famine which drove Naomi from home (1:1-2); the bereavements which brought her back with just a daughter-in-law (1:5-19), as she thought, empty (1:21); the 'chance' of their arrival at harvest (1:22) which threw Ruth and Boaz together (2:3) – who but the Lord would devise such a strange and wonderful sequence? People we wouldn't choose, experiences we wouldn't want, events we did not plan ... and all are part of a detailed providence, to bring the chosen king to Jerusalem (4:22), and the Messiah to the world (Matt. 1:1-17).

- But we must not overlook that the outworking of the Lord's purpose, though pre-planned and irresistible, is not an unfeeling Juggernaut, on its way regardless of individuals, trampling on feelings. 'When Naomi was finding life bleak and pointless,

Ruth chose to stand by her mother-in-law ... Tragedy in Moab led to a happy ending in Bethlehem ... God overruled events to bring love and security to those who trusted him ... weaving their lives into his purpose for the world ... at work in the ordinary affairs of daily life, fulfilling his promises to his people' (Baldwin).

THE LOVE STORY

• The book of Ruth is a beautifully told love story, a story to be read in its own right, which keeps the readers in suspense by the device of 'foiled climax'. Naomi succeeds in throwing Boaz and Ruth together (3:1-11) and we readers are excited and satisfied that, since she is ready to marry him and he only too willing to marry her, things have reached a happy ending. Unlike, of course, a novel reflecting today's customs, the happy couple do not there and then leap into bed. Ruth is a virtuous woman (3:11), and Boaz' part is to honour that virtue.

Consummation therefore waits – one of the special bitter-sweetnesses of the engagement period, as every biblically informed couple knows.

THE KINSMAN-REDEEMER

But there is more, a legal impediment (3:12), and this too must be honoured, for in all his dealings and providences, the Lord must remain 'just', true to himself and therefore to his own requirements. This brings us to the theological high spot in the book of Ruth, the law of the next of kin. Its background legislation is found in Leviticus 25, Numbers 35 and Deuteronomy 25.

When a person fell into financial hardship, and was obliged to sell either family land or even himself, or when someone was murdered, the immediate next of kin had the right to take as his own the financial problems or the duty of family vengeance. Deuteronomy extends this principle to the case of a childless widow. The point here is not loss of life or land but the disappearance of a man's name. It fell, then, to the nearest brother to accept the widow as his wife for the purpose of maintaining his brother's name and claim. Naomi was involved in the former set of circumstances – sale of family land in time of poverty (4:3-4); the childless Ruth is involved in the latter (4:5).

From the narrator's point of view, all this provides the delightful tension of Ruth 3 and 4, the 'will-he-won't he?' of suspense. But theologically, the point is that the Hebrew word for the next of kin is go'el and, in the Old Testament, the Lord is the go'el, the 'Kinsman-redeemer', the divine Next of kin, of his people. We can therefore

look at Boaz and see the Lord, the one who accepts the right to take
and bear as his own all that spells ruin, loss, hurt and difficulty to us.

Some references:
The verb *ga'al*, to redeem, used of the Lord: Exodus 6:6, 15:13; Isaiah
43:1; 44:22-23. The participle used as a noun, the 'kinsman-redeemer':
Psalm 19:14; Proverbs 23:11; Isaiah 41:14; 49:7, 26; 54:5.

Further reading
B. Davis and A. Luter, *Ruth and Esther* (Christian Focus, 2003)
J.G. Baldwin, *Ruth*, in New Bible Commentary (IVP, 1994)
D. Atkinson, *The Message of Ruth*, The Bible Speaks Today (IVP, 1983)
D.A. Leggett, *The Levirate and Goel Institutions in the Old Testament* (Mack, 1974)
B. Webb, *Five Festal Garments* (Apollos, 2000)
M.D. Gow, *The Book of Ruth* (Apollos, 1992)
L. Morris, 'Ruth', in *Judges and Ruth*, Tyndale OT Commentary (IVP, 1968)
D. Jackman, *Judges, Ruth* (Word Books, 1991)
R.L. Hubbard, *The Book of Ruth*, (Eerdmans, 1988)
H.H. Rowley, 'The Marriage of Ruth', in *The Servant of the Lord* (Lutterworth, 1954)

Samuel himself is portrayed as the king-maker, used by the
Lord to anoint Saul and David (1 Sam. 10:1; 16:13). David
passed the kingdom to Solomon (1 Kings 1:30), establishing in this way that within the Davidic dynasty it was not
necessarily the eldest son who succeeded his father. But, as
we have seen, when the historian's spotlight fell on these
men neither the loveable but insecure Saul, nor the charismatic David, nor the hugely gifted and privileged Solomon,
proved to be the king envisaged in the Judges-ideal.

The Search Continues
When Rehoboam threw away his patrimony, and the kingdom
divided between Israel to the north and Judah to the south,
the historian insists that we keep both kingdoms under examination. This is not just because, like all the prophets, he is unwilling to acquiesce in a sundering of what the Lord planned
as a unity (compare 1 Kings 18:31); it is because he is putting
a question to history: Has the ideal king yet appeared?

In Judah, the kings of David's line sat on the Lord's
throne (1 Chron. 29:23), and for nearly five hundred years
followed each other in ordered succession within the Davidic
covenant (Ps. 89:3).

In Israel, kings came and went by their own abilities, sometimes establishing short-lived dynasties but for the most part themselves as episodic as the Judges.

The history is written in exclusively personal terms. In Judah the question asked was how the king measured up to the Davidic norm (1 Kings 15:3, 11; 2 Kings 14:3; 16:2; etc.). In Israel the question was whether he had broken with the disastrous pattern whereby Jeroboam I had forfeited the promise of continuance (1 Kings 11:35-38; 12:26-30; compare 15:34; 16:2-7, 19, 26; etc.).

A Single, Dominant Interest: Messianic History

It is easy to misunderstand and therefore to belittle the sort of history we find in Kings. It is solely concerned with the single person of the king, and, even within that limitation, frequently tells us little about him. But all this is explained when we see that it is 'Messianic history'. This historian has only one question to ask. Is this the needed ideal king? When we understand this, we are no longer surprised when the fifty-five-year reign of Manasseh merits but eighteen verses! (2 Kings 21:1-18), and tells us nothing except that he 'did evil in the sight of the LORD'. That is all we need to know: the hunt for the Messianic King is on, and neither the covenanted house of David with its orderly succession nor the charismatic monarchy of Israel with its strong natural leaders seems capable of producing him.

Rather than criticise such history, we should be moved by it – moved even to tears as each monarchic line in turn runs into the sand and disappears (2 Kings 17, 25), but moved also to wonder and responsive gratitude when, with the changed fortunes of Jehoiachin (2 Kings 25:27) after thirty-seven years, the Lord allows us to see that the promises to David are still alive.

The question the Kings' historian was asking history still awaited an answer: Where is the Messianic King to be found and when will he come?

Further reading
J. Bright, *The History of Israel* (SCM, 1960)
B. Tuchman, *Practising History* (Ballantine, 1981)
D. Bebbington, *Patterns in History* (IVP, 1979)
D.R. Davis, *No Falling Words* (Joshua) (Baker, 1988)
—*Such a Great Salvation* (Judges) (Christian Focus, 2006)
—*Looking on the Heart* (1 Samuel) (Christian Focus, 2009)
—*Out of Every Adversity* (2 Samuel) (Christian Focus, 1999)
—*The Wisdom and the Folly* (1 Kings) (Christian Focus, 2008)
—*The Power and the Fury* (2 Kings) (Christian Focus, 2009)
J. Hayford, *Taking Hold of Tomorrow* (Joshua) (Regal, 1989)
B. Webb, *The Book of Judges* (Sheffield, 1987)
M. Wilcock, *The Message of Judges*, The Bible Speaks Today (IVP, 1992)
J. Baldwin, *1 and 2 Samuel*, Tyndale Old Testament Commentary (IVP, 1988)
D.J. Wiseman, *1 and 2 Kings*, Tyndale Old Testament Commentary (IVP, 1993)

THE BOOKS OF CHRONICLES

CONTENTS
An outline of the books of Chronicles establishes how they mesh in with the rest of the Bible histories:

A. 1 Chronicles 1–9. Genealogies, on the one hand reaching back to Adam, on the other hand extended at least till the return from exile, with particular reference to the genealogy of David.

B. 1 Chronicles 10–29. The reign of David, culminating in his plans for the Temple.

C. 2 Chronicles 1–9. The reign of Solomon, especially the building of the Temple.

D. 2 Chronicles 10–36. The kings of Judah, from the disruption of the kingdom until the Exile and return.

DATE AND AUTHORSHIP
Chronicles is anonymous. Likewise there is no sure indication of how long after the return from Exile the author lived (2 Chron. 36:22-23, 539 BC). 1 Chronicles 3:17-24 traces the genealogy of Jeconiah (= Jehoiachin, 2 Kings 24:6-12; 25:27-30) through six generations, bringing the date of the authorship down into the fifth century. There would seem to be no great point in recording this extension unless, perhaps, as Wilcock suggests, the sons of Elioenai were known to the author. Fundamentally, the Chronicler intended an historical sweep from Adam to his own day.

SELECTION OF MATERIAL
In such a colossal sweep of history, selection is all the more to be expected, but this does not mean that the Chronicler decided on the story he wanted to tell and then made the facts tell it, or that, in default of

finding suitable facts, he fabricated them. It only means that, as he pondered the past, he discerned principles and purposes in history and allowed the flow of his story to underline them.

Compared with Samuel and Kings, he omits events here (for example, 2 Sam. 11) and adds facts there (1 Chron. 23–26). He had his sources (1 Chron. 29:29), and he had his purposes. As Dr Tuchman says, if the historian will 'submit himself to his material instead of trying to impose himself on his material ... the material will ... speak to him and supply the answers'. It is necessary to say this in the light of the poorly considered remarks of many commentators who denigrate the Chronicler as an historian. Like all biblical historians, the Chronicler did not stop to preach sermons. The assumption (as in Stephen's speech in Acts 7) is that, for those with eyes to see, the facts tell their own story.

PURPOSE
To discern the purpose of this history we must note the facts the Chronicler selected, and the emphases he made, asking 'Had he preached a sermon, what would he have said?'

- 'God is working his purpose out as year succeeds to year.' In the difficult and disappointing circumstances of the return from Babylon, the Chronicler's people needed to be helped to look back, to see where they had come from, and therefore how special they were as the chosen people, the descendants of the fathers. They needed the reminder of the unfailing purposes of God, his changelessness in the face of so much human recalcitrance, his perseverance through generation after generation. He is the God who never gives up.
- David captures the lion's share of the Chronicler's space.

    1. Nothing is recorded of the history of the northern kingdom, only of David's house, the covenant line. The omission of Israel does not disinherit them, but serves to focus on the central line of salvation history, Abraham to David. This is where the returnees – and all subsequent generations, and we – must take our stand.

    2. Within the reign of David, the Chronicler's great interest is on the king and Temple. This is what kings are 'all about': they are to express the Lord's rule over his people, and to secure for the people the ordinances of mercy and reconciliation whereby they may live with the Lord at the

centre of their lives. This is, of course, the heart of the Messianic history of the Old Testament and the Chronicler wrote in this way in order to keep hope alive.

- Though the Chronicler writes distinctive and colourful history, along with the writers of Judges and Samuel-Kings, he has learnt from Deuteronomy the moral lesson that obedience is the key to blessing and disobedience the recipe for punishment and disaster.

Further reading
C. J. Barber, *1 and 2 Chronicles* (Christian Focus, 2004)
M. Wilcock, *The Message of Chronicles*, The Bible Speaks Today (IVP, 1987)
R.L. Braun, R.B. Dillard, *Chronicles* (Word, 1986, 1987)
M.J. Selman, *1 and 2 Chronicles*, Tyndale Old Testament Commentary (IVP, 2 vols, 1994)
R.L. Pratt, *1 and 2 Chronicles* (Christian Focus, 1998)

6

Joshua to Kings:
The National Portrait Gallery

The great sweep of history in Joshua–Kings which we have been considering in broad terms brings together a fascinating array of characters. It is concerned with persons rather than with the sort of events, movements and policies that form the focal points of today's narrative histories. This is because of its basic Messianic orientation. Every next king might be the expected king who would fulfil the Judges-ideal and bring his people into a perfect society.

In this sense, then, Joshua–Kings is like the catalogue of a portrait gallery. Catalogue in hand, we can walk around and be alerted to the identity and salient features of the subject and to significant aspects of the portraiture itself. Space, of course, only allows us to offer a brief selection of these great portraits, and in each case to make, so to speak, only a précis of their catalogue entries.

Recording and Approving

Before embarking on our tour of the pictures, we must recall that the Bible does not necessarily approve what it records. In general, the historians do not step aside from their narratives to point morals. For this reason Joseph's comment that to acquiesce in the desires of Potiphar's wife would be to 'sin against God' (Gen. 39:9), and the historian's interjection that 'the thing that David had done displeased the LORD' (2 Sam. 11:27 NKJV) are out of the ordinary. Usually we are left to observe the benefits of the good and the ill-fruits of the bad, and to draw our own conclusions. The New Testament finds examples (1 Cor. 10:6) and instruction (Rom. 15:4) in the Old, things to avoid as well as things to copy. Hebrews 11 encourages us to look to the great names of the Old Testament as exemplifying the way of faith, but it does not throw a covering of approval over all that they did.

JOSHUA: THE SUCCESS OF AN UNLIKELY SOLDIER

From his earliest appearances in the Bible Joshua is presented as a man needing tender loving care. He was certainly not a 'strong, natural leader'. With the prospect of his taking over from Moses, the Lord twice directed Moses to 'encourage' (literally, 'strengthen') him (Deut. 1:38; 3:28), and twice (once publicly, Deut. 31:7, once privately, Deut. 31:28) Moses did so. Joshua's unsure approach to life – and to his enormous responsibility as Moses' successor – was, indeed, something everyone seemed to recognise: the Lord himself used Moses' words three times (Josh. 1:6-7, 9) and the people, too, were aware that their new chief needed stiffening in his resolve (Josh. 1:18).

So how did this trembling general manage to succeed so brilliantly?

The Book and the Man

The message of the book of Joshua and of the life of Joshua are the same. The promise of God – that is, the power of the word of God – prevails over every human factor: the death of Moses (1:2), the frailty of Joshua (1:6, 9), defection, disobedience and defeat (7:7-8, 10, 20-21; 8:1); the power of the enemy (10:8). Thus the book can end by recording that the Lord did what he promised (21:43-45; 23:14). The Lord gave the word and the Lord kept the word.

Military Success
The word secured the advance into Canaan (2:8-11) and the breakdown of Canaannite morale (5:1; 9:24; 10:1-2).

Joshua Himself
His brilliant career was wholly due to his doing what the Lord said to him.

- He was already practised in the presence of God (Exod. 24:13; 32:15-17; 33:11);
- He was commanded to pay daily attention to the word of God (1:8);
- He staked his reputation on God keeping his word (3:8-13);
- He saw to it that the people kept the word of God as it had come to him (4:8, 10);
- He took it for granted that what the Lord said he would also do (11:6-7).

Jericho
The incident at Jericho (5:13–6:21) is a paradigm of the whole life of Joshua. Like any responsible commander, Joshua went forward to view his problem for himself (5:13). Siege warfare was a novel experience, for his earlier command had been in the open field (Exod. 17:8-16). Jericho was also the first test of his sole leadership. Furthermore, since Jericho was the gate into Canaan, the whole enterprise of invasion began or ended there. But what Joshua saw was not the immensity and importance of his task but the sufficiency of his God, the Lord dressed for battle.

Joshua asked the obvious question but received a far from expected answer (5:13-14). For the crucial issue is not whose side the Lord is on but who is on the Lord's side. Joshua promptly put this matter beyond doubt: 'What does my Lord say to his servant?' Were it not for this fundamental com-mitment, Joshua would not have learned the divine strategy against Jericho nor enjoyed the Lord's intended victory.

The Weakness of Strength: Ai and the Gibeonites
Biblically, the corollary of, 'when I am weak, then I am strong' (2 Cor. 12:10 NKJV) is, 'When I am strong, then I am weak.' Abraham, so strong in faith, failed through a lapse of faith (Gen.12:10-20; 20:1-18). Moses, the meekest of all (Num. 12:3), failed through losing his temper (Num. 20:10-11). And Joshua, the man of the word of God, registered his two failures when he acted without the divine word:

1. Without the Lord's direction (contrast 7:2 with 8:1), Joshua sent a selected force against Ai, and reaped the bitter fruits of trusting human wisdom (7:3). It always takes a total commitment of all our resources to stand against the enemy (8:1), but no resource is sufficient unless it acts at and upon God's word.

2. When the Gibeonites came with practised deceit-fulness, Joshua again followed human wisdom: they 'took note of their provision and did not ask counsel at the mouth of the LORD' (9:14-15).

The Last Word
Joshua's final speech leaps across the centuries to address us as powerfully as it addressed his contemporaries: he would have us live by what he, the unfit leader, learned of leader-ship, the irresolute soldier learned of victory – clear, decisive commitment (24:14-15), worked out in obedience to the word of the Lord (24:25-26).

GIDEON: GOD'S POWER, FOUND, USED AND ABUSED
Gideon, one of the two judges selected for special mention, was a freedom fighter. Like Samson (Judg. 13–16), his career (Judg. 6–8) is recorded in some detail, and, like all the judges, he left his people as he found them. At the start, they

were defeated (6:2), frustrated (6:3), ruined (6:4), helpless (6:5) and, worst of all, under divine displeasure (6:7-10); and when he died (8:33-35) they 'turned again' to seek other gods, remembering neither the Lord and his deliverances nor Gideon and his good services.

In the case of Samson, we observe his inability to take anything seriously, and find ourselves unsurprised that no lasting achievement resulted. But Gideon is so attractive that we want him to succeed. He captures our hearts – this small man (who else could use a flail in a winepress? 6:11), with his self-doubts and honest questions (6:13-15), his nervousness (6:27), and uncertainty (6:36-40), his need for support and reassurance (7:9-11), yet also his resoluteness (7:15), perseverance (8:4), and humility in victory (8:22-23).

Gideon in Summary

Three verses provide the frame around the portrait of Gideon:

1. *Judges 6:34*: Gideon was empowered by the Lord, literally, 'The Spirit of the Lord put on Gideon as a garment', 'clothed himself with Gideon'.

2. *Judges 8:22*: Gideon, the man of power, so acted that he saved his people and subdued his enemies.

3. *Judges 8:27*: somehow, after all, the Gideon who was so powerful for the Lord against Israel's enemies succumbed to self-importance, allowing himself and his ephod to become a corrupting national focus, leading to the religious (8:33) and social (9:1–10:57) collapse of Israel.

Coming to Power

Gideon came to the moment of empowering by way of two altars (6:24, 26).

The first altar represents Gideon's awareness of entering into a relationship of peace with the Lord. His comparison of present with past (6:13) and his honest self-appraisal

(6:15) made him wonder if this interview was only imagination (6:17). But the fact that he actively sought reassurance
on the point indicates that he was not unready to accept
the Lord's surprising will for his life (6:18). The angel's response betrayed his identity, and Gideon was overwhelmed
by a sinner's peril in coming face to face with God (6:21-22).
The Lord's immediate response of 'peace' was matched by
Gideon's first altar, his embracing of the peace with God of
which the Lord had spoken.

The second altar expresses bold, if cautious, commitment
(6:25-32), earning for Gideon public recognition as one taking a stand for the Lord (6:32).

The incoming of the Spirit (6:34) matches what the
New Testament speaks of as the 'filling' of the Spirit (e.g.
Acts 2:4a; 4:8; etc.) – a specific empowering for a specific
task, not once for all but repeated as the Lord may will.
The occasion was a renewed Midianite invasion (6:33),
and Gideon was ready, a man at peace with God, personally
committed in sole loyalty to the Lord, and empowered.

Using Power

How gently the Lord now dealt with his chosen and empowered man! Neither conversion nor the indwelling Spirit
necessarily changes the human temperament. Extroverts become converted extroverts; introverts, converted introverts;
melancholics, converted melancholics; and, in Gideon's
case, an insecure man needing reassurance (compare 6:17)
remained insecure. But if it was reassurance he needed, the
Lord met him at that point (6:37-40). The substantial truth
here is that *the power of God must be used to do the will of God*,
and Gideon needed to be certain of the Lord's will lest he
launch into action only to find that the Holy Spirit was no
longer on his side.

A more testing experience awaited Gideon: *to do the
work of God in God's way* (7:1-8). Human logic would have
promoted further recruitment beyond the thirty-two thou-

sand who first responded (7:3), for, after all, the Midianites and their allies were innumerable (6:5). The Lord, however, said, 'Not so.' Gideon's enjoyment of the power given to him depended on the spirit of trust which accepted that the Lord's thoughts are not ours nor our ways his (Isa. 55:8). Power is linked with the trust and obedience that does God's work in God's way.

Divine graciousness again enters the story and, by implication, indicates that Gideon did not find it easy to acquiesce in the reduction of his grand army to a paltry three hundred. The Lord allowed him to overhear a Midianite conversation which revealed that already the enemy had conceded defeat (7:9-14). The timid Gideon was able to take a resolute lead (7:15) and bring the matter to a successful conclusion (7:22).

Three Truths Are Exemplified in Gideon's Use of Divine Power:

- The humility of the victor. It is part of the Lord's plan for his people's conquest of the forces of the world that they unite in his cause. We see this in action as Gideon summoned all Israel to share with him in the victory (7:23-25) and, marvellously, when he replied with such gracious self-forgetfulness to the bumptious Ephraimites (8:1-3).

- The enjoyment of the Holy Spirit's empowering is in the context of costly, disciplined and demanding effort (8:4). The Holy Spirit does not marginalise us while he does the work; he mobilises us for conflict and disciplined perseverance.

- Through the Lord's gentle care for his timorous servant, Gideon became resolute and firm in leadership, able to take action both against dangers within the church (8:15-17), and against even the most intimidating foes outside (8:18-21).

Power Abused

We have noted the sad declension of Gideon's last years and its ill-consequences. On the one hand there was Gideon's public testimony in a 'politically correct' disavowal of kingship (8:22-23). But on the other hand, his outward correctness was, it seems, at variance with his heart, for he called his son Abimelech, 'My Father is King.' Not for nothing does biblical wisdom instruct us to 'keep our hearts with all diligence for out of them life issues' (Prov. 4:23).

SAMSON: BEGINNING AND NOT FINISHING

Samson could never resist a girl and he could never resist a joke. In his jaunty way, confident in his amazing strength, he could walk right into Philistine country (16:1), yet immediately capitulate to a girl he chanced to meet (16:1). And when the *amour* was over, the other side of his nature exerted itself – his sheer impishness. Any other equally strong man would simply have kicked down the gates and left, but not Samson! Oh no! The chance was too good to miss. He picked up the gates with all their attendant bits and pieces and left them on a hilltop forty miles away (16:3).

Samson was God's plan and God's man. But with sad realism the Lord knew Samson would never get beyond beginning (13:5). His strength was not in his physique (else why should Delilah be puzzled about its source, 16:5-6?) but its source was supernatural (14:6, 19; 15:14). He was as truly 'filled with the Spirit' as ever Gideon before or Peter after him, but uncontrolled lust and undisciplined buffoonery set limits to what he would do for God, or God would do through him. He exemplifies promise unfulfilled; great strength vitiated by small bondages; public commitment and secret failure; and what he was at the end – blind, bound, and, especially, 'making sport' (16:21, 25) – he had been all along.

The Serious Mind

Did Samson ever take anything *seriously*? Paul urges the 'serious' mind – no humourless solemnity but the thoughtfulness which gives things their proper worth and weighs decisions. The adjective is *semnos* (Phil. 4:8; 1 Tim. 3:8, 11; Titus 2:2) and the noun *semnotes* (1 Tim. 2:2; 3:4; Titus 2:7). But Samson allowed his capacity to be lighthearted (not an error in itself), to have a laugh (certainly not wrong) and to play the fool (not a bad thing in its place) to get out of hand. Otherwise would he, a Nazirite, have wilfully insisted on a Philistine bride (15:3), chosen the road through the vineyards (14:5) and carelessly defiled himself with a dead body (14:8)? But he did not take his vow seriously.

The brackets round the threefold Nazirite vow (Num. 6:2-8) call for separation (v. 2) and holiness (v. 8). The three stipulations are:

1. *No alcohol*, for the Lord must be the joy of the one taking the vow (vv. 3-4; compare Ps. 104:15);

2. *Uncut hair*, symbolising the consecration to the Lord of the outgrowth and vigour of life (v. 5);

3. *Purity and loyalty*, to keep far from all that defiles (v. 6), in order to give primary devotion to the Lord (v. 7).

Was this Samson? His wedding feast is specifically called a 'banquet of wine' (*misteh* 14:10) – and, even so, he had to spoil it by his jokey approach to life (14:12), and then proceed to further defilement with the dead (14:19) – and after all that, off he marched in high dudgeon! What childishness and petulance – and no *semnotes*! No seriousness of mind that weighs priorities, thinks of the consequences and holds to great objectives.

The Downfall

In the end, of course, flippancy caught up with Samon. In the case of Delilah (16:4ff.), as earlier in Gaza (15:1), and before that in Timnah (14:1) and in the vineyards (14:5), Samson should not have been there in the first place. It is hard to think that Samson deliberately sought temptation, but he certainly took no steps to avoid it (compare 1 Tim. 6:11; 2 Tim. 2:22). He frequented places where it was to be found, and toyed with it when it came. But was he so thoughtlessly frivolous that he was willing to go along with Delilah's probing about his strength? Did he really think that there would be no end to the divine patience when finally he played fast and loose with his Nazirite vow? Apparently, yes.

The Lord's Strange Instruments

Of course, we cannot but laugh with and at Samson. His name is related to the Hebrew word for the 'sun', and at best he had a sunny disposition which anyone of us might desire as a Christian asset. Amazingly, however, even when his sunny outlook deteriorated into superficiality, he was still in the Lord's hand, still used for the Lord's purposes (13:25; 14:6, 19; 15:14). It is the illustration of the horse and rider all over again. Samson chose to be a fool; very well, the Lord would direct his foolery and use it for the purpose of justice and deliverance.

But was it meant to be otherwise? What would Samson have been and done if he had taken his vow seriously and channelled all his sunniness into joyful holiness for the Lord? As C.S. Lewis makes Aslan say, 'We are never told what would have happened.' But what Samson made of himself the Lord nevertheless used. This is both the tragedy and the comfort of the portrait of the Lord's great fool.

SAMUEL: PRAYING AND PREACHING

We look at the portrait of Samuel and say, 'Oh to be such a person!' He inherited a situation of despondency (1 Sam. 4:21; 7:2), defeat (4:10; 7:3) and religious corruption (2:12ff.; 7:4), and he lived to see defeat transformed into victory (7:12-13), and people coming back to God (7:2-6).

Birth and Boyhood

The delightful stories of Samuel's early years underline the two features which predominate through his adult life.

Hannah

Samuel was born in answer to prayer and given a name which recorded that prayer is answered. His mother Hannah dominates the narrative of 1:1–2:10. She was childless and her sorrows were exacerbated by Elkanah's second wife, Peninnah. They were also not helped by the bluff chauvinism of Elkanah who could only say, '*Am* I not better to you than ten sons?' when Hannah needed him to say, 'Are *you* not better to me than ten sons?' (1:8 NKJV).

But she brought her grief to the caring God of Israel and – marvellously! – once she had made her prayer, before it was answered one way or the other, she felt her heart to be light, and, 'her face was no longer *sad*' (1:18 NKJV). The prayer was answered as she wished, and she called her son 'Samuel', 'Heard by God'. From that time onwards Samuel could not even say his name without being reminded that God hears and answers prayer.

God's Call

From birth Samuel was given to the Lord (1:11, 28) in Nazirite consecration. From his earliest days he worshipped the Lord (1:28); he was preoccupied in holy things (2:11, 18; 3:1), and grew up in the Lord's presence and favour (2:21, 26). But for all this Samuel 'did not yet know the LORD' (3:7). There was a personal dimension which had not yet been his experience, but it came to him by divine initiative and gracious persistence on that night when the Lord spoke his name and summoned him to personal faith (3:2-10).

God's Word

The stated context of Samuel's experience of conversion is important. The story begins by recording, 'In those days the word of the LORD was rare' (3:1). The comment that

'Samuel did not yet know the LORD' (3:7) is amplified by
the words, 'The word of the LORD had not yet been revealed
to him.' When the Lord spoke Samuel's name and elicited
a response of listening (3:10), he at once gave him a word to
pass on (3:11-18); and this became a pattern: people learned
to acknowledge Samuel as a prophet to whom and through
whom the Lord spoke (3:19-20).

The Man of Prayer

Samuel's biblical reputation (Ps. 99:6; Jer. 15:1) matched his
contemporary reputation (1 Sam. 7:8; 12:19): he was a man
of prayer. He saw intercession as his primary ministry to his
people. They needed to be led into a fresh commitment to
God (symbolised by the outpoured water, 7:6a; compare
2 Sam. 23:16; Lam. 2:19) and to renewed penitence (7:6b),
and he would bring this about by his prayer for them (7:5).

Samuel also saw and found prayer to be the way of victory
(7:9-10). Verse 9 affirms a principle: when the Lord's people
come to him in self-offering (v. 9a, a 'whole burnt offering',
compare Gen. 22:2, 12) and their commitment issues in
prayer (v. 9b), the Lord answers (v. 9c). Verse 10 applies
this principle to a specific situation. Samuel was engaged in
the offering when the attack came, but he saw it as more
important to seek God than to counter-attack. The worship
and its consequent intercession continued, and the answer
came in direct divine action (v. 10b). The victory was won
by prayer.

This was typical of Samuel's reaction to the diverse circumstances of his life: in disappointment (8:6), perplexity
(8:21) and anger (15:11), his first response was to pray – and
he ended his ministry as he began it (12:23), seeing it as
a sin against the Lord to stop praying for his people.

The Man of the Word of God

Samuel's commitment to the word of God is all of a piece
with his commitment to prayer: it was in the place of prayer

that he received the word he was to pass on (8:6-7, 21-22; 15:11b-16). Furthermore, his ministry of God's word started with himself. Displeased though he was with the proposal that Israel become a monarchy, when the Lord so directed him he bowed to the Lord's word (8:21-22). He accepted without question what the word of the Lord said to him (9:15, 23), and, though the institution of monarchy was against his personal desires, nevertheless, when Saul's kingship floundered, Samuel did not gloat: 'Samuel distressed himself over Saul' (15:35). His *mind* (8:6-7), *will* (9:15, 23) and *heart* (15:35) were captive to the word of God. In this, too, Samuel ended as he began (3:18, 20, 21–4:1), by bringing the word of God to Israel (12:1-25).

Unchanging Truths

In a fundamental way the situation at Samuel's death was totally changed. The episodic rule of the Judges had become the institutionalised rule of the king. The people, as Samuel knew, had sought this change in order to have the benefit of a permanent ruler to care for them – and, presumably, his standing army for their defence. Samuel's strange prayer for a visitation of storm in harvest (12:16-18) bore directly on this point. No human expedient to gain security changed the fundamental reality that it was to the Lord they must answer and to him they must look for their welfare. It was in this context that Samuel ended as he had begun: the ongoing obligation of the leader to pray for his people (12:23) and their unchanged obligation to serve the Lord in truth (12:24).

SAUL: LOVABLE AND TRAGIC

King Saul was rightly a much-loved man. His strange jealousy of David can easily mar our appreciation of one whom David himself called 'lovely and pleasant' (2 Sam. 1:23), but so indeed he must have been. Just think how there was not a whisper of criticism when the towering Saul (1 Sam. 9:2) failed to fight with the giant Philistine, but instead gave his armour to a mere boy. In such a David-orientated history this silence can only speak of the affection in which Saul was held – as does the alacrity with which the people of Keilah (notwithstanding their debt to David) sent to inform Saul of the whereabouts of their king's enemy (23:11-12, 19; 24:1; 26:1). Saul had an easy capacity for attracting loyalty, and people spontaneously risked their lives for him (1 Sam. 31:11-13). Well has he been called 'the Beloved Captain'.

What Went Wrong?

Why did the Spirit of anointing (10:5) leave Saul and an evil spirit from the Lord (16:14) trouble him? In psychological terms, Saul was insecure, lacking a proper sense of self-worth, and insufficiently aware of his God-given gifts and calling. To others this was probably part of his attractiveness – they would have called him 'unassuming'. We see it in his first reaction to Samuel (9:20-21), or in his keeping quiet about the kingship (10:15-16), or hiding among the baggage (10:21-23), or in the way he took criticism in his stride (10:27). But the worm in the bud of self-deprecation is self-doubt which, if allowed, becomes a spreading cancer.

Tripping at the Second and Third Hurdles

The Lord brought Saul to kingship with many reassurances:

- When Saul met Samuel, he found the prophet already alerted by the word of the Lord to the coming of the chosen king (9:17-21);

- The private anointing was quickly followed by outward (10:2-6) and inward (10:9) confirmations;

- The lot (10:20-24) was, as Proverbs (16:33) says, 'cast into the lap, but the whole disposing of it is of the LORD.'

Testing, however, is always the way to maturity (Rom. 5:3-5; James 1:1-2). If God gives gifts he gives also that which tests his gifts (compare 1 Kings 3:12-13). If Saul was to 'grow into his job' he must be tested. Samuel gave forewarning of two such tests: a test of acting (10:7) and a test of waiting (10:8).

The First Test
Saul passed this test magnificently when a timely divine enabling (11:6) lifted him out of obscurity into the public arena (11:7-8) and on to national acclaim (11:14-15).

The Second Test
It could seem unfair in that Samuel did not explain what he meant by 'waiting at Gilgal' (10:8), but Saul (13:8) understood it fully. When he failed to wait (13:9), he forfeited the hope of founding a dynasty (13:13-14).

God's Tests
It is not for us to question either the procedure or its outcome. It is the way of divine providence that we grow to maturity by facing tests and making choices. Furthermore, only the gracious God himself, who desires our maturity, knows the significance of each test and the appropriate benefit should we pass, or loss should we fail. The example of Saul warns us not to question the ways of God, but to take sensitive care over even our least obedience, for we cannot tell what issues are involved.

Saul does not seem to have taken the dynastic threat seriously (20:30-31), or learnt the lesson of his second testing in order to be better prepared for what was to come.

The Third Test
This was a command to destroy Amalek (15:1-3), and again Saul failed to obey, sparing Agag (15:8-9) and the best livestock. Samuel's response was uncompromising: Saul was no longer the Lord's king (15:22-23); the Lord must seek another (16:1-13).

The Years of Darkness

Saul's repentance sounded genuine (15:24), though the way it is rephrased in 15:30 could raise a doubt: Was he sorry for sin or sorry for being found out? Only God knows. But what is evident in the heartbreaking story is that Saul became mentally unstable (16:14ff.), and slipped progressively into paranoia with its attendant delusions.

- He began to entertain suspicions instead of facing the truth (17:55–18:8).
- He gave place to an envious, grudging spirit (18:8-9).
- He schemed for another's downfall (18:17; 19:1).
- He retreated into self-pity and a persecution complex (22:7-8).
- He came to the place where he could only intermittently recognise the truth (24:16-22; 26:17-21, 25).
- In the end, he even turned to powers of darkness (28:5-7).

Lighten our Darkness

The Old Testament is clear about communicating with the dead: its possibility and its impermissibility. It was one of the spiritual perils of Canaan against which incoming Israel was warned (Deut. 18:9-13; compare Lev. 19:31; Isa. 8:19-20).

The dangers of such practices are not detailed, but neither are they hard to guess. The witch at Endor apparently had the power to bring the actual Samuel to Saul at his request, though this does not mean that every spirit claimant has the same power. Once the 'spirit world' is entered, no further control is possible over the activities of deceiving and foul spirits. The Bible, however, is clear on two points: folly and sin.

The folly of spiritism is that the dead, as far as power is concerned, are weaker than they were on earth. For this reason they are sometimes called 'the shadowy ones' (e.g. Isa. 14:9-11). And as far as wisdom is concerned, they know

no more than they did on earth. The Samuel who came from
Sheol to speak to Saul was the same Samuel he knew on
earth, saying the same things, knowing nothing more.

The sin of spiritism is that it is turning from the divine to
the (deceased) human, and from the one and only God to
inferior spirits. Further (as Isaiah 8:19-20 says so dramatically) it is departing from the clear word of God to the 'chirping
and mutterings' of the darkened room.

Peace for Saul

One thing, however, Samuel could affirm which Saul could
at best guess: 'Tomorrow you and your sons *will be* with me'
(1 Sam. 28:19 NKJV). Dear Saul! He forsook the way of obedience and walked deeper and deeper into the valley of deadly
darkness, but the Lord never deserts those to whom he has
given a new heart (10:9). He brought Saul out of despair, delusion and failure to where 'the wicked cease from turmoil,
and the weary are at rest, and those in bondage take their
ease' (Job 3:17-18).

DAVID: THE KING WHOSE HEART WAS RIGHT AND WHOSE HEART WAS WRONG

David is one of the most complex characters in the Bible,
one of the most colourful and lovable – and one of the most
exasperating. It is easy to see why he excited such devotion;
it is just as easy to feel disenchantment. But whatever his
qualities as a person, as a king, he proved a failure – he failed
to govern his kingdom, and was unable to govern his family,
because he did not govern himself.

This is not to say that he was not a great king or unworthy
to serve as a standard of comparison for his successors. It is
only to note that in the Bible not even its greatest characters
get the whitewash treatment, and that, in the case of David,
the historian asked the same question he was to ask of the
sons of David for the next four hundred years: Is he the king
whom we need?

David Ascendant

The story from the secret anointing (1 Sam. 16) to David's accession to the united throne of Judah and Israel (2 Sam. 2:4; 5:1-3) is a window into the wonderful works of the Lord. It teaches that what the Lord purposes – in this case, David's kingship – will inevitably come to pass, but that the pathway from initiation to fulfilment may be one we could never have foreseen or, at any given point, necessarily have fathomed.

Here was a man in whom the Spirit was mightily present (1 Sam. 16:13), but for whom nothing seemed to go right, and that through no fault of his own. As for Jesus (Matt. 3:16; 4:1) and for the Christian believer (Rom. 7:23; 8:5-7; Gal. 5:17) so for David: the presence of the Holy Spirit means conflict.

Success

When we find, following the secret anointing, that David was providentially brought to the king's court (1 Sam. 16:21) and then, by killing the giant, into the public arena (18:7), into favour with Jonathan (18:1) and, by marriage, into the royal family (18:20ff.) while, at the same time, Saul was obviously failing, it is easy to assume that David would soon be king. But our logic is at once baffled.

Distress

David was brought close to the throne only to experience suspicion (1 Sam. 18:11-12), secret opposition (1 Sam. 19:1), open enmity (1 Sam. 19:9-10) and a narrow escape from death into the life of a hunted outlaw (1 Sam. 19:10–26:25). Then, perhaps not surprisingly, buoyancy of spirit and faith in the Lord's protecting power both failed, and he slipped over the border into Philistia and the service of Achish (1 Sam. 27:1-6). Where then was his throne?

But there was more to come. When the Philistines went to war with Saul, even Achish had to dismiss David (1 Sam. 29:9-11), and when he returned to the only place he

could call home, Ziklag, he was to find it sacked by the Ama-
lekites and his family gone (1 Sam. 30:1-6). David had now
reached rock bottom for, in their desperate grief, even his men
turned against him. Yet it was from the ashes of Ziklag that David moved to become king of Judah (2 Sam. 2:1-4; Ps. 113:7-
8). The Lord's ways are undeniably odd (Isa. 55:8), but they
are sure. What he purposes he most certainly accomplishes.

David Reigning
There was no need for David to engage in the long war with
the sad rump of Saul's kingdom (2 Sam. 3:1). Was it by war that
he had become king of Judah or by divine sovereign grace? It is
obviously hard to become king and then to avoid doing what
kings do! But David had no call to fight for what the Lord had
promised him. Nor had he any call to use Michal as a pawn in
his ambitions (2 Sam. 3:12-16) – making her the cover for Ab-
ner's treacherous visit – and then treat her in such an utterly
unhusbandly and beastly way (6:20-23) just because she voiced
a wifely and understandable word of caution. Yet how magnificently the Lord kept faith with David, pledging him an unending throne and dynasty (2 Sam. 7:1-29), giving him rest from all
his enemies round about! But then ...

David Declining
But then came the Ammonite Wars, not of David's seeking
(2 Sam. 10–11) but, as it turned out, a crucial test for the
king. Before this, David's leadership was never in dispute;
after it, his leadership was never undisputed.

Bathsheba
The wording of 11:1 says it all: 'when kings go out *to battle*,
... David sent Joab.'(NKJV). He neglected his duty (compare
15:3-4). He also pampered his body, taking to his bed in the
afternoon (11:2) in contrast to the disciplined concern of
Uriah (11:11) for his fellow soldiers. The downward slope
brought David to the moment of uncontrolled, indulged
passion. 'He saw a woman bathing' (11:2) – that was a mere
happenstance. 'The woman was very beautiful to look at'

(11:2) – that was the king's choice. He possibly could not help seeing: he could help looking – and 'the thing that David did displeased the LORD', one of the very few times when Bible history pauses to pass a moral judgment (11:27).

Consequences

Repentance is like fetching back a stone one has just thrown into a pool. The stone can be fetched back but the ripples go on spreading. Divine mercy, movingly and marvellously, accepted David's repentance (12:13, compare Ps. 51). But the Lord did not choose to stop the ripples. What David sowed he lived to reap. He opened the door to sexual immorality and murder.

- Amnon, his eldest son (3:2), raped his half-sister, Tamar (13:1ff.).

- Absalom, Tamar's full brother, killed Amnon (13:28-29), and fled (13:38). What a tangled web! – and the king's own behaviour tied his hands, for there is no harsher or more unanswerable riposte than, 'Who are you to talk?'

- Absalom (15:1–18:33) brought rebellion within the royal house.

- Sheba the Benjamite (20:1ff.) rebelled from outside.

- David himself behaved with extraordinary lack of wisdom in the matter of the Gibeonites (21:1-14).

- David made a disastrously selfish choice after he had provoked the plague (23:2-3, 14-15).

The end. David's life just tumbled into ruin, and he ended up in the indignities of extreme old age (1 Kings 1:1-4), a pawn in the hands of power-hungry interests within the palace (1:5-53), and the author of the horrifying vengefulness of his 'last will and testament' (2:1-11).

The history of David is every bit as heartbreaking as that of Saul. At his best, how great he was, how large-hearted (2 Sam. 9), but only the morally perfect can be the Messiah. Great David's greater Son was still to come.

Further reading
J.A. Motyer, *Treasures of the King* (IVP, 2007)
Paul Gardner, Ed., *Who's Who in the Bible* (Marshall Pickering, 1995)
D.R. Davis, *No Falling Words* (Joshua) (Baker, 1988)
—*Such a Great Salvation* (Judges) (Christian Focus, 2006)
—*Looking on the Heart* (1 Samuel) (Christian Focus, 2009)
—*Out of Every Adversity* (2 Samuel) (Christian Focus, 1999)
—*The Wisdom and the Folly* (1 Kings) (Christian Focus, 2008)
—*The Power and the Fury* (2 Kings) (Christian Focus, 2009)

SOLOMON

Solomon had the greatest opportunity to be the ideal king Israel needed. With the donation of heaven-sent wisdom, the inherited subjection of all external threat, and, for much of his reign, an unchallenged supremacy over his people, he also enjoyed the gifts and circumstances for the longed-for ideal to be realised. His failure is all the more culpable, and, while he bequeathed to the future the perfect religious focus of the first Temple, no future king was compared with him as the model to be followed. This is the extent of his failure.

With Solomon the possibility of the 'Judges ideal' of Messianic kingship being fulfilled came to an end. As we saw, the king whom the author of Judges desired would solve the religious, social, moral and national problems of the people. Saul achieved success religiously (1 Sam. 28:9) but failed to achieve national unity; David brought the nation together around his own person and the new capital city of Jerusalem, but failed morally (2 Sam. 11), whereupon his family, his kingdom and his own character disintegrated. Solomon, famed as well as chosen to be the builder of the house, corrupted the house with false gods (1 Kings 11:4-8). After this the incompetent Rehoboam fractured the kingdom and, though it took centuries to become apparent, the hope that David promised had already been lost in the sands of time.

The fact is that no gift of God comes without accompaniments which test its reality. In Solomon's case, the gift he asked for brought with it gifts he might have asked for but did not (1 Kings 3:11-13) – the riches which would test his ability to manage and control his own life, and the honour which would test the reality of his primary honouring of the Lord. But riches brought a character-testing abundance under which Solomon broke – thirteen years to build his own house but seven spent on the Lord's house (1 Kings 6:38–7:1); and international acclaim led to the fantastic folly of his marriages of political convenience. Saul, who so effortlessly commanded the affection of his people, failed where he was strong – both doubting the affection in which he was held and failing to exercise his personal magnetism; David of the loving heart gave his love in dishonourable and disreputable ways; Solomon failed in wisdom.

7

PSALMS:
THE SINGERS AND THEIR SONGS

The book of Psalms as we know it was not brought together until after whatever date may be assigned to Psalm 137 (that is, when the Exile was still a fresh memory), but for us it is the most natural thing to move from David, 'the most delightful singer of Israel' (2 Sam. 23:1), to the book which he initiated and which depends so heavily on his contribution. It is here more than anywhere else that we find the real David, and understand why he was the man after the Lord's heart (1 Sam. 13:14).

But in respect of the leading ideas and sentiments of the Psalms, David and his successors are as one, with one pervasive aim: to bring life in all its variety and complexity into the presence of the Lord, to tell him about it, and to come to see it from his perspective.

THE CAVE AND THE WINGS
Psalm 57 is an example. The introductory title places David in 1 Samuel 22:1. He is a fugitive from Saul, and, to begin with, completely alone. Think of his first night in the cave: doubtless he was actually in the midst of lions and could

hear the beasts hunting their prey. But they reminded him of the even more dangerous hunters Saul had deputed to track him down (v. 4). Yet as he lay awake in the darkness, it was not the rock of the cave he saw above him but 'the shadow of Your wings' (v. 1 NKJV).

There is the whole perspective of the Psalms. No matter whose hands we fall into, it is the Lord's hands we are in; no matter what darkness looms over us, it is his overshadowing – the 'shade of his hand outstretched caressingly' (Francis Thompson); and no matter how great the plight, the way of prayer is still open, offering the most effective solution to our needs.

TAKE IT TO THE LORD

The Psalmists address us at points of need and often points of failure. Where we tend to draw back and question God, they moved forward into him; where we retire hurt, telling ourselves how awful life is, how disappointed, ill-used and disillusioned we are, they had the discipline, determination and good sense to 'take it to the Lord in prayer'.

Psalm 34 is a psalm about prayer and its effectiveness. It is also an interesting example of a psalm which has headings relating to the life of David. There are fourteen of these psalms and their headings are to be taken seriously. The headings form part of the Hebrew text as we have received it, and in Hebrew Bibles with verse numbers they rank as verse 1.

In the case of Psalm 57, we saw how illuminating it is to note the parallelism between 'in the cave' and 'in the shadow of Your wings', the one as the real situation and the other as the true. Yet without the heading we would never have linked Psalm 57 to 1 Samuel 22. The Israelites do not go in for narrative poetry in the sense of poems describing events. The poets meditated on events and experiences, and distilled essential truths, principles and lessons into their poems.

Meditations on What Happened

The heading to Psalm 34 is a striking example. At first sight it conflicts with the incident in 1 Samuel 21:10-14 to which the heading refers. In the story, David extricated himself from a tricky situation by cleverness and deceit, but in the psalm his deliverance is due to prayer: 'I sought the LORD, and he answered me and delivered me from all my fears ... This poor man cried and the LORD heard him and saved him out of all his troubles' (vv. 4, 6). What do we say, then? That both are true? That the Lord helps those who help themselves? Or that it was the wangling that did it, and prayer is no more than a pious gloss?

Psalm 34 does not describe the Achish-situation but meditates upon it so as to draw out the truth displayed and the lesson learnt: as David looked back he saw into the reality of what had happened. He had unthinkingly brought himself into a life-threatening situation, for the courtiers of Achish soon realised what a pawn in their game such a notable prisoner could be. But from this it was not, after all, his wangling that saved him, but, 'poor man' that he was (crushed, downtrodden, at the bottom of the heap), he prayed and the Lord worked a full deliverance. Therefore, in this acrostic psalm, which attempts to provide an A to Z on handling life's crises, he counsels the voice of prayer to God (vv. 4, 6, 10, 15, 17) and the voice of honesty to man (vv. 11-14).

GOD-CENTRED PRAYING

This, then, is how the psalms view prayer, for Psalm 34 is typical. But it is typical also in that its emphasis is on the Lord and his merciful deliverances, not on the intercessor and his needs. So much biblical praying is taken up with 'telling God about God', rehearsing, repeating and dwelling on what he is.

Psalm 44 is as public and national as Psalm 34 is private and personal, but the doctrine and practice of prayer are the same. It could well have been composed for a Day of

National Prayer in a time of crisis: there is a sense of divine alienation (v. 9), and the experience of defeat (v. 10), with loss of life and prisoners taken by the enemy (v. 11). But before any petition is voiced, verses 1-3 recall the greatness of the Lord's past acts, and verses 4-8 make a creedal profession of his sovereign kingliness (v. 4), the victory that he will give (v. 5) and the trust he merits (vv. 6-8). Within the structure of the psalm, the God of the past (vv. 1-30) is balanced by the God of the future (vv. 23-26), so that the whole presentation is dominated by who and what the Lord is to his people. This is what the Psalms describe as 'blessing' the Lord.

'Bless the Lord'

The verb (barak, blessing) in its various forms is used forty-four times in the Psalms (e.g. 18:46; 72:18; 96:2; 100:4; 145:1-2, 10, 21). The thought, of course, lies very close to that of praise, but two such distinct verbs should not be confused in translation. So what does it mean to 'bless' the Lord?

When the Lord 'blesses' us, he reviews what we are and notes our needs so as to meet them. This is what we want him to do when in prayer we ask him to 'bless' our friends – to review (how they are placed), take note (of their needs) and respond.

When we 'bless' God, likewise, we review what he is in order to take note of his glories, and respond in wonder, love and praise. It is for this reason that in the Psalms – and in other Bible prayers (for example Neh. 9:5-38; Dan. 9:4-19; Acts 4:24-30) – dwelling on who and what God is preponderates over asking, for how can we match our petitions to his will unless we first 'bless' him, allowing the glories of his person, attributes, character and acts to pass before our minds?

'YOU WHO HEAR PRAYER' (Psalm 65:2)

The Psalms teach us how to bring all life before God and to be determined about it.

In *Psalm 143* David faced persecution and life-threaten-ing enemies, and brought it to the Lord, praying in turn for his own renewed vitality, the end of his trouble and the de-struction of his enemies (vv. 11-12).

In *Psalm 142:4* the problem is loneliness – but the solu-tion the same.

By contrast, *Psalm 145* shows us how exhilaration and abounding joy are enhanced by 'blessing' the Lord's name (v. 1) – and what a glorious, heart-filling array of the divine at-tributes the psalm gathers together! But note, too, how 'bless-ing God' (vv. 1-21a) slips into an intercession (v. 21b). What could be more appropriate to the glory and immensity of this God than that 'all flesh' should 'bless His name', that is, come to know all he has revealed himself to be?

Psalm 88 is one of the most moving psalms in the whole collection. It is the only psalm without any note of hope, the product of a time of apparently terminal and prolonged ill-ness, and, appropriately to its mood throughout, it ends with the bleak word 'darkness' (v. 18). The three sections of the psalm, each beginning with a renewed appeal to the Lord (1-9a, 9b-12, 13-18), deal in turn with life without com-fort, death without hope and questions without answers. But prayer is still the way when all hope has gone: the sufferer in all his darkness is still the intercessor!

CURSES IN THE PSALMS

What about all those imprecations the Psalmists hurled at their enemies? There are about thirty places in the Psalms where the Psalmists want their enemies to be held guilty (5:10), their arms broken (10:15) or their way dark (35:6). They ask for the sudden death of their enemies (55:15), their teeth to be broken (58:6) and their children made fatherless (109:9). It is a grim catalogue and it is no wonder that com-mentators have turned to the seemingly obvious 'solution' – that this, after all, is the Old Testament, and Jesus has lifted us to a higher morality. This, however, will not do.

The Context of the Imprecations

- First of all, such a solution is not true to the Old Testament where we are instructed to love, and forbidden to take vengeance (Lev. 19:17-18), where we find deeds of kindness to enemies (1 Sam. 30:11-13), a reputation for undeserved mercy (1 Kings 20:30-31) and an example set of non-retaliation (Ps. 7:3-5; 35:12-13).

- Secondly, this simplistic solution is untrue to the very psalms in which the imprecations occur for, in every case, alongside the so-called difficult verses lie others which reveal a deep, even covetable spirituality.

Psalm 139 is a case in point. The imprecations occur in verses 19-22, but the previous verses are full not only of the most exalted theology – a God who knows all (vv. 1-6), pervades all (vv. 7-12), controls and predetermines all (vv. 13-16) – but of profound devotion, a beautiful, confident, restful trust in a God who surrounds (v. 5), leads and sustains (v. 10), plans with perfect prescience (v. 16), thinks thoughts of matchless preciousness (v. 17), and who is blessedly inescapable (vv. 7-12).

It is not the Psalmist who is in two minds but the commentators. Even Kirkpatrick, whose commentary is so generally helpful and who finds the imprecations 'the very opposite of the spirit of the Gospel', writes regarding Psalm 139 of 'the duty of keeping alive in the human heart the sense of burning indignation against moral evil' and finds this 'as much a part of the Christian' as of the earlier dispensation. (p. 791).

We may take a more positive approach:

- The imprecations are all prayers. They, too, are examples of 'taking it to the Lord in prayer'. There is no suggestion that the Psalmists intended to take any personal action against their foes in word or deed (35:13ff. would suggest the opposite). Prolonged, uncaused, oppressive and deadly enmity was their lot, but they did not respond in kind. They prayed about it.

- We have no liberty to read a spirit of personal vengeance into the prayers, for the Psalmists prayed with the 'perfect hatred' of Psalm 139:22. The fact that possibly we ourselves could not say such words without entertaining matching thoughts is a comment on us rather than on the Psalmists. They were living – as we are enjoined to live – in Romans 12:19-20.

PSALM 137:8-9

Typically of the so-called Imprecatory Psalms, the context in which the 'offensive verses' (vv. 8-9) occur is one of sensitive and developed spirituality. This should warn us against rushing hastily into an adverse judgment regarding the way the psalm ends, with its apparent commendation of a loathsome infanticide.

'Happy' has prevailed as a translation from the King James Version to the New International Version, and this is the heart of the problem. But the difficulty belongs to the translators rather than to the psalm itself.

The Hebrew (*'ashrey'*) is capable of three meanings:

- Its foremost meaning is 'under God's blessing' (as, for instance, 32:1).
- It also means 'personally fulfilled' (as, for instance, 1:1)
- The word also means 'right', 'doing the right thing in given circumstances' (as, for instance, 106:3; Prov. 14:21).

The third meaning accords more exactly with the base-meaning of the word than the other two. The Psalmist, then, does not ask that this fate should befall Babylon. This is not a prayer-imprecation like the others. Nor does he even express the wish about the way things are in God's world, according to the exact justice of God. This is what Babylon gave, and it is 'right' that this is what Babylon should get.

The Spirit of Christ

We must nevertheless ask how such prayers stand in the light of the Christ who prayed, 'Father, forgive', and chose rather to commit himself and his cause to God the Judge (1 Pet. 2:23; compare 4:19 and Isa. 49:4).

The question is proper, but it represents a selective view of the Lord Jesus. We must remember that it was he who pronounced a sevenfold 'woe' on his opponents (Matt. 23), who spoke of fearing One who could destroy body and soul in hell (Matt. 10:28), and from whose wrath none will be able to hide (Rev. 6:14-17). Before the throne, the prayer for vengeance was not rebuked but accepted, to be answered in its own time (Rev. 6:9-11). It would seem, then, if we are to model ourselves on the Lord Jesus, that the prayer we pray is a matter of spiritual sensitivity, and of praying the right prayer at the right time.

Realism

A fact central to our problem with the imprecations is revealed in Psalm 143:11b, 12a. Why is it that we would be comfortable with praying verse 11b in a time of trouble, and yet find ourselves offended by verse 12a? The answer is that verse 11b is non-specific and verse 12a is realistic. In David's situation, whatever it was, he obviously could see no other solution than the destruction of his enemies, and the same may well be true today when we pray for Christians in areas of persecution: their deliverance can often only come through the overthrow of their oppressors. When we pray, then, in our bland way, 'Lord, because you love what is right, bring them out of trouble', we are in fact praying, 'Because you love them, destroy their torturers.' In the same way, we would rather not pray, 'Lord, in flaming fire render vengeance to those who do not obey the gospel', but it is part of the unspoken realism accompanying a prayer we love to pray, 'Even so, come, Lord Jesus' (2 Thess. 1:8; Rev. 22:20).

Exact Divine Retributive Justice

As a generation, we are weak in a sense of moral outrage. Our culture loves to be 'cool'. The background to the Psalmist's realism in prayer is something we need to recapture: a sense of the holiness and wrath of God and the outrageousness of sin. The strong reactions expressed in Psalm 139:19-22 are but the obverse of the psalmist's awareness and commitment to the holiness of his God, (compare 17:13; 56:7; 141:10).

Furthermore, the Lord's holiness works out in ways he has himself revealed. Two biblical principles will be found to cover all cases where the Psalmists utter imprecations:

1. The Lord is faithful to his principle of exactness in the administration of justice (Exod. 21:23-25; Lev. 24:19-20; Deut. 19:21). The law, 'an eye for an eye', called the *lex talionis*, was given to the judge on the bench, not to direct him on the application of punishment but on its assessment. The punishment must exactly match the crime, no more, no less. Divine justice works with this same exactitude and the Psalmists did not hesitate, when it was right, to ask for it. It was the equivalent of praying, 'Your will be done.'

2. Deuteronomy 19:19 enunciates the principle that the false accuser must receive in retribution whatever he had purposed should happen to the one he falsely accused. Psalms like 69 and 109 are no more than this principle spelt out in intercession.

'SINGING SONGS OF EXPECTATION'

A very large group of psalms is concerned with the king. It is, for example, easy to see Psalm 2 as a coronation anthem.

Psalm 45 announces its occasion as a royal wedding.

Psalm 21 is David's own meditation on the privilege of his kingship.

Psalm 89 recalls the Lord's promises to the House of David and his successors.

Psalm 110 reflects on the union of priesthood and kingship in Melchizedek.

From the Real to the Ideal

When we think of the actual kings of David's line and even of David himself we have either to say that the portrait of the king in the Psalms is outrageous flattery, or that the Psalmists were expressing an ideal, holding up before each succeeding king a mirror of the true, alive with expectation that every next king might be the king for whom the people of God were longing, the king first expressed in the Judges-ideal.

There is much in the movement from the real to the ideal, the actual to the expected, that we cannot trace out. Nathan (2 Sam. 7) promised David an enduring house, but when did this promise modulate into the expectation of an ideal, individual and eternal king? Certainly it had done so by the time of Isaiah (9:1-7; 11:1-16; 32:1-8; 33:17-24).

It used to be a commonplace among Old Testament specialists that it was the collapse of the monarchy at the time of the Exile (586 BC) that provided the soil from which hope grew: for either the end of the monarchy spelled the end of the promises, or else, if they still held good, they would ultimately come to realisation. The commentators who adopted this view would feel that the Isaiah passages, for example, must be dated in and after the Exile.

But insofar as disappointment provokes re-evaluation, we surely do not have to wait for the Exile. Saul, David and Solomon all failed the Judges-test at one point or more, and there is no reason to doubt that the agonised question, 'Where is the king we need?' could have been asked during their reigns. It was certainly an urgent question under every subsequent king, south and north. The Royal Psalms express a longing hope and a living Messianism. Just as Deuteronomy 18:9-22 created the hope that every next prophet might be a prophet like Moses, so the Royal Psalms indicate that every next king was greeted by the same eager expectation.

Melchizedek

Psalm 110 stands out amongst the Royal Psalms in the way it reaches back into the past (to Gen. 14:17-20) and (as we see by hindsight) prepares for the future (in Heb. 4:14–7:28). It is only in these three places that the mysterious figure of Melchizedek appears, yet we have clues to follow which enable us to group the three references into a coherent picture.

- In Genesis 14 Abram becomes in principle king of the world. He has conquered the world rulers from the east (Gen. 14:1-16), and as he returns two kings meet him. As befits the conqueror, Abram sends the king of Sodom packing but, as it were in the same breath, acknowledges the superior kingship and true priesthood of Melchizedek: the former by paying him a tenth of all the spoil, and the latter by identifying Melchizedek's God, 'God Most High, the Possessor of heaven and earth', as none other than Yahweh himself (v. 22). The king of Salem is a true king, exercising a true priesthood based on a true theology.

- Salem and its kings resurface during Joshua's southern campaign when he faces Adoni-zedek, king of Jerusalem (Josh. 10:1). Almost a millennium after Abram, the same kingship reigns in the same city, for Adoni-zedek is a name or title of the same formation and meaning as Melchi-zedek, the former meaning 'Lord / Sovereign of righteousness' and the latter 'King of righteousness'.

- Jerusalem was sacked (Judg. 1:8) but not occupied (Judg. 1:21) in the wars of occupation, and does not figure again in the story until David takes the city, makes it his capital and royal seat – and himself (presumably) becomes Melchizedek, king of Salem. This would account for the otherwise inexplicable statement that 'David's sons were priests' (a literal translation for 2 Sam. 8:18), that is to say, not in the Aaronic priesthood, for that would be illegal and impossible, but within the royal priesthood their father possesses as king of Salem, 'the order of Melchizedek'.

- This is the context of Psalm 110 in the life and thinking of David. In this psalm we see David bringing together his acquired royal priesthood and his developing awareness (stated in Psalm 89:22-25, 30-33) that the Lord's (literally) 'never-failing loves' (Psalm 89:1, 49) for David involved universal sway (89:24-27) and an unending dynasty (89:28-29). In Psalm 110 David's 'Lord' reigns as king over his enemies (vv. 1-3), and in his unending priesthood (vv. 4-7) judges the nations.

Hebrews (5:1-10; 7:1-28), therefore, was neither fudging an important issue, nor engaging in special pleading, but re-introducing a biblical truth when it validated our Lord as 'priest after the order of Melchizedek.'

THE COMPILATION OF THE BOOK OF PSALMS

The process of compilation of the book of Psalms can only be surmised, and there is much we do not, indeed cannot, know.

1. There is no need to doubt that David was 'Israel's sweetest singer' (2 Sam. 23:1), nor to question his authorship of the psalms ascribed to him.

2. It is logical to assume that a religion so concentrated on the Jerusalem Temple would stimulate the collection of songs old and new:
   - The pilgrim feasts (Deut. 16:16) could well have prompted the collection of the 'Songs of Going Up' (Ps. 120–134).
   - If there was, as is likely enough, a special Festival of Kingship, it could have prompted Psalms 93–100.
   - Solomon's Temple could have supplied the impetus for at least the earliest collection of Davidic Psalms.
   - The major efforts at reform were Temple-centred, doubtless bringing their own prompting to revise the hymn-book.
   - Each guild of Temple singers probably had its own hymn-book.

LIFE, FAITH AND GOD

Faith may expect great things in the future, but life never looks like that! The realism of the Psalms is illustrated by comparing the opening psalms of the 'Five Books' into which the Psalter is divided. As to the 'books' themselves, this division is very ancient, reaching back at least to the LXX which could have been started in the third century BC. The fivefold division may have been modelled on the five books of the law, to give a matching compendium of song. We do not know if it was happy chance or intention that divided the Psalter at 42, 73, 90 and 107, but the sequence is full of meaning:

Psalm 1 expresses the faith that all must be well for those who walk with God and love his law.

The paired *Psalms 42–43* faces the fact that life is often quite the reverse of this faith, bringing tears (42:3), mockery (42:3), loss (42:4) and suffering (42:7), but at the same time it counsels hope in God (42:5, 11; 43:4).

Psalm 73 concurs: the disparity of life is often such as to make the righteous despair (vv. 2-3, 12-13), but there is the hope of glory (vv. 23-24), the presence of God in the heart (v. 36) and refuge found in him (v. 28).

Psalm 90 picks up Psalm 73:26: in all the vicissitudes of earthly pilgrimage, God is unchanging (vv. 1-2) and bestows a satisfying mercy (v. 14).

Psalm 107 reviews aspects of our pilgrimage to Zion (vv. 4, 10, 17, 23), and advocates the way of prayer as the way of deliverance (vv. 6, 13, 19, 28), as well as calling for confidence in the transforming power of God (vv. 33-43).

This, then, is the mix: faith is constantly tested in the concrete realities of life, but persists, strengthened by God's present help, confident in his control of present and future, looking on to an eternal hope, and bringing every experience and vicissitude of life to him in prayer.

DEATH AND LIFE

As in 1 Thessalonians 1:3, so in the Psalms, patient, persistent well-doing is spurred by hope. For the Psalmists, this hope had a twofold foundation.

Fellowship with the Living God

1. Fellowship with God continued from this life into the life after death.

- In *Psalm 16* David has experienced some undisclosed brush with death that makes him probe the question of security. He enjoys a present security in his 'possession' of God (vv. 1-8), but this security has also an eternal dimension (vv. 9-11). Beyond Sheol (the place where the dead lived on), he discerns a 'path of life' into the full joy of the Lord's presence (v. 11).

- In *Psalm 17:14-15* David draws a contrast between his foes (v. 14) and himself (v. 15). He speaks ironically of the 'satisfaction' that awaits them, the full requital of what they have done. By contrast he, too, will be 'satisfied', but with the visible presence of God ('gaze upon your face ... likeness') which lies beyond his 'awaking', that is, to new life after death (compare Isa. 26:19; Dan. 12:2).

- *Psalm 49* may owe its position in the Psalter to the last words of Psalm 48: 'He will guide us unto / against death.' In support of this faith, Psalm 49:15 cries out, 'God will redeem my soul from the hand of Sheol, for he will take me.' The psalm focuses on the perennial problem of life's inequalities, particularly the fortunes and hopes of the wealthy (vv. 6, 10, 16). Verses 1-12 can be summarised by saying that death levels all. No earthly wealth can find the ransom price (v. 7) to buy death off. All alike die (v. 12).

But verses 13-20 penetrate further, right into differing destinies after death. For the ungodly, Sheol becomes their sheep pen (v. 14a) and Death their shepherd (v. 14b). Earthly relationships are reversed and 'the upright', those who are right with God, have the dominion (v. 14c). For them God has found a ransom price (v. 15a, the same verb as in verse 7, *padah*); Sheol cannot retain them (v. 15b). God 'takes' (verb *laqah*) them, that is, to himself, as once he 'took' Enoch (Gen. 5:24), and Elijah (2 Kings 2:1, 3, 5, 9, 10).

- The same verb (*laqah*) is used again in the climax of *Psalm 73:23-24*. Once more the Psalmist is troubled by the inequality of life as he finds it. He exercises himself in the way of holiness but only meets one trouble after another (vv. 13-14), whereas the spiritually careless die without pain (v. 4, literally, 'there are no bonds/pangs in their death'), live without worry (v. 5), enjoy plenty (v. 7), and complacently flout the authority of God (v. 8).

- Only in the Lord's sanctuary is the problem solved (vv. 16-17), and the solution is this: what to the human eye is a painless death (v. 4) is actually the slippery slope to destruction (v. 18), terror (v. 19), and rejection by God (v. 20).

By contrast, the Psalmist possesses an immediate and constant enjoyment of God's presence ('I *am* continually with you', v. 23a NKJV) and of his upholding (v. 23b, compare v. 2), a future confidence based on the assurance that a divine plan is shaping his life (v. 24a), and an ultimate entrance to 'glory' (v. 24b).

2. The kingship of the Lord
This is alluded to widely in the Psalms, and may even have been the focus of an annual Festival of Divine Kingship (rather like our Ascension Day).

The Eschatological God

Psalms 93–100 offer a focus of Old Testament thinking about the kingship of the Lord. If there was a Festival of Kingship, this was its hymn-book.

The collection starts with the Lord's reign as the Holy One over all creation (Ps. 93) and moves progressively to the vision of all peoples acknowledging him (96:8-9). Ultimately, he will judge the peoples (96:10) and bring creation back to its proper joy by judging the world (96:11-13; compare 98:5-9). In the Old Testament this is the royal 'judgment' which sets everything to rights by making and implementing the right decisions.

This is the Old Testament expectation of new heavens and a new earth, and its way of saying, 'Even so, come, Lord Jesus.'

Further reading

J.A. Motyer, 'Psalms' in *New Bible Commentary* (IVP, 1994)
—*Treasures of the King: Psalms from the Life of David* (IVP, 2007)
—*Journey: Psalms fot Pilgrim People* (IVP, 2009)
—*Life 2: The Sequel. What Happens when you die?* (Christian Focus, 1995)
E. Lane, *Psalms 1–89,* (Christian Focus, 2006)
—*Psalms 90–150,* (Christian Focus, 2006)
M. Ross, *The Light of the Psalms* (Christian Focus, 2006)
D. Belcher, *The Messiah and the Psalms* (Christian Focus, 2008)
T. Moore, *God's Prayer Program* (Christian Focus, 2005)
J. Day, *Psalms,* Old Testament Guides (Sheffield, 1990)
T. Longman, *How to read the Psalms* (IVP, 1988)
F.D. Kidner, *The Psalms,* 2 vols, Tyndale Old Testament Commentary (IVP, 1973/5)
M. Wilcock, *The Message of the Psalms,* The Bible Speaks Today (IVP, 2001)
A. Harman, *Psalms* (Christian Focus, 1998)
A.F. Kirkpatrick, *The Psalms* (CUP, 1910)
W.A. VanGemeren, 'Psalms' in F. Gaebelein, Ed., *The Expositor's Bible Commentary* (Zondervan, 1991)

'DEATH' IN THE PSALMS

The fundamental Old Testament position is that the dead are alive. They live on in Sheol (Num. 16:33). Theirs is necessarily a somewhat diminished life, for they have left part of themselves, the bodily part, behind: nevertheless they live on – to be met (Gen. 25:8) and recognised (Gen. 37:35; 2 Sam. 12:23). Job anticipated Sheol as a place of rest (3:17-19), and if, on the one hand, the Old Testament considered Sheol the destination of the sinner (Prov. 7:27), on the other hand, it entertained a blessed hope for those who were right with God (Ps. 17:15; 49:14-15; 73:23-24).

DEATH AFTER DEATH?

Some verses are often understood to indicate absence of hope after death: 6:5; 30:9 and 88:10ff. fall into this category and, at first sight, seem to present unrelieved darkness. But consider a parallel hermeneutical situation: Psalm 7. The heading to Psalm 7 places it in the period when David was in danger from Saul. When, therefore, in verse 8, he speaks of 'my righteousness' we know that he is not claiming sinless perfection, but believes that in relation to Saul and the things of which he has been accused, he is in the right – and, indeed, has done nothing wrong. In other words, within any psalm its statements must be contextualised and only universalised if that context suggests or demands it. In the same way, in the three psalms mentioned above, the Psalmist believes himself to be dying under the wrath of God and it is in this situation that he expresses personal hopelessness.

PRAISE FOREVERMORE

Regarding Psalm 115:17, we note that verse 18 envisages praise 'forevermore'. It would be wrong, then, to interpret verse 17 as meaning that for everyone praise stops at death. Behind the psalm lies a deadly crisis which would have silenced the earthly praise of the Lord (v. 17) but for divine intervention.

Further reading

J.A. Motyer, *Life 2: The Sequel. What Happens when you die?* (Christian Focus, 1996)

8

ELIJAH AND ELISHA:
A RESOUNDING 'NO'

The first reference to a prophet in the Bible is Genesis 20:7, where Abimelech is instructed by the Lord to take his problems to Abraham because 'he *is* a prophet and he will pray for you.' There does not, however, seem to be anything in the title 'prophet' as such to forge a link with intercession. Insofar as the word for prophet (nabi) is understood, it is passive in form and probably means 'one sent'. Genesis 20:7 suggests that by the intention of God the person sent from him to others also carries their needs back to him.

From the time of Moses onwards, prophets wove their way in and out of the history of the Lord's people, not predictable in their appearing nor indeed explaining themselves: simply individuals who were bearers of the word of the Lord to the people of the Lord.

MOSES: THE NORM AND THE EXPECTATION
The unique Moses (Num. 12:6-8), the norm against which all subsequent prophets were to be compared

(Deut. 34:10), created the expectation of the ministry of prophets in Israel.

Testing a Prophet: By his Message

In Deuteronomy 13 Moses sketches the situation where a prophet arises and validates his claims by supernatural signs. In such a situation, Moses warned, the validation of the prophet is not in his signs but in his message, and the question they must ask is not, 'Has he shown a sign from heaven?' but, 'Does his message conform to or diverge from the truth of "the Lord your God who brought you out of the land of Egypt and redeemed you from the house of slaves"?' (13:5-6, 13).

Thus Deuteronomy 13 proposes a theological test for the prophet: Is he true to the Exodus / redemptive revelation of God?

Testing a Prophet: by Fulfilment

Moses offers a second test of prophetic validity (Deut. 18:20-22). The implication here is that prophets will arise in the course of Israel's history; each must be awaited with eagerness in case he should be the promised 'prophet like Moses' (John 6:14; 7:40) but each must pass the test of the fulfilment of his predictions for the unfulfilled word cannot be what the Lord has spoken.

PROPHETS AND SIGNS

The Bible does not encourage a preoccupation with what is loosely called the 'miraculous'. Neither Old Testament Hebrew, nor, indeed, New Testament Greek offers a word quite equivalent to our word 'miracle'. Both speak of 'wonders' (Deut. 13:1; Acts 2:22), that is, acts or events that cause amazement, or make people stop in their tracks (Luke 11:14), and 'signs' (Deut. 13:1; John 2:11), that is, acts or events which point away from themselves, calling attention to something or someone else.

The words most usually translated 'miracle' are, in the Old Testament, *pele'* which, in a broad sense, corresponds to our idea of supernatural, belonging outside the ordinary range of experience (Exod. 15:11; Ps. 78:12; compare the adjective 'hard' in Gen. 18:14, that is, 'beyond available power'), and, in the New Testament, *dynamis*, a 'power' – expressing the same basic idea as *pele'*, that here is something involving a power beyond the usual.

The supposed philosophical objection to miracles as fracturing the laws of nature has always been based on the erroneous assumption that we 'know the laws of nature', but it also overlooks the fact that, supremely in the case of the Lord Jesus, the frame of reference proper to him is not the frame of reference in which we live. It would certainly be a 'miracle' if some mere human raised Lazarus from the dead, but to use the word 'miracle' of Jesus is quite misleading: rather it stands to reason that the Son of God raises the dead – but naturally, when he does so we feel this is a *wonder*, causing us to stop in our tracks, a *sign* pointing away to a truth about him, and a *power* at work beyond the usual.

KEY DATES		
Kings of Israel:		
874	Ahab	1 Kings 16:29–22:40
853	Ahaziah	1 Kings 22:51–2 Kings 1:18
852	Jehoram	2 Kings 3:1-27
841	Jehu	2 Kings 9:1–10:36
814	Jehoahaz	2 Kings 13:1-9
798	Jehoash	2 Kings 13:10-25; 14:8-14
	The Elijah stories	1 Kings 17–2 Kings 2:12
	The Elisha stories	1 Kings 19:19–2 Kings 13:20

Speaking God's Words

But signs and wonders are not evenly spread through the Bible. The God of providence is much more in evidence than the God of miracle. We have only to think of the huge tracts of history covered by genealogies to see that for the most part God has quietly, unobtrusively and secretly worked his purposes out. Even in the case of prophets this is so.

- In Judges 6:8 a prophet suddenly confronted the people with typical Exodus reminders and rebukes.
- Gad (1 Sam. 22:5; 2 Sam. 24:11) and Nathan (2 Sam. 7:1; 1 Kings 18–45) ministered to David, directing and correcting, and Nathan took a leading part in the palace revolution that brought Solomon to the throne, but as far as is recorded their ministry was not marked by any overtly supernatural act.
- Moses performed signs (Exod. 4:1-9; 17:1-7; etc.), but after him, it was not until Samuel that such signs once more made their appearance (1 Sam. 7:10; 12:17-18).
- After Samuel signs disappeared until the ministry of Elijah and Elisha.

The Function of Signs

Signs marked and called attention to the great turning points of salvation-history. Moses was the unique foundation-layer; in Samuel prophetic ministry of the word of God was restored to Israel after a dead period (1 Sam. 3:1, 19, 21–4:1), and Samuel was used by the Lord to institute kingship. Elijah and Elisha were raised up to utter a resounding 'No' to a fatal national apostasy, and to set in train that astonishing flowering of prophetic ministry which we still treasure in the books of the prophets.

THE CLASH OF CULTURES

Canaan had been a new experience in every way for incoming Israel. Leaving wilderness isolation to become a nation among nations had brought with it a clash of cultures. Deuteronomy 11:10-11 puts its finger on the point where this clash will become crucial: What is the basis of prosperity in an agricultural economy? The problem hardly arose in Egypt where the perennial Nile guaranteed both the proverbial fertility of the soil and an unbroken water supply. Therefore, said Moses, you sowed your seed and watered it with your foot. All you had to do was kick away the small mound of soil damming the irrigation channel which brought the Nile into your fields and water flowed without end! Not so in Canaan where dependence on rainfall (Deut. 11:11) introduces the novel element of looking in faith to the God who gives the rain.

Baal
Traditionally in Canaan the god who gave the rain was Baal, the god of fertility for land, animals and humans. But Moses revealed an alternative economic theory: if they obeyed the law of the Lord their God they would be blessed in the fruit of their bodies, of their land and of their cattle (Deut. 28:1-4), and the Lord would in particular 'give the rain of your land in its season to bless all the work of your hand' (28:12). There was not only, therefore, a clash of deities or a clash of religions but, very practically, a clash of economic systems.

In the Time of the Judges – Compromise
The book of Judges reveals to us that the sin of compromise beset Israel from the start. They compromised with the local inhabitants (1:21, 27-36), and it was then but a short step to forsake the Lord and serve Baal (2:12-13). Yet it was conscious compromise – compromise with a guilty conscience – for Israel knew where its true allegiance lay, as is evidenced by the unquestioning Yahwism of the Song of Deborah (Judg. 5), or the reply of Gideon (Judg. 6:13).

After the Division of the Kingdom – Apostasy
It was especially in the newly founded northern kingdom of Israel (1 Kings 12) that compromise was taken to the next stage.

Jeroboam 1 (931–910 BC) authorised a syncretism, centring his innovative religion on the Baal-system of the bull, and actually identifying this as 'the God who brought you out of the land of Egypt' (1 Kings 12:28-29). Yahweh was no longer, so to speak, co-existing with Baal; he was himself seen as a Baal.

Ahab (874–852 BC), forty years later, at first continued the 'sins of Jeroboam' (1 Kings 16:31), but under the influence of his wife Jezebel, herself a Baal-worshipper, he went further. He built in Samaria, a 'house of Baal' with all its religious furnishings (1 Kings 16:32; compare 2 Kings 10:17-27), and supported Jezebel in exterminating Yahweh's prophets (1 Kings 18:4), and in relentless pursuit of Elijah (18:10).

Things were now very far beyond either hedging one's economic bets by dabbling in Baalism, or even Jeroboam's 'new theology' of making Yahweh a Baal. Ahab and Jezebel turned the situation into an either/or. Israel's rulers were intent on replacing Yahweh with the Baal of Ekron.

ELIJAH AND ELISHA

Elijah (1 Kings 17–2 Kings 2) and Elisha (2 Kings 2–13) were very different in personality and approach but, facing the same religious and spiritual situation, they made the same response to it, and left the same legacy: the unique and non-negotiable truths of Yahweh and Yahwism.

God's Contrasts

Taken together, Elijah and Elisha illustrate two contrasting dimensions in the work of God.

- Elijah majored on great public demonstrations, the prophetic voice addressing the nation (1 Kings 18), confronting the king (1 Kings 21). Fire from heaven was his chosen proof of answered prayer (1 Kings 18:24) or of the dignity of the Lord's prophet (2 Kings 1:10).

  Elisha, so to speak, lived close to the earth. His demonstrations were local and for the most part merciful provisions for known needs (2 Kings 2:18-22; 4:1-7, 36-37, 38-44).

- Where Elijah commanded crowds (1 Kings 18:19), Elisha dealt with individuals (2 Kings 5:1).

- Elijah (rightly but also typically) executed the false prophets (1 Kings 18:40); Elisha (typically) sent home the invading army in peace (2 Kings 6:21-23).

All such contrasts are, of course, relative and not absolute. Elijah also ministered domestically and individually (1 Kings 17:17-24), and Elisha played his part (and with Elijah-like frankness!) on the national scene (2 Kings 3:13ff.). But the essence of the contrast is accurate: there are two avenues of prophetic ministry, and two distinct approaches to national crises: the public, denunciatory and dramatic, and the local, individual and low-key. Each man in his own way, in obedience to God, played a key role in saying 'No' to apostasy and maintaining the testimony to the truth.

God's Servants

God's two great witnesses had this in common: they came in their distinctive ways into public ministry from the privacy of the Lord's fellowship. Twice each man used the same oath of confirmation: 'As the LORD lives before whom I stand' (1 Kings 17:1; 18:15; 2 Kings 3:14; 5:16). Like all the Hebrew 'tenses', the perfect tense, 'stand', here is rich in nuances. It reflects choice ('I have taken my stand'), commitment ('I have determined to stand') and an established state of affairs ('I do indeed stand'). The position is that of a servant awaiting orders (compare 2 Kings 5:25; Isa. 6:8).

Behind the public man, therefore, was the private man, spiritually 'waiting on God', enjoying the presence of God, only moving at the divine word (compare 1 Kings 17:2, 5, 8, 10; 18:1), and therefore a man of confidence in action and of authority in ministry.

ELIJAH
Elijah came to the place where he uttered his resounding
'No' to Baalism through a carefully planned apprenticeship
with God.

Elijah's Apprenticeship (1 Kings 17)

Before (literally) 'show yourself' (1 Kings 18:1) there was 'hide
yourself' (17:3), a three-year secret divine schooling (Luke
4:25; compare James 5:17). The tests were progressive.

- In the *first test* (17:2-7), obedience was made easier
  in that Elijah was sent back home across Jordan
  (17:1, 3). But even so, the call to trust God's word
  was far from easy, for Elijah was committed for his
  support to a wady (17:3) – a stream dependent on
  rainfall – and to scavenging birds not notable for
  charitable ways. But he trusted and obeyed and
  was provided for. The apprentice was learning the
  power of the word of the Lord over needs, things and
  circumstances.

- The *second test* was more demanding (17:8-16), for
  Elijah, still committed to a totally uncertain source
  of support (17:9), was now sent out of his own land
  into enemy territory: to 'Zarephath which belongs
  to Zidon', that is, into the land of Jezebel's father
  (16:31) and, as the map shows, under the very nose
  of this powerful foe. When Ahab's messengers came
  to Zidon seeking him (18:10), Elijah in Zarephath
  may very well have watched them go by. But he
  was there by obedience and in a spirit of trust in
  the divine word, and he learned the lesson that the
  Lord rules the hearts of people (17:10-11), and is
  powerful in every place and over all the power of
  the enemy.

- The *third test* was hardest of all (17:17-24) for it
  touched on the mysterious power of death itself: Does

the power of the Lord extend here, too? Furthermore, Elijah faced it without any preparatory word of command. The test was supremely one of confidence in the Lord: Had he learnt enough of the tender care and concern of the Lord to know that he would interest himself in this need? Had Elijah learnt enough of the power of the Lord to believe that even death is subject to him? Through this test he discovered the power of prayer and the reality of a prayer-answering God.

What lessons, then, did Elijah carry with him when he was called to leave his hidden years?

1. When he walks in obedience to the Lord he will be provided for.
2. The Lord is equally in charge in every place and is the master of things, circumstances, people, enemies and even death itself.
3. Prayer is answered.

Elijah on Carmel (18:1-46)
Elijah obeyed a command and received a promise (18:1). As he obeyed, he discovered that the Lord was on his side, stage-managing the whole exercise, for, though he was commanded to 'show himself to Ahab', it was in fact Ahab who was put at the disadvantage of approaching Elijah (18:16). Elijah's answer (18:18) is a superb demonstration of the unaggressive authority of the man who comes from the presence of God.

The Contest
On Carmel itself, following the lesson learned in his apprenticeship, Elijah proposed a prayer-contest. The point at issue was not fire from heaven but (18:24 NKJV) 'the God who answers by fire'. Does Baal answer prayer? Elijah knew that the Lord does.

First, then, the prophets of Baal practised their religion (18:26-28). Baal was the impersonal force which was thought to energise life on earth. One could no more pray to Baal than to pray to electricity or to the contemporary form of Baalism, 'market forces'. All Baal's devotees could do was:

1. Try to make him look their way awhile;
2. Perform on earth some action similar to what they wanted Baal to do in heaven. Crying out (18:26, 28), then, was designed to catch Baal's attention. They did not ask for fire from heaven to ignite their sacrifice; they simply made what they hoped would be attention-catching cries. This was the essence of Baal 'worship'.

Since Baal was the god of fertility, Baal worship required the performance of human acts of fertility in the hope that Baal would see and catch on. This is called 'sympathetic' or 'imitative magic'. The Baal-prophets required a down-pouring fire, and they had to do their best to imitate what they needed. As they leapt around their altar they therefore made blood pour down over their bodies, trying in this way to replicate down-falling fire and dancing flames.

Elijah's Victory

1. Elijah started with a deliberate rejection of imitative magic (18:33-35), hence the water: the very last thing an imitative magician would dream of doing. The prophets of Baal must have been aghast that someone who desired outpoured fire would so deliberately and repeatedly pour out the very reverse! Elijah was making a theological statement: Yahweh is not that sort of God; his responses are not extracted from him by magic. He is a personal and caring God whose ear is open to his people's cry.

2. Consequently, Elijah turned to the simplest of prayers. In Zarephath he had learned the effectiveness of putting the whole case to the Lord (17:20, 22), and what he had learned in secret he relied on in public. His requests were twofold. He asked that by answering prayer:

   a. the Lord would affirm himself as 'God in Israel' (18:36) and therefore the proper object of his people's devotion, as distinct from a foreign import like Baal;

   b. he would affirm himself 'as God', the only God in contrast to pretenders and nonentities such as Baal.

   The prayer is as notable for its brevity as for its simplicity, for the power of prayer is not located at the point of departure – the human mind that devises it, the human tongue that voices it or the human energy that lends it urgency – but at the point of arrival, the ear of a prayer-hearing God.

3. Elijah set about the eradication of Baalism from Israel by his immediate execution of the prophets (18:40). Before we leap to condemn him for an act of savagery, we need to ask ourselves if we really see theological and religious falsehood as a serious matter. Do we share Elijah's conviction that life-and-death issues are involved for individuals, nations and churches if error is allowed to flourish unchecked? Elijah, with these convictions, acted appropriately to his own times. We readily allow that such a remedy would not be appropriate today, but equally readily we should covet for ourselves the conviction which animated Elijah, the decisive commitment to the truth and abhorrence of error which he possessed.

4. Elijah, having obeyed the Lord's command, waited confidently for the fulfilment of his promise (18:1).

The posture indicated in 18:42 is not necessarily one of prayer; it is certainly one of submissive waiting. So the attendant was sent back seven times, and with the appearance of even such a tiny cloud, Elijah recognised the time of the promise of rain.

ELISHA

Elisha, too, had his apprenticeship, but of this we are told nothing. All we know is that he joined Elijah after the latter's nervous breakdown and restoration (1 Kings 19:1-21) in the reign of Ahab, and was with him to witness his 'ascension' (2 Kings 2:1-12), apparently in the reign of Jehoram.

Elisha's Hidden Years

Ahab began to reign in 874 BC; Jehoram began his reign in 853 BC. If it were possible to be sure of the dates (or even the identity) of the Benhadad whose invasion is recorded in 1 Kings 20 this would provide a *terminus ante quem* for the beginning of the great partnership, but certainty is elusive. The suggestion that this was Benhadad II who acceded in 860 BC certainly suits the feel of the biblical narrative.

By the time of the Carmel incident (1 Kings 18) and certainly by the time of Naboth (1 Kings 21), Ahab and Jezebel had a very firm grip on royal power, suggesting a possible date around 865 BC. This would mean that Elisha had a dozen or so years as Elijah's junior – enough time to become his own man, to take the affectionate and almost playful attitude to Elijah that 2 Kings 2:1-6 reveals, and to be confident enough in their relationship to ask for the 'double portion' of the first-born son (2 Kings 2:9; Deut. 21:17).

It would be guesswork to ask what Elisha might have learned by 'being there' during the events of 1 Kings 21 or 2 Kings 1, though the similarities between the two incidents of restoring the dead (1 Kings 17:17-24 and 2 Kings 4:8-27) reveal a history of sharing and instruction by the older prophet. We are on firmer ground, however, in following Elisha as he went with

Elijah to Jordan and in seeing how he reacted when his master was 'taken away from his head' (2 Kings 2:3, 5).

- *He was a prophet in his own right,* confident in his personal relationship with the Lord. The secretive Elijah kept back the information of his departure, but when the 'sons of the prophets' came to break the news to Elisha he was ahead of them. He knew already.

- *He had a sensitive awareness of other people.* From the start, Elijah was 'God's loner', Elijah contra mundum. In 1 Kings 17:1 he simply leapt out of obscurity to confront the king, bringing and needing no one with him. Even after the faithful Obadiah revealed that there were one hundred other prophets of the Lord (1 Kings 18:4), he still said 'I only am left' (1 Kings 18–22). Maybe he scorned them for hiding in their caves, but if so he was forgetful that he had been keeping his head below the parapets in Zarephath! In the nervous crisis of 19:1ff. he left his servant in Beersheba while he headed out into the wilderness alone, and, reaching Horeb, it was still 'I only am left'. Typically, therefore, Elijah was going to die alone, and Elisha was too sensitive to intrude on the older man's privacy by saying that he already knew what the end of this road would bring. Silent and undemanding, he accommodated himself to the other's weaknesses.

  The same was true when the 'sons of the prophets' wanted to send a search party out to find Elijah (2:17-18). Elisha knew that there was no need to do this but he also knew that for their part they needed to do it, and he acquiesced in what would quieten their anxieties. This could be called 'learning by contrast' – at least it shows that during the hidden years Elisha saw that there was another way of going about things besides Elijah's more confrontational methods.

- *Elisha was aware of the function of the prophetic office and the resources needed to fulfil it.* Watching the departing Elijah he addressed him as 'the chariot of Israel and its horsemen'. In other words the prophet was the real defence force against Israel's enemies and the real counter-offensive against threat. Elisha began his solo ministry by fulfilling this double function but he knew that if he was to do so it would only be by receiving a double portion of Elijah's spirit.

  It is easy to enter into Elisha's feelings at this point: the feelings of everyone with a 'lower key' temperament in the shadow of a towering figure such as Elijah, the feelings of every more introvert or melancholic servant of God in comparison with the dominant extrovert. Did Elisha ever say to himself, 'It's all very well for Elijah to go bouncing into the king's presence, shouting the odds!'? The spirit of Elijah was the Spirit of the Lord, and Elisha knew his need.

- *Elisha knew and was prepared to trust the power of the Lord as he had watched it at work in and through Elijah.* He had seen Elijah as he went into heaven; he believed that he was now endowed with the first-born's double portion, and in that faith he smote the waters of Jordan and crossed back like another Joshua to capture and possess the land. Could this have been the deeper thought in the Lord's mind in bringing Elijah home to die in Transjordan – that by doing so Elisha would have to make his personal commitment to the prophetic office as Israel's chariot and horsemen, to retake the land for God?

Elisha's Work – His 'No'

Like Joshua (Josh. 5:13ff.; 7:2; 8:9, 12, 17) Elisha's first port of call was Jericho (2 Kings 2:18-22) and his second Bethel (2 Kings 2:23-25). In the presentation of the Elisha-stories, these two incidents are set apart from the long series which begins at 4:1 by a war-narrative (3:1-27) in which Elisha was only an incidental participant. Chapter 3 has, of course, its own quota to add to the portrait of Elisha, but it also serves to isolate these two initial acts. In the first a curse is removed, in the second a curse is imposed, and together they reflect the balance of Elisha's theology and ministry, and his role as the defensive and offensive chariot and horsemen of Israel.

God's Blessing: Jericho (2 Kings 2:19-22)

This town had been put under a curse by Joshua (6:26), and it is typical of the increasingly apostate reign of Ahab that in his time Hiel the Bethelite rebuilt the cursed city (1 Kings 16:34) – though he did so, as Joshua forecast, at the expense of his children. Is it the implication that he himself killed his sons as consecration-offerings marking the beginning ('foundations') and completion ('gates') of the enterprise? Or that, flouting the word of God, he came under direct divine judgment? If the former, then the Jerichoites live to see that no human expedient, however costly, suffices to satisfy the wrath of God. If the latter, then those who took up residence in Hiel's new city were flying in the face of God's displeasure.

The new citizens of Jericho lived to rue the day they moved there, for residence proved that, lovely though the site was, the 'water was bad' and the land brought nothing to full growth (v. 19). The verb here is *sakal* which in its simple form means to be 'bereaved' (Gen. 43:14) and, in its transitive form, is used of spontaneous abortion in animals (Gen. 31:38), of people 'robbed of their children' by hostile action (Gen. 42:36; 1 Sam. 15:33) and of a vine failing to produce mature fruit (Mal. 3:11). There was something about Jericho that was inimical to health: abortions were common and crops uniformly stunted.

When Elisha acted to counter this situation it was in a true prophetic manner with actions symbolic of the word of God. He was not a magician working by intrinsically potent rituals. The rectification was the work of God who says, 'I have healed.' But the acts were symbolically important.

A *new dish*: 'new' (v. 20) is only used in ritual contexts in Leviticus 23:16 and Numbers 28:26, both of which refer to new beginnings with God, celebrated on what we know as the day of Pentecost. Very likely, Elisha required a 'new dish' for this same symbolic reason. He was giving Jericho an opportunity to start anew with God.

'*Salt*' may well have a double meaning. On the one hand, it was used as a contaminating agent, destructive of fertility (Judg. 9:45; Ezek. 47:11). With this use in mind, we can see Elisha following the example of Elijah in publicly contradicting a theology of sympathetic magic – the reverse of what a prophet or priest of Baal would have done. But, on the other hand, salt was an invariable component of sacrifice (Lev. 2:13; Ezek. 43:24) and an unexplained covenant symbol (Lev. 2:13; Num. 18:19; 2 Chron. 13:5). Elisha was bringing Jericho out of the sphere of the curse and into the circle of covenant blessing.

God's Curse: Bethel (2 Kings 2:23-25)
One side of the prophetic office, then, was to bring people within the sphere of divine blessing and favour, as, for example, Elisha was later to do for Naaman the Aramean (2 Kings 5:1-19). The other side was to visit the curse of God on apostasy (as Elisha did, later, in the case of Gehazi, 2 Kings 5:20-27). Arguably, Bethel lay on Elisha's obvious route back to his headquarters at Carmel (compare 4:25), but he could not have been unaware of an inevitable 'stand-off' as the new prophet came to confront the old apostasy (1 Kings 12:28-29).

The meaning of the word 'youths': the older translations (King James Version and, astonishingly, the Revised Version) have served Old Testament readers wretchedly in portraying this incident as a chance encounter of a bald prophet with a cheerfully teasing group of children. It was anything but this. In verse 23 the mockers are called (literally) 'small young men' (*n'arim q'tannim*). Jonathan took a 'small young man' (*na'ar qaton*) with him as a servitor (1 Sam. 20:35), not a 'little lad' (KJV), but a junior member of his staff. The same words are used of Joseph's teenage sons in Genesis 48:16, 19. Regarding the different word (*y'ladim*) in verse 24, much the same is true. Rehoboam, in his forties at the time of his accession (1 Kings 14:21), consulted with the *y'ladim* who were his contemporaries – in other words, the younger age group as compared with the old courtiers who had served his father. The words used, then, must be translated appropriately to their context.

In the light of all this, a very different scenario emerges. News that Elisha had succeeded Elijah would have reached Bethel, and the priests there would have made plans to strike the first blow before the new man was confidently secure in office. They therefore arranged a 'reception committee' of 'young louts' (v. 23). The chant of 'bald head' remains without sure explanation. Commentators have noted that, even were Elisha bald (unusual for so young a man), the would-be muggers could not have known it, for he would not have been out and about with uncovered head. It is not impossible that youngsters (then as now) invented nicknames by opposites – for example, calling the bald 'hairy', the over-tall 'shorty'. Did Elisha, then, wear his hair notably long (compare 2 Kings 1:8), and was this because of a Nazirite vow (Num. 6:5)? If so, then the shouts of his tormentors were an appropriate expression of derision from the Bethel mob, a pointed mockery of his consecration to Yahweh.

This is, of course, supposition, but the situation in which Elisha found himself was a real crisis. If he stood to make a fight of it he had no hope: his ministry would have ended before it had begun. If he ran for cover, he sacrificed forever the possibility of an effective ministry against the Baalists. Like the Psalmists, he made his need a subject for imprecatory prayer and left the outcome to the Lord (v. 24).

The Powerful God

The question, therefore, is not that old chestnut, the supposed 'moral problem' of a God who sends she-bears to savage toddlers, but whether those who venture out in the Lord's service have on their side a God who will stand by them in need and danger, or one who will desert them when they need him most. And Elisha was certainly in need. If the she-bears caught forty-two assailants, how many got away? To think of a gang of one hundred or one hundred and twenty would not be excessive. In such circumstances, would we not long for a God of power to step in on our side?

This is no passage for ivory-towered comment but reflects the cruel reality of an often desperately hostile world in which a god of fashionable political correctness is a waste of time. In fact, the holy Yahweh decided to kill none of the assailants but to leave forty-two bully boys on the streets of Bethel, carrying for life the scars which proved their and their god's powerlessness before the God of Israel and his servants the prophets.

Further reading

D.R. Davis *The Wisdom and the Folly* (1 Kings) (Christian Focus, 2008)
–*The Power and the Fury* (2 Kings) (Christian Focus, 2009)
A.W. Pink, *The Life of Elijah* (Banner of Truth, 1991)
Lance Pierson, *Elijah: Standing for God in a Hostile World* (IVP, 1989)

9

Amos and Hosea:
Voices in the North

The northern kingdom of Israel lasted for nearly two hundred years until, following the politically successful reign of Jeroboam II (died 753 BC, 2 Kings 14:23-29), thirty years of dissolution terminated in the fall of Samaria to the Assyrians in 722 BC (2 Kings 17).

The Fall of Samaria
It all began with a great promise rashly squandered. Through the prophet Ahijah, the Lord, while affirming his unchanged commitment to David, promised Jeroboam I 'a sure house' on condition of obedience (1 Kings 11:29-38). Jeroboam, however, who saw religion only as a political adjunct to his monarchy, flouted the Lord's law, and became a forerunner to a line of kings who continued in 'the sins of Jeroboam the son of Nebat' (for example 1 Kings 15:26, 34; 16:26, 31).

There were twenty kings in all (six of them in the last thirty years) with five dynasties of varying length. Eight kings were assassinated. Nevertheless, when a second Jeroboam came to the throne in 782 BC, the kingdom enjoyed a late flowering. He was no exception to the melancholy chorus in that he continued in the sins of his namesake (2 Kings 14:24), but he came to a kingdom brought to its knees by the preceding five-king dynasty of Jehu and the Lord's mercy was such that he enabled Jeroboam to restore Israel to its Solomonic boundaries (1 Kings 14:25-28). Along with this territorial enlargement came wealth, but not equally shared. While the commercial classes grew richer, the poor became increasingly deprived and oppressed (Amos 2:6-7; 4:1; 5:11; 8:5-6).

AMOS AND HOSEA

Into this situation the Lord sent two prophets, Amos and Hosea, mounting a rescue mission of mercy, a final warning of the abyss ahead. In Amos there is still a sense of a strong, central government (e.g. 7:10ff.), and a stable, even if unequal, and corrupt society. Hosea, however, (7:1ff.), reveals a society breaking up under dissolute leadership. We may therefore place Amos somewhere around the mid-point of Jeroboam's long reign (c. 760 BC), but Hosea in the last years (c. 750 BC) of the strong king and on into the break-up of the kingdom.

Contrasts and Similarities

G.A. Smith sponsored a contrast between Amos and Hosea as respectively the voices of law and love. The substantial truth behind this contrast is that Hosea (3:1; 11:1, 4; 14:4-5) explicitly refers to the Lord's love for his people whereas Amos does not. Also Hosea gives the impression of a more emotional nature than Amos. But the distinction between the prophet of law and the prophet of love can easily be overdone, and there is much more to unite than to distinguish them.

1. They were both prophets to the North.

- Amos (1:1), a farmer from Tekoa, south of Bethlehem, combined shepherding with producing cattle-feed (1:1; 7:14), and it may have been the markets of Samaria that brought him north in the first place.

- Hosea tells us nothing of his origins – the reference to his father (1:1) gives nothing away – but he
  does move very freely among the details of life in
  the North, and probably he was a northerner both
  by birth and by residence. Was he, perhaps, a baker
  by trade? When he bought Gomer back (3:2), he
  paid in both cash and in kind, and the 'kind' a baker
  would have in stock, while in 7:4-8 he shows famil-
  iarity with baking. But he does not say and we cannot know.

  Both prophets show themselves to be politically
  and religiously aware of northern life, as well-informed
  in current affairs as in the history of their people.

2. Both show a concern for the South (Amos 2:4-5; Hosea 1:7; etc.).
This sort of interchange is common in the pre-exilic prophets: Micah's prophetic word concerns 'Samaria and Jerusalem' (1:1, 5), and he frequently addresses his oracles to 'the
house of Jacob' (2:7; 3:1); Isaiah, the Jerusalem prophet, includes Ephraim in his purview (9:8–10:4; 28:1-6).

To make an issue about a northern prophet concerning
himself with the South or vice versa fails to note that in
prophetic thinking the division of the kingdoms was
a punitive expedient (1 Kings 11:29-39), without prejudice
to the Lord's promises to David (1 Kings 11:32, 36, 39). Elijah
gave vivid expression to this when he built the Lord's altar
on Carmel of 'twelve stones, according to the number of the
tribes of the sons of Jacob, to whom the word of the Lord
came, saying, "Israel shall be your name"' (1 Kings 18:31
NKJV). In this way he courageously affirmed their true reality
as a twelve-tribe confederation, united in ancestry (Jacob),
revelation (the word of the Lord) and spiritual status (Israel).
Amos and Hosea would have concurred.

3. Both look back to the Mosaic foundation.
Like all the prophets, Amos and Hosea belong to the line
of Moses.

- Hosea, unlike Amos, refers explicitly to the Lord's covenant with his people (6:7; 8:1), and when, in chapters 11–14 (see below), he needs to affirm the Lord's unchangeable relationship with his people, he abandons the marriage-metaphor of chapters 1–10, in favour of Exodus-sonship (11:1; Exod. 4:22).

- Amos has his feet equally firmly set on the Exodus (2:10; 3:1-2), and while his general approach lacks the emotional throb of Hosea, his reference to the Lord 'knowing' his people (3:2) includes the loving intimacy of the marriage bond (Gen. 4:1).

4. *Both prophets are rooted in the Davidic traditions, and look forward to a coming Davidic restoration.*

- Hosea 1:11 refers to the expected Davidic king, linking that royal expectation with the Exodus-motif of 'going up from the land' (compare 12:13; Micah 2:13): they will come out of bondage to an alien king into liberty under their (true) 'head'. The reference to David is explicit in 3:5, linked with a reverent return to the Lord in the 'latter days'.

- The Davidic references in Amos (9:11-15) have been a matter of dispute among the commentators but mistakenly so. As we have seen, in the Old Testament there is a distinct flow of covenant thinking whereby the universal covenant of grace vouchsafed to Noah (Gen. 6:17) comes into closer focus in the covenant of election with Abraham (Gen. 12:2-3; 15:18; 17:1-2; 22:15-18), modulates into the covenant of redemption with Moses and Israel (Exod. 2:24; 6:1-7; 24:4-8), and is then subsumed under the Davidic covenant.

As always with cumulative revelation, the earlier covenants are not lost in the latter but carry their truth and their promises forward until the seed of David becomes the bearer of the full covenant reality. It was theologically natural, therefore, for the prophets not only to be aware of their standing in the line of Moses but to be heralds of the coming David – as, for example, when Ezekiel holds together the kingship of David, the covenant of peace and the Lord's sanctuary in the midst of his people (37:24-28). Thus Amos and Hosea were not 'both' Mosaic and Davidic but were Davidic because they were Mosaic.

5. They were both writing prophets.

Both Amos and Hosea have bequeathed to us a written deposit of their ministry. Theirs is the earliest prophetic writing apart from Elijah's letter in 2 Chronicles 21:12-15. Unlike Jeremiah (36:2), they do not record any divine command to become 'writing prophets', and their adoption of this course may have arisen from no reason beyond the fact that they both exercised extended ministries compared with the episodic oracles of earlier prophets like Nathan (2 Sam. 7), Gad (2 Sam. 24) or Ahijah (1 Kings 11:29ff.).

It is unreasonable to suppose that men confident that their words were the very words of God, and finding themselves with an increasing body of divine revelation, should either fail to record it, or optimistically commit it to the uncertainties of oral transmission, or even bequeath it to followers without directions for safeguarding its integrity.

It is commonplace among Old Testament specialists today to suppose that each prophet had his own 'school' or discipleship-group, and that this group not only preserved his teaching but expanded it to meet new situations. The books of the prophets, then, would be accretions around a nucleus.

The only evidence we have of such a 'school', however, is Isaiah 8:16-20, but it should be carefully noted that when Isaiah committed his teaching ('law') and 'testimony' to them, it was as a sealed deposit which they were to preserve (v. 16) and live by (v. 20), not a few jigsaw pieces round which they would gradually assemble a larger picture. Certainly books such as Amos and Isaiah have come to us in such a balanced and crafted form that it is much more difficult to think of them as the product of an ongoing school than of the named prophet.

KEY DATES		
Kings of Israel:		
782–753	Jeroboam II	2 Kings 14:23-29
753–752	Zechariah	2 Kings 15:8-12
752	Shallum	2 Kings 15:10-15
752–742	Menahem	2 Kings 15:14-22
	The Assyrian	
	king called Pul is	
745–727	Tiglath-Pileser	2 Kings 15:19
	III	
742–740	Pekahiah	2 Kings 15:26
740–732	Pekah	2 Kings 15:25-31; 16:5;
		2 Chronicles 28:6-15; Isaiah 7:1
732–722	Hoshea	2 Kings 15:30; 17:1ff.

Within these dates, Amos and probably Jonah can be placed about 760 BC, Hosea about 750 BC. We know nothing of Amos except in the reign of Jeroboam II. The references to Judah scattered in Hosea are best explained on the assumption that he emigrated (or went as a refugee) to Judah and put his prophecies into their present shape there.

The accession of Tiglath-Pileser marked the start of Assyria's serious bid for imperial power, and spelled the end of the independence of the small Palestinian states.

AMOS: THE INTRUSIVE CALL OF GOD
We know nothing of Amos except what is revealed in his book. But happily he is informative about his call to be a prophet. With Isaiah (6:1), Jeremiah (1:4) and Ezekiel (1:3–3:28), he records a divine intrusion, an initiative of God, breaking the pattern of the past and setting a new course for the future.

Opposition

The clash with the priest Amaziah (Amos 7:10-17), in which Amos records his call, is a revelation of the influence the prophets exercised. Today their books are not always the most popular reading, but the fault is ours. In their day they had the ear of the nation; they were the opinion-makers to such an extent that Amaziah feared for national stability if Amos were not checked.

Amaziah reported the prophet to the king (v. 10) and then himself attacked Amos (vv. 12-13). While the word 'seer' is not itself belittling, Amaziah, nevertheless, adopted a denigratory approach. He feigned not to know Amos' name, reminded him that stipends were better in Judah (v. 12) and rubbished his message as unsuitable for the Chapel Royal (v. 13).

To these sneers Amos replied in turn: as regards being in it for the money, he was content as a farmer, but it was the Lord who had determined otherwise (vv. 14-15); as regards a message unsuited to high-class society, the word of God would demonstrate its authority, even over Amaziah himself. The priest may have thought he could prohibit the word (v. 16), but events would demonstrate otherwise (v. 17).

The Call (7:14-15)

> No prophet I,
> Nor a prophet's son.
> Indeed a stockman I and a fig-producer.
> But Yahweh took me from attending the flock
> And Yahweh said to me:
> Go, be a prophet to my people Israel.

The contrast between the past (lines 1-3) and the future (lines 4-6), between the threefold 'I' (the will of man) and the double 'Yahweh' (the will of God) – what Amos was by human lot and what he became by divine intention – comes out strongly in this baldly literal rendering. Amos did not choose prophesying as a business (line 1), nor was he training under a senior prophet (line 2, compare 2 Kings 6:1); Yahweh intruded on a settled and busy life (lines 3, 4), and imposed his sovereign will (lines 5, 6). This is what makes a prophet.

The Prophet's Work

In verses 16-17 Amos defines a prophet's work: first through the lips of Amaziah: 'Prophesy not ... do not distil your word', and then in his own rejoinder: 'Thus Yahweh has said.' The work of the prophet is to speak. His word is as heaven-sent as gently dropping rain, and it is the inescapable word of the Lord. In the traditional 'thus says' the verb is in fact always perfect in tense, emphasising that the prophet is the bearer of what 'Yahweh has (already) decided.'

AMOS: THE BOOK AND THE MESSAGE

We only know what Amos said by what he wrote. Every preacher, however, will realise that the prophet must have actually said a great deal more than he recorded. It is unlikely that Amos 1:3 to 2:16 is a sermon, since it can be read aloud in about four minutes, leaving the hearers no time to focus on what the preacher is saying. It also contains too much material, too tightly packed and too closely argued for the hearers to grasp and retain. Preaching requires repetition, recapitulation, enlargement and explanation – not in the interests of clarity (a single statement should be crystal clear), but in the interests of communication, so that the hearers may take in what is being said, dwell on it, assimilate and remember it.

Like all the prophets, Amos has left us maybe the carefully prepared notes from which he preached, or maybe the distilled essence of the word of the Lord subsequently crafted for preservation.

Announcing, Reasoning and Forecasting

The outline offered (see boxed feature) sees Amos' book as based on the literary feature of 'inclusion', that is to say, the beginning and ending of the individual sections of the book are indicated by matching 'markers'. Thus the roaring lion (1:2; 3:8) marks off the first section; the surrounding enemy (3:9-11; 6:14) brackets the second; and the contrast between the annihilation that will not happen (7:1-6) and the restoration that will happen (9:11-15) defines the third. In addition, the whole book is embraced by the inclusion of a Zion-centred world judgment (1:2) and a Zion-centred world renewal (9:11-15).

Amos' 'text'

Amos 1:2 summarises Amos' message. It speaks of impending judgment. The roar (*sha'ag*) is that of the already-pouncing lion (compare Judg. 14:5). It is directed against all creation from the lush valley bottoms where the shepherds pasture their flocks right to the top of Carmel – a Hebrew idiom of inclusiveness expressed by contrast. The roar is the roar of Yahweh from his mountain home in Zion: literally 'Yahweh from Zion keeps roaring, and from Jerusalem he utters his voice.' The words 'Yahweh' and 'Zion' combine to focus on the holy God in his holy place, and this prepares the ground for the ensuing message of inescapable, just judgment. But Zion was also the place of propitiation where the appointed sacrifices provided 'a way back to God from the dark paths of sin'. It was the chosen seat of David, the place of the promise. Therefore, the word contains a seed of hope, a question mark. Is the roar of judgment Yahweh's last word?

Monotheism

Amos did not, of course, invent monotheism, which is as old as biblical thinking (e.g. Gen. 18:25), but his theology of 'governmental monotheism' dominates his book. In 1:3–2:3 he reviews the surrounding pagan nations and pronounces them answerable to Yahweh, the only God of all the earth. Yahweh's governmental rule extends from Damascus (v. 3) in the north-east to Gaza (v. 6) in the south-west, from Tyre

(v. 9) in the north-west to Edom (v. 11) in the south-east and out to the two eastern nations of Ammon (v. 13) and Moab (2:1).

Condemnation
Amos groups the places in pairs:

- Damascus and Gaza have practised inhumane cruelty, the former in war, the latter in commerce;
- Tyre and Edom have betrayed brotherliness;
- Ammon and Moab have outraged the unborn, the dead and the helpless who deserve respectful protection.

All these are today called 'crimes against humanity', that is to say, they need no further sanction than that of the human conscience. In a day preoccupied with human rights, Amos makes us face human wrongs, and voices his condemnations on the assumption that because people are human they should 'just know' that such things are culpable.

For the most part, the actions Amos denounces have gone unrecorded in human history-writing but he insists they have been recorded in heaven, and their perpetrators will answer to the God of Israel. They are things which (even) God, the ever-patient, cannot overlook. These people have sinned in other ways ('three transgressions') and he has kept silent, but now they have committed the 'fourth sin', and in consequence all their sins must be brought to book.

The Unforgivable Sin
In his world review Amos has circled round the land of Israel beginning with the unrelated heathen (Damascus, Gaza, Tyre), coming nearer home with the brother-nation Edom (Gen. 25:30) and the cousin-nations Ammon and Moab (Gen. 19:37-38). But when he turns on Judah (2:4-5) and Israel (2:6-16) to announce their joint condemnation (3:1-8), he enters a different world. Certainly they, too, have committed crimes against humanity (2:6-7), but there is, in

their case, another and primary target for divine judgment: this is the 'fourth sin' of Judah (2:4). Judah has:

- Spurned the law (teaching) of the Lord;
- Disobeyed his statutes (unchangeable decrees);
- Followed human tradition.

Israel has:

- Embraced unacceptable religious practices (2:8);
- Opposed those who wished to live for the Lord (Nazirites) (2:12; Num. 6:1-8);
- Silenced the voice of prophecy (2:12);
- Having experienced redemption (2:9-10; 3:1-2) they have not lived as the redeemed. They possessed divine revelation but turned from it.

True Religion

Amos has been given the undeserved reputation of 'a bull at a gate' among the prophets, as if he were no more than a denunciatory demagogue. Nothing could be further from the truth. We shall never enter Amos' mind until we learn to read his book quietly, often tearfully, but always as a reasoned statement of a case.

Thus, in section one (1:2–3:8), no nation is condemned without reasons being adduced. This continues in section two (3:9–6:14) where the judgment heralded in 1:2 ff. is to be executed on Israel by the inescapable invader (3:11; 6:14).

- Amos backs up this threat by reminding his hearers of the reality of divine lordship in the fine print of history and in the created universe. The Lord who threatens punitive historical disasters in fire (1:4, 7, 10, 12, 14; 2:5) and in military catastrophe (1:5, 8, 14-15; 2:2-3, 14-16) actually directs all the forces of nature and history to his own moral ends – famine (4:6), drought (4:7-8), blight (4:9), epidemic (4:10a), military losses (4:10b) and defeat (4:11). See also 5:8-9 and 9:5-6. Nothing is accidental or purposeless. Nothing happens except 'the Lord has done it' (3:6).

• Amos justifies the threat by exposing:

a.   Their devotion to false religion (4:4-12; 5:4-25; 6:3-8).

b.   Unreality in religion. The moral and spiritual purpose at which the Lord's historical actions (4:6-11) were aimed is stated five times (4:6, 8-11): 'Yet you have not come right back to me.' This is Amos' first exposure of unreal religion. So punctilious were they in observances that sacrifices every day and tithes every three days (instead of annually and triennially, 1 Sam. 1:3; Deut. 14:28) were an apt caricature of obsessive ritualism (4:4), but behind it all lay a self-pleasing spirit, a religion of 'what we find helpful' – in Amos' words, 'this is what you love' (4:5). But there was no repentance, no turning to God, no entering into a personal relationship with him. Consequently, Amos says what must have shocked his hearers to the core: 'Come to Bethel and rebel' (4:4). Religion without repentance is rebellion against God.

In 4:4 Amos focuses on the ritual of religion as supposedly sufficient; in 5:5 (his second reference to Bethel) it is religion to the exclusion of the moral transformation true religion should produce: 'justice and righteousness' (5:7), moral standards in public life (5:10), concern for the poor (5:11), personal integrity (5:15). In summary, it is religion without morality (5:21-24), and it comes under divine judgment.

c. Complacency. Amos concludes his diagnosis by observing a third aspect of a religion that is under divine judgment: the careless complacency that follows when religion is divorced from repentance and morality (6:1-6).

The Day of the Lord

Amos did not, of course, invent the concept of a 'day' when the Lord would intervene decisively. He refers to it (5:18) as part of popular religion, currently understood in terms of complacent expectation. The people thought that just as in their past there had been a divine act of redemption, so the future would bring a divine rescue. As they had been centrally favoured in the former, they would be centrally favoured in the latter.

'Not so,' says Amos. When he refers to the Exodus in 3:1-2 he follows it up with the surprising conclusion that therefore God will punish them. The act of God in the past is the guarantee of divine disciplines in the present and future. Much is required of those to whom much has been given.

When Amos refers to the Exodus in 9:7, he sees it, considered simply as an event, as of no more significance than any other divinely promoted historical migration. Just as religion cannot be equated with ritual act, so divine favour cannot be equated with the historical act. When the Lord comes on his 'day', he will come as the holy one whom they have forgotten, and there will be no escape from his judgment.

Locusts, Fire and Plumb line

The final section of Amos (7:1–9:15) opens with three visions.

1. In 7:1-3 Amos is allowed to see the preparation of a coming dearth of such proportions that 'little Jacob' will perish. In answer to prayer the Lord

promises that no such all-destroying judgment will happen.

2.   In 7:4-6 the vision moves from land to sea, from food to fire, from the natural (locusts) to the super-natural – the fire is so fierce that it consumes even the 'great deep'. In answer to prayer this judgment, which would have obliterated 'little Jacob', is also forsworn.

The locusts and the fire are two contrasting judg-ments (totality by means of contrast), a 'doubling' be-cause the thing is determined by God (Gen. 41:32). But the doubled divine promise in answer to prayer rules out the possibility of such divine judgment as would prove to be the end of 'little Jacob'. The first two main sections of Amos, however, have argued that judgment is inescapable and justly due! So how are things going to work out? The answer lies in the third vision (7:7-8).

3.   Amos sees the Lord standing (literally) 'beside a plumb line wall with a plumb line in his hand'. From the start, the builders have the plumb line to guide their work, and the finished wall must face the same test. When Moses laid the foundations of Is-rael's religion it contained two elements:

   a. The obligation of the redeemed to obey the divine law;

   b. The provision for the redeemed of the blood of sacrifice to accompany their pilgrimage and to cater for their lapses from obedience.

   This is the twin-cord plumb line which the people possessed from the beginning, and by which they will be tested at the end: the demands of the law and the ordinances of grace; the call to obey and the invitation to forgiveness; the proper balance of a religion of morality and penitence. In the light of this, Amos alerts the people to the certainty and severity of coming judgment (8:1–9:7). But, he insists, this judgment will be as discriminating as the use of a sieve (9:8-10). It is the complacent sinners (exposed in 4:4–6:6) who will find no hiding place. They are the ones who have failed the plumb line test by discounting the life of obedience and perverting the means of grace.

David and the New World

The 'inclusion-pattern' of Amos shows just how exactly in place is the bright hope expressed in 9:11-15. It is nonsense to insist that Amos is only a prophet of judgment. How could the 'Yahweh-and-Zion-prophecy' of 1:2 be without hope? Yahweh is eternally the redeemer (Exod. 3:15). Zion is a place of sacrifice for sin. But it is also the throne of David, and it is this great Zion theme that Amos now puts forward as he balances the judgments that will not happen (7:1-6) with the glories that will:

- The coming king (9:11), his world-empire (9:12), the new creation (9:13);
- The restored people (9:14);
- Their eternal security (9:15).

AMOS IN OUTLINE
A. 1:2–3:8 The roar of the lion: universal condemnation
a¹ The lion's roar: the voice of the Lord 1:2
b¹ Against pagan nations 1:3–2:3
b² Against the chosen people 2:4–3:2
a² The lion's roar: the voice of the prophet 3:3-8
B. 3:9–6:14 A surrounding enemy: judgment applied
a¹ The shattered kingdom 3:9-15
b¹ The leading women 4:1-3

c^1 Religion without repentance 4:4-13
c^2 Religion without reformation 5:1-27
b^2 The leading men 6:1-7
a^2 The shattered kingdom 6:8-14

C. 7:1–9:15 The Lord, sovereign in judgment and hope
a^1 The final judgment which shall not be 7:1-6
b^1 Discriminating judgment: the plumb line 7:7-9
c^1 The inescapable word 7:10-17
d The Day of the Lord 8:1-14
c^2 The inescapable judgment 9:1-6
b^2 Discriminating judgment: the sieve 9:7-10
a^2 The hope that will be 9:11-15

HOSEA: THE IMPERCEPTIBLE CALL OF GOD

Hosea's book is different from Amos' not only in content and style but also in presentation. To say that Hosea is 'emotional' is not to deny emotion to Amos. Far from it, except that in Amos emotion is held in check and the message is presented as a reasoned argument. In Hosea emotion dominates. Consequently, his style is homely and sometimes even frantic rather than quiet and magisterial, and his book (to use a description in a private communication from F.D. Kidner) more a 'wild' garden than a piece of cultivation. Very broad beds of plants can be seen but within those beds unexpected plants flower and some stray from one bed to another.

How It Started

Hosea opens his book with a long meditation on how he found himself to be a prophet of the Lord (1:2–3:5). Commentators argue about Hosea's marriage, with differences focused at two main points:

1. *What does 'a wife of harlotry' (a literal translation of 1:2 NKJV) mean?* Was the girl Hosea married a working prostitute? Or did he marry a girl who subsequently deserted her husband and became a prostitute? Or is 'prostitution' used here in a figurative

sense typical of Hosea, a girl caught up (in whatever way) in Israel's disloyalty to the Lord?

2. What is the relationship between 1:2-9 and 3:1-3?
Is it Gomer who is being bought by the husband she had (presumably) deserted? Or is this a second symbolic act commanded by the Lord?

Did Gomer Desert Her Husband?
Taking the second question first, it is difficult to see how Hosea could be replicating the Lord's love for Israel (3;1, 'as the Lord loves') if he had not previously been deserted by the girl. Simply to buy and house a prostitute with whom he had no previous link re-enacts nothing: to make 3:1-3 a 'figure of the true' requires him to seek one who had earlier spurned the love that now pursues her. This is precisely what 3:1 commands: literally, 'Go, love again the/your wife', where grammatically the adverb 'again' is correctly linked not with the auxiliary verb, 'Go', but with the main verb 'love'.

What Sort of Person Was Gomer?
Maybe we cannot be certain of the answer to this question. Some commentators take the moral high ground and are outraged at the thought that the Lord should direct Hosea to marry a working prostitute. Yet such a command would well put Hosea in the compromised situation in which the Lord found himself (if we may so say), allied in his 'marriage' with a people from the start unfaithful, and whom, from the start, he knew to be so.

On the other hand, Hosea, linked in so many other ways with Jeremiah, seems to share also Jeremiah's view of early halcyon days in which Israel walked with God (e.g. Jer. 2:1-3; Hosea 11:1, 3-4), though the perfection did not last long (Jer. 2:4ff.; Hosea 11:2). This would suggest a good marriage which went sour, and, in this connection, many note that only in the case of the first-born, Jezreel, is paternity explicitly ascribed to Hosea (1:3, 6, 9).

The question cannot be resolved by asking what 'a wife of harlotry' (1:2 NKJV) means because the identical phrase is used of the children. If, in the case of Gomer, it means 'a woman of known immorality', how could Hosea be commanded to have children of known immorality? But if, in the case of the children, it means the subsequent discovery of their alien paternity, we at least have a perspective from which to understand the essential substance of 1:2–3:5: that it is Hosea's meditation upon a situation in which he finds himself, and within which he cannot escape the conviction that it has all come about by the word of God and within the will of God.

Hosea and Gomer
In these chapters, then, we find Hosea looking back over six or seven years of increasingly harrowing experience. He fell in love with a girl named Gomer and sensed divine permission to marry her. If she had a racy past, then, like many since, he felt confident that a good marriage, a loving husband and her own home would change her ways. If there was nothing morally questionable about her, then he had all the normal high hopes for the future. But it was not to be so. Either after the birth of her three children, Gomer suddenly deserted him for another man, or during the four or five years after the birth of his first son, Hosea became aware that he was being cuckolded. Yet out of love for his wife, he said nothing, and accepted her illegitimate offspring as his own by giving them their names.

But when Gomer went off with her lover(s), Hosea took his agony to the Lord in a new way. Had he been mistaken from the beginning? Had he misunderstood the Lord's will for his life? Was he wrong to acknowledge as his own a family he knew or suspected were not? And what about the sinister-sounding and unusual names he had given them?

Meditation brought confidence but surely not comfort. Martin Parsons, the first minister I ever heard preach about

Hosea, called him 'the prophet with the broken heart', and rightly so. But it had all been the word of God, right from the moment he had considered marrying at all. He was in this pickle, with an unfaithful wife, possibly two out of three children not his, and three oddly named kiddies, all by the will of God: he and they alike were 'acted oracles'. In their time and situation, they were 'the word made flesh'.

Hosea the Prophet

So Hosea found himself to be a prophet – not because, like Amos, he was commanded to drop everything and start preaching (Amos 7:11), but because imperceptibly he had 'become' the word before he started to share it with others.

Double Meanings and New Beginnings

Both in respect of his children and of his marriage, Hosea found that his personal anguish involved him in theological perplexity. The three names seemed to spell finality (1:4-9), whereas the promises of God (1:10a) said otherwise. There must, therefore, be a further story, reversing the meaning of the names (1:10b-11; 2:1, 22) and reconstituting the marriage (2:14-23). Since it was the transformed marriage that would reverse the fortunes of the children, Hosea gives most space to it in his recorded meditation.

Chapter 2 is built around three 'therefores' (vv. 6, 9, 14). They all, of course, reflect the logic of God.

- Responding to his 'wife's' adulteries, the Lord will first visit upon her *frustration*, non-fulfilment, the dissatisfaction of a life of sin (2:6-7a). The Lord foresees, however, that this will prompt only a self-seeking repentance (2:7b).

- 'Therefore' he acts in *deprivation* (v. 9) and *punishment*: 'I will hedge' (v. 6) becomes 'I will punish' (v. 13).

- Another 'therefore' is still to come (v. 14). If the 'therefore' of frustration was followed by the 'therefore' of destruction, whatever can a further 'therefore' bring? Divine logic reflects the divine nature, and the third 'therefore' brings fresh love (v. 14), new beginnings (v. 15), true responses (v. 16), a changed heart (v. 17), another covenant (v. 18), an eternal relationship (vv. 19-20) and the reversal of all the doom inherent in the three names (vv. 21-23).

Waiting in Hope
Hosea knew that all this glory lay in the undated future. What, then, about the interim, the waiting time? In his meditation another word of God came to him: he must go on loving Gomer (3:1) because that is what the Lord is like with Israel, and since there is no other way with a prostitute than finance, he must buy her back to himself (3:2, compare 2:7b-8). After that, they must wait together for what the future will bring.

All Hosea's sensitivity is now revealed: he will keep Gomer indefinitely (3:3a, 'many days') during which time 'you will not be a prostitute nor have a husband' (3:3b), and Hosea imposes the same discipline on himself: 'also I towards you.' For so it will be for Israel: infidelity commits them to an indeterminate period in which they will lose nationhood ('king and prince'), and be deprived of religious benefit – the legitimate ('sacrifice ... ephod') as well as the impermissible ('pillar ... teraphim') – until the bliss forecast in 2:14-23 becomes a reality in true penitence, their proper king and the richness of the 'latter days' (3:5).

Hosea's Message (chs. 4–14)
The analogy of a wild garden is very apt for Hosea 4–14. Beauty lies in profusion rather than in orderliness, and in the marvellous way every colour blends with every other. Yet amid the free flow of Hosea's thoughts there is an underlying cohesion.

A Dialogue
Chapters 4:1–14:9 consist of alternating passages in which Hosea speaks of the Lord in the third person and speaks as

the Lord in the first person. Thus in 4:1-3 Hosea reports the Lord's charge against his people while in verses 4-9 the Lord speaks for himself: 'I will destroy' (v. 5), 'I will forget' (v. 6), 'I will punish' (v. 9). Maybe there is a clue to the integration of this quasi-dialogue which has yet to be discovered.

The Three 'Therefores'
There is, however, another orderliness which reveals Hosea's message. As we have seen, the prophet's meditation in chapter 2 passed through three phases, marked by the 'therefores' of divine logic (2:6-8, 9-13, 14-23), dealing respectively with frustration, punishment and the surprising horizon of hope. This meditation is in fact a paradigm for the rest of Hosea's book.

1. Chapters 4:1–8:10: frustration, the hedged-up way
In this section:

- They 'eat and do not have enough' (4:10);
- 'stumble in their iniquity' (5:5);
- Seek the Lord but do not find him (5:12);
- Try unsuccessful cures (5:13);
- Suffer an unacknowledged ageing process (7:9);
- Act without common sense (7:11);
- Sow the wind, reap the whirlwind (8:7).

Hosea teaches that all this frustration has come upon them because they 'did not know'. Chapters 4:1–8:10 major on this as the root of the ills of the people of God: basic to everything is the knowledge of God, and to fail to grasp that knowledge or, having grasped it, to forsake it, is the parent of frustration: lawless living (4:1-3), breakdown (4:6a, 14), a broken relationship with the Lord (5:6b), a spirit of disloyalty to God (5:4). The knowledge of God is at the heart of a sound relationship with him (6:3; 8:2), and it is what he desires (6:6).

2. Chapters 8:11–10:15: punishment

This section focuses on coming retribution: 'I will take away' (v. 9) ... 'uncover' (v. 10) ... 'cause to cease' (v. 11) ... 'destroy' (v. 12) ... 'punish' (v. 13).

The note of punishment is not lacking in 4:1–8:10 (compare 4:9; 5:10, 14; etc.), but it becomes explicit in 8:11–10:15:

- A 'return to Egypt' (8:13; 9:3, 6);
- 'Fire' (8:14);
- Bereavement to the last man (9:12);
- The death of children (9:16);
- The breaking down of altars (10:2);
- Spoil carried to Assyria (10:6);
- Desperate pleas for protection (10:8);
- Enemies gathering (10:10);
- Plundered fortresses (10:14);
- The death of the king (10:15).

3. Chapters 11:1–14:8: hope

In 2:14-23 the third 'therefore' proclaims the surprising logic of hope. It is interesting that while the heart of this passage is the new marriage covenant and an eternal betrothal (vv. 16-20), the concluding verses promise the reversal of the dire meaning of the names of Hosea's children (2:21-23). This is the theme of 11:1–14:8 where Hosea abandons the marriage motif in favour of the sonship motif.

This final section of Hosea's book is built around assertions of the Lord's changeless love for the 'son' he brought out of the land of Egypt (11:1, 8-9; 12:9, 13; 13:4-5, 9-10, 14; 14:4-5). These passages are in tension with interleaved passages which focus on the failure of the Lord's 'son': his speedy defection (11:2), deceitfulness (11:12; 12:1), innate duplicity (12:3, 7), provocation (12:14), forgetfulness (13:5) and iniquity (14:1).

In this way we see even more clearly than in 2:14ff. that the ground of hope is in the Lord and not in us. Right up to Eschaton, the Lord's people remain a failure – and would remain so were he not to intervene to heal (14:4) and to water us with the dew of new life (14:5). Only then are we able to respond with a true acknowledgement and loyalty (14:8).

Sonship

Why is it that both in the preview (2:14-23) and in the widescreen presentation (11:1–14:8) sonship comes to predominate? Probably because, as a relationship, sonship is indissoluble. The son may dishonour his father but the relationship itself cannot change. Such a relationship Hosea had with his children, and such a relationship the Lord has graciously constituted with his elect. Exodus 4:22 is but the shadow of which the substance is Ephesians 1:4-5.

Further reading

J.A. Motyer, *The Message of Amos*, The Bible Speaks Today (IVP, 1984)
D.A. Hubbard, *Joel and Amos*, Tyndale Old Testament Commentary (IVP, 1989)
—*Hosea*, Tyndale Old Testament Commentary (IVP, 1989)
H.W. Wolf, *Amos the Prophet* (Fortress, 1973)
B. Fyall, *Teaching Amos* (Christian Focus, 2006)
G.V. Smith, *Amos* (Christian Focus, 1998)
F.D. Kidner, *The Message of Hosea*, The Bible Speaks Today (IVP, 1981)
D. Stuart, *Hosea-Jonah* (Word, 1987)
H.D. Beeby, *Grace Abounding* (Eerdmans, 1989)

THE DESIGN OF HOSEA'S 'WILD GARDEN'

A 1:2–2:23 Hosea's meditation:
  a¹ Hosea's sorrows; the Lord's sorrows (1:2-8)
    b Tension: do the promises of God prevail? (1:10–2:23)
    the children's names: promises kept (1:10–2:1)
    the marriage (2:2-5): the Lord's 'logical responses'
      frustration (2:6-8)
      judgment (2:9-13)
      hope (2:14-20)
    the children's names: blessing and response (2:21-23)
  a² Hosea's love; the Lord's love (3:1-5)

B 4:1–14:8 The elaboration of the logic of God
  a The Lord's charge against Israel (4:1–8:10)

    b The Lord's coming chastisement (8:11–10:15)
        c The undimmed hope (11:1–14:8)

A² 14:9 Hosea's call to meditation

10

Isaiah:
Jerusalem's Crisis

War is a crisis; the collapse of a family business is a crisis; a loved one diagnosed with a terminal illness is a crisis. The common factor in these three very different situations is that they define crisis as a threatening event. And, of course, this is correct. The twentieth century saw the whole world in crisis in two wars of global dimensions, bringing crisis-situations to families and individuals.

But another point of view is put forward by the prophet Isaiah: the crisis is not in the event only but in the way people react to it, whereby the event – which need not necessarily be earth-shaking in itself – becomes their crisis.

ISAIAH'S COMMISSION
When the Lord called Isaiah to be a prophet (Isa. 6) he gave him a strange-sounding commission:

> [9] Go and say to this people:
> Go on hearing but fail to discern;

> Go on perceiving but do not understand!
> Make this people fatheads!
>
> [10] Dull their ears and blindfold their eyes
> in case they should see with their eyes,
> hear with their ears,
> discern with their minds,
> and turn back and find healing.

Verse 9 is Isaiah's message and verse 10 his ministry: his message is to tell the people not to understand, and his ministry is to guarantee that they will not.

The frequent use of these verses in the New Testament (Matt. 13:14-15; Mark 4:10-12; Luke 8:10; Acts 28:26-27; Rom. 11:8) makes them of wide biblical importance, but it is through the prophet that we must discover their meaning. The man to whom the commission was given understood what it required of him.

The Meaning of the Commission

In 28:7-13 Isaiah records how the religious and political leaders of the day scoffed at his message:

> [9] Whom will he teach knowledge?
> Whom will he make to discern the message?
> Kiddies taken off milk, weaned from the breast!
>
> [10] For he goes, 'Za, za, za, za, ka, ka, ka, ka!
> There, little one! There, little one!'

In their eyes Isaiah would have made a good pre-school teacher. Why didn't he go and run a play group? Whatever the varieties of translation of their words in verse 10, this is the implication: a message of utter simplicity – no use, of course, in the 'real' world where the political sophisticates lived – but you couldn't accuse him of obscurity! Even a child could understand it.

KEY DATES

Almost in parallel with the long reign of Jeroboam II in Israel, Uzziah / Azariah gave Judah a period of peace and rising prosperity (2 Kings 15:1-7) but towards the end of his reign, and more forcibly in the time of Jotham his son, the shadow of Assyria began to loom, provoking the great Jerusalem Crisis.

791–740　　*Uzziah / Azariah.* Co-regent with his father until 767 (2 Kings 4:18-21; 2 Chron. 25:27–26:1), sharing the throne with Jotham after the events of 2 Kings 15:5; 2 Chronicles 26:21-23

750–732　　*Jotham.* Co-regent with Uzziah until 740, and with his son Ahaz for some period in the 730s (2 Kings 16:1-20; 2 Chron. 28:1-27).
　　　　　　The ministry of Isaiah and Micah (Isa. 1:1; Micah 1:1)

732–716　　*Ahaz* bartered away Davidic sovereign indepen-dence by a foolhardy alliance with Assyria, Isaiah 7:1-18. Never again did a son of David enjoy inde-pendent sovereignty

716–687　　*Hezekiah,* having been co-regent with his father from 729 (2 Kings 18:1–20:21; 2 Chron. 28:27–32:33; compare Isa. 36–39).

Isaiah was a master of language, and his whole book exhibits the same clarity. It would seem therefore that Isaiah under-stood his commission, not, as it might seem, as a call to be-wilder, but as a responsibility to make the truth unmistakably plain (as Jesus did in his use of parables, e.g. Matt. 21:45).

A Warning of a Crisis

Seen in this light, the wording of the commission is not a pro-gramme to follow, or a target to aim at, but a warning of the crisis the people face. It is the hardening of Pharaoh's heart all over again. Every rejection of truth hardens the heart; repeat-ed rejections of the truth bring progressively more determined resistance to the truth until the point is reached (known in advance only to God) when the next rejection will prove to be final, and the heart is irretrievably hardened.

But when people prove obdurate in the face of the truth, there is no way of winning them to a different mind but to tell them the same truth again, with ever greater efforts to make it plain. The danger inherent in this is that the next rejection of the truth could prove fatal.

It was at such a time, then, that Isaiah ministered. Decisions would be made, and a point of no return would be reached. Yet the only way Isaiah could hope to mount a rescue was to declare the truth once more, even though 'once more', as he was forewarned, would mean 'finally'.

AHAZ AND HEZEKIAH: THE TESTING OF FAITH

The point of no return for Judah was reached in stages, in the reigns of Ahaz and Hezekiah. History was the anvil on which faith was tested and the decisions hammered out.

1. Ahaz: Cynical Unbelief

In 745 BC Tiglath-Pileser III came to the throne of Assyria in Nineveh, and determined to make the Assyrian Empire a reality.

Treaties

While Tiglath-Pileser was taken up with securing his rule in the east, the Palestinian states of Aram and Israel felt the threat of coming events, and came together in the collective security of a defensive treaty (Isa. 17:3).

Even as early as the time of Jotham (Ahaz' father, 2 Kings 15:37), possibly still in the 740s BC, these northern powers began to exert pressure southward to bring an unwilling Judah into their West Palestinian Treaty Organisation.

Invasions

When Judah remained recalcitrant, incursions were replaced by invasion. The first invasion met with success, but for some reason stopped short of attacking Jerusalem itself (2 Chron. 28:5-8; Isa.7:1).

Panic

Isaiah 7:2 takes up the story at the point where news from the North spelled an imminent second invasion (2 Chron. 28:17-18), and panic ensued: literally, 'The house of David was told, "Aram has swarmed into Ephraim", and his heart and his people's heart swayed this way and that like forest trees sway in the wind' – Isaiah's vivid way of saying they got into a flap!

The Real Danger

Part of the reason for alarm was the stated purpose of this invasion – the end of David's dynasty in Jerusalem (7:6). But Isaiah saw that the real danger to the dynasty was not the northern powers: they were on their way out (7:4, 'two smouldering fagends'), and the Lord had spoken against their enterprise (7:7, 'It will not be realised; it will not happen'). The real crisis was in the king himself: would Ahaz believe or reject the divine promises? For 'If you will not stand by faith you will not stand at all' (7:9), or, in a blunt attempt to reflect the gloriously rhyming Hebrew, 'If you will not trust, you will surely go bust.'

The issue was crucial, to such an extent that the Lord was, so to say, ready to move heaven and earth to bring Ahaz to faith (7:11). But, in default of faith, the long reign of David was over. When the ten northern tribes withdrew their allegiance (1 Kings 11–12) David was left with the small royal enclave of Judah (1 Kings 11:34-36), but now even sovereignty itself was at risk (7:17).

Politics or Faith

2 Kings 16 brings us to the heart of this crisis of politics and faith. The astute Ahaz saw a way to make Assyria's plans work in his favour. If they could be persuaded to bring forward their westward move into northern Palestine, the treaty powers must fall and would no longer be a threat, while Ahaz would be safe under his alliance with their conqueror. Isaiah,

however, saw that to ally with Assyria was to take a tiger by the tail (7:17). Imperialists do not have allies, only puppets!

ISAIAH IN OUTLINE

A. 1–37 *Isaiah and the contemporary kings*
   a. 1–5 Author's Preface: the 'anatomy' of Judah, backdrop to the ministry of Isaiah
   b. 6–12 Isaiah in the time of Ahaz: his call (ch. 6). Ahaz refuses the way of faith: the parallel prospects of Judah (7–9:7) and Israel (9:8-21), coming disaster and glory (10:1-34; 11:1-16) and the saved community (ch. 12)
   c. 13–27 Isaiah's world-panorama: the glorious prospect on a world-scale, compare 19:24-25; 23:18; 27:12-13
   d. 28–37 Isaiah in the time of Hezekiah: the Assyrian invasion and the Lord's victory

B. 38–55 *Isaiah, Hezekiah: coming need and provision*
   a. 38–39 Hezekiah refuses the way of faith: exile foretold
   b. 41:1–42:17 Comfort, for Israel and for the Gentile world
   c. 42:18–44:23 Israel's double need, enslavement and sin (42:18-25), and the Lord's double promise: deliverance (43:1-21) and forgiveness (43:22–44:23)
   d. 44:24–55:13 The Lord's two agents: Cyrus the deliverer (44:24–48:22); the Saviour from sin (49:1–55:13)

C. 56:1–66:24 *Isaiah, the returned community and the final state*
   a. 56:1-8 The comprehensive Sabbath people
   b. 56:9–59:14 Aspects of a community in need
   c. 59:15–63:6 The Lord's response in salvation and vengeance
   d. 63:7–66:9 Aspects of the community to come
   e. 66:10-24 The comprehensive Sabbath people

---

2. Hezekiah: Playing with Fire

The best way to harmonize what we are told about Hezekiah's dates is to suppose that he was co-regent with his father, Ahaz, from 729 BC and became sole ruler in 716. The practice of co-regency could be necessitated by the older king's incapacity (2 Kings 15:5), but it seems also to have been practised as a way to secure the succession for the king's chosen nominee, and to avoid replicating the confusion of David's last days (1 Kings 1).

Ahaz' Legacy: Hezekiah's Frustration

Following Ahaz' refusal to trust the Lord's promises, and his consequent reliance on his own political astuteness and Assyria's 'good faith', real Davidic kingship disappeared for good. Kings still reigned for another century in Jerusalem, but only by permission. They enjoyed appearance but not reality. Understandably, Hezekiah chafed under this loss of sovereignty, and was ready more than once to join in anti-Assyrian alliances in order to recover his independent kingship. His final and greatest attempt to rebel and to re-establish his sovereignty focused on the death of Sargon and the accession of Sennacherib in 705 BC. The ancient conglomerate empires were held together by the centralised authority of the emperor. Uncertainty following the death of the emperor created a transient power vacuum into which would-be rebels were always prompt to step.

At this point Judah lay between the might of Assyria to the north and the would-be might of Egypt to the south. Hezekiah and his politicians were all too ready to listen to the siren voice that promised Egyptian aid if only the Palestinian states would front an anti-Assyrian rebellion.

The Real Issue

The issue was again really one of faith. Isaiah 28 lies at the heart of it. Envoys had been sent to secure Egyptian aid and had come back from Pharaoh with their piece of signed paper. To them, a treaty with Pharaoh and the covering power of Egypt was a guarantee of success. To Isaiah, they had only signed their own death warrant: 'We have made a covenant with Death and with Sheol we have agreed a common vision' (28:15). Thus he retranslates their achievement and exposes its true consequences.

But, all the while, real security lay at hand, neglected: 'Behold I lay a foundation-stone in Zion, a tested stone, a precious cornerstone, securely founded: the believer will not panic!' (28:16). Whether this foundation stone was the city itself as the locus of the divine presence, or the Davidic monarchy with all the Lord's promises to David, the issue for Hezekiah was the same as that faced by Ahaz. *Where there are divine promises the only proper course is to trust them*: hence the command to Ahaz (7:4), 'Take care to do nothing/to be quiet', and the assurance to Hezekiah, 'in returning (to the Lord) and rest (upon the Lord) you will be saved; in quietness and trust will be your might' (30:15).

Hezekiah's Besetting Sin

The incident Isaiah records in chapters 38–39 is chronologically earlier than the events in 36–37 – which makes Hezekiah's 'playing with fire' all the more astonishing. Hezekiah was a good-hearted man, capable, as Isaiah 38:9ff. shows, of spiritual exaltation. But he longed (understandably) for a real kingship, something that was outside his ability, exceeded his available power, and, saddest of all, involved him in abandoning the way of faith. It happened like this.

Prayer and Promises

Diagnosed with a terminal illness (38:1), Hezekiah discovered the power of prayer (38:2). In answer to prayer the Lord gave him two promises (38:5-6).

- The desired promise of extended life;
- The gratuitous offer of a further and surely much desired promise of political liberation and restoration: 'Out of the grip of the king of Assyria I will deliver you and this city'.

When the Lord then literally did 'move heaven and earth' (38:7-8, compare 7:11), it was in dramatic confirmation of this double promise: the king would live, and also he would become at last a real king, free of overlordship. But there is no such thing as untested faith.

Enter Merodach-Baladan!

He came unheralded into Bible history but he was a large figure in the contemporary world. Depending on one's point of view, he was either a terrorist or a freedom-fighter, with an inextinguishable passion to see Babylon free of Assyria, a nation once again. He had already experienced considerable success, reigning as king of Babylon from 721 until Sargon of Assyria drove him out in 710.

Looking forward to the power-vacuum that would follow Sargon's death, Merodach-Baladan now began his preparations. He took the chance offered by Hezekiah's sickness and recovery to send a congratulatory present and a letter (39:1). We only know the content of the letter from Hezekiah's reaction (39:2). But what could provoke a display of wealth and armed readiness (39:2) except an invitation into an alliance with a view to a co-ordinated east-west rebellion?

The choice before the king was plain. He could reply, 'Please excuse me. I have no need to rebel. My God has given me promises of deliverance and restoration.' But he did not do this. Like his father before him, he abandoned the way of faith for the way of works.

'Babylon', Said the King

Isaiah came to Hezekiah with questions, not pronouncements, and it was not till Hezekiah said, 'Babylon' (39:3) that Isaiah forecast destruction (39:6). This is important, because it means that in this incident we see all the values and procedures of Old Testament prophecy: a message arising from a situation and spoken to that situation.

1. Isaiah did not snatch the idea of Babylon out of the air by some sort of spiritual intuition. The text for his sermon was given to him by the king, and he preached it.

2. Isaiah did not bring in any time factor. If someone should say that this was an impossibly long-distance prediction in that the exile to Babylon was still a century away, or that comfort (40:1) that is nearly two centuries away is cold comfort indeed, we need

to remember that it is we who are contributing these timings by hindsight. In Isaiah's day Babylon had already once held the balance of power with Assyria in Mesopotamia, and could do so again. A Babylonian threat (39:6-7) and a Babylonian comfort (40:1) were far from remote and far from inapplicable. What Isaiah did, therefore, was to allow an undated threat and an undated hope lie in counterpoint.

ISAIAH: THE PROPHET OF FAITH

There is thus a consistent emphasis running through Isaiah 1–39:

- The Lord has given promises to his people;
- Where there is such a promise, the response of the Lord's people is simply to trust the Lord to keep his word.

The Continuing Need to Prophesy

We can, however, trace the faith-principle further into the Isaianic literature. The fact is that the events of Isaiah 39 obliged the prophet to continue prophesying. We can think of Isaiah returning from the palace to face questions from his disciples. They would want to know how the message of wholesale deportation of the royal house (39:6-7) affected the royal promises Isaiah has already revealed (7:14; 9:1-7; etc.). Were these wonderful promises still to be conserved (8:16), or should they now be torn up? How did the predictions of royal glory relate to predictions of royal termination? Isaiah would be a strange man indeed if he had not himself faced these tensions created by his Babylonian prophecy.

- Isaiah 39 prompts Isaiah 40–55. The Qumran Isaiah Scroll reads straight through from what we call the end of chapter 39 into what we call chapter 40. It has no break, no versification, no chapter division, no gap in its text. To read Isaiah like this is to be startled by the promptness with which the word of comfort follows the message of doom: 'The period of duress' ('warfare') is limited and will end, and sin will be pardoned (40:2). What is now required, therefore, is the *patience of faith*, for the captivity will yet be undone by Cyrus (44:24–45:8), and sin remedied by the Servant (52:13–53:12).

- Further, Isaiah 1–37 prompts Isaiah 56–66. Through his awareness of what Cyrus would do, Isaiah could face the certainty of the returned community. But knowing that a change of address – Babylon to Palestine – is not the same as a change of heart (48:20-22), he sees the returnees in pre-exilic terms: cursed with inadequate leadership and poor government (56:9–57:21), and helplessly struggling with personal inadequacy and sin (59:1-15a).

Isaiah 2:2-4 and 11:6-9 had promised a united, transformed world (compare 19:23-25), but the return from Babylon brought no sign of this. He also promised a glorious David (9:1-7), but this had not happened either. What then? Were these promises only a great 'might have been'?

As Isaiah looked forward he saw these needs met in the figure of the Anointed One with his work of transformation, salvation and vengeance (59:21; 61:1-3; 61:10–62:7; 63:1-6). The new heaven and new earth would yet come (65:17-25).

Back in their land, the *trusting faith* called for in Isaiah 6–37 and the *patient faith* of 40–55 now had the added dimension of the *obedience of faith* in prospect of full salvation (56:1).

FAITH WELL-FOUNDED: THE MESSIANIC TRIPTYCH

Faith is not the fatalism which credulously 'trusts' that everything turns out for the best, nor is it a leap in the dark. Rather, faith is a leap into the light, for faith is conviction based on truth, and action based on evidence.

Isaiah provided a ground for faith in his threefold Messianic portrait:

1. The King

The promise of a Davidic restoration implied in 1:26-27
began to take substantial shape with the announcement of
Immanuel (7:14), though the enigmatic brevity of the announcement may have raised questions rather than provided answers. Was the name to be taken seriously – a birth of
God, or some unique presence of God in the birth of the
boy? And was his birth imminent, as the Assyrian references
in Isaiah 7 suggest?

The developing prophecy brings the answers. The idea
of an immediate birth is transferred to Isaiah's own son,
Maher-shalal-hash-baz (8:1-3), and Immanuel, moved
into the undated future (9:1), becomes the bearer of the
great fourfold name of 9:6, whose second component,
'Warrior God', gives the Child the same title as Yahweh
himself (10:21). He is a Davidic King (9:7; 11:1), perfect in character (11:2-3) and rule (11:4-5), in a perfect
(11:6-9), united world (11:10-16). He reigns in righteousness over a righteous society (32:1-6), and is the 'beautiful king' bringing security and the forgiveness of sins
(33:17-24).

2. The Servant of the Lord

The security of Israel in the Creator God (40:12-31) leads
to a contrasting exposure of the plight of the heathen (41:1-
29). Their idol-gods are nothing and do nothing (41:21-24).
They are themselves without direction. The heathen are
without help or revelation of truth, empty, and makers of
empty gods (41:28-29).

- *The Servant's task.* It is on to this stage that the
  Servant steps with a task to bring 'judgment/justice'
  to the whole earth. The translation 'justice' suggests

social amelioration, equality, the righting of wrongs, and the word (*mishpat*) allows this meaning, but, contextually, it is not the most suitable. The word 'judgment' is used often (e.g. Deut. 5:1) as one way of describing revealed truth: what the Lord has 'judged to be right', and has revealed as such to his people. Against the background of Gentile ignorance (41:22, 29) this is the appropriate meaning here. The Servant will counter the needs of the Gentile world by furnishing worldwide revelation.

- *Who is this Servant?* But is he the Servant Israel of 41:8 – the Israel who, as heir to the Abrahamic promise (Gen. 12:1-3), was to bring all nations into their blessedness? Isaiah 42:18-25 tells us otherwise: this Israel is blind (v. 19), imprisoned (v. 22) and spiritually insensitive (vv. 20, 25). How can such a servant bring truth, light and liberty to the world? By 48:20-22 Isaiah has become so aware of national Israel's need (e.g. 48:1-8, 22) that, when the Servant appears for the second time (49:1-6), it is with a rewritten job description: to Israel first and then to the world (49:5-6).

- *The Servant revealed.* By contrast with a despondent, unresponsive people (49:14ff.), the Servant is revealed as accepting suffering with buoyant, responsive, obedient faith (50:4-9). In the sequence of the Servant Songs the importance of 50:4-9 is that it matches Exodus 12:5 – the Lamb of God must be perfect. In consequence of this moral perfection, the Servant is qualified to be the substitutionary sin-bearer of 52:13–53:12, and it is on the basis of this saving work that the invitation to rejoice (54:1) and feast (55:1) go out to Zion (54:1-17) and to the whole world (55:1-13).

THE AUTHORSHIP OF ISAIAH

Three in one or one in three? The case for the multiple authorship of Isaiah is taken as read by the majority of Old Testament specialists, and yet it rests on very unimpressive foundations. Of course, it is true that the first impression of Isaiah 40–55 is of difference, and this is usually focused on two points, literary style and geographical/social location.

STYLE
The argument from style is particularly weak.

1. To claim that different style points to, suggests, proves different authorship is plainly silly. Timothy Dudley-Smith writes hymns, letters and is an editor and notable biographer with a fastidious prose style. Is he then three people? Is Timothy the letter-writer – for so he sign his letters: Dudley – a rather romantic name – the hymn-writer; and Smith (? short for 'word-smith'?) the biographer?

2. The high poetic style of Isaiah 40–55 has already appeared, for instance, in chapter 35, and will reappear in chapters 60–63. Unless (as some insist, without proof) these chapters also are denied to Isaiah, we have to note that a mixed style – rhythmic prose and high poetry – mark the whole literature.

This can be related to a hypothetical but not fanciful scenario. As an old man, Isaiah lived on into the 'police-state' times of Manasseh. At that point it would be prudent to circulate his messages by the written word, hence the incredibly wonderful poetry. Such a time also would give the old man opportunity, in retirement, to edit the whole literature.

LOCATION
But what about the difference of location in 40–55? Candid examination shows that though these chapters have a Babylon-locus, they are not the product of an eyewitness. The picture of the exiles (for instance, 42:18-25; 52:2, 5) is contradicted by Jeremiah 29. No prophet actually living in Babylon could have so described the situation – nor spoken of the fall of Babylon as in 46:1-2; 47:1-15. Throughout chapters 40–48 the author is using types and stereotypes in imaginative poetry – motifs of captivity and of the fall of a city, true in the inward spirit of the thing but not descriptive of the outward circumstance. In these chapters Babylon is only mentioned by name four times and can

hardly be said to dominate the scene. Babylon, in the first half of the sixth century BC, could not be constructed, socially or politically, from Isaiah 40–48. And, incidentally, all references to scenery, trees and weather reveal an author in the midst of the Palestinian countryside.

THE STUMBLING-BLOCK OF THE PREDICTIONS
But *could* and *would* a prophet actually look forward one hundred years beyond his time to the Exile, and nearly two hundred years to the return? Of course, the very foundation-stone of the claim that chapters 40 to the end were by one or more authors lies in uncertainty at least and often outright denial of predictive prophecy. O.T. Allis is correct in finding the origin of the division of this supremely great literature in nineteenth century and earlier rationalism.

- As to 'could', there can be no doubt of the Bible's answer. Prediction is one of its clear claims. Indeed, Isaiah 40–48 is outstanding in using the fact of prediction and fulfilment to prove that Israel's God is the only God. If Isaiah could predict the undated coming of the Messiah, there is no reason why he could not reach forward two hundred years to the return. A man must not be penalised for being good at his job.

- As to 'would', Isaiah 40–48 is introduced (40:1) as a word of 'comfort' to those just threatened with coming captivity in Babylon (39:1-8). Critics of Isaiah's authorship ask: 'What comfort is it to say, "Never mind, in two hundred years it will be all right"?'

But in answer:

a. The two hundred years is our contribution, by hindsight. Isaiah mentions no time factor, only that the people are doomed to exile but will return.

b. The Babylon of Isaiah's day was a world power which had already demonstrated its ability to hold the balance of power with Assyria in Mesopotamia. To predict an exile to Babylon and a return was well within the practical politics of the prophet – and a real word of the Lord to his contemporaries.

The Isaianic literature is, in fact, one great wondrous panorama of the ways of the Lord with his people, his purposes for the world and his final victory.

THE SERVANT OF THE LORD

Isaiah's passages on the Servant have provoked sustained, specialist enquiry: Who is this figure intended to be? The four passages in which the Servant is described or in which he testifies of himself are: 42:1-4 (with 5-8); 49:1-6 (with 7:13); 50:4-9 (with 10-11); and 52:13–53:12 (with 54 and 55). These are usually called 'The Servant Songs'. The bracketed references are 'tail-pieces' or concluding comments attached to the passages.

WHO IS THE SERVANT?

Since the foundational work of Bernard Duhm in 1892, three lines of interpretation have been pursued:

- The autobiographical, the prophet is speaking of himself;
- The historical, the prophet has some particular, already known individual in mind;
- The national, the Servant is a personification of either the nation, Israel, or of the ideal Israel was meant to be.

There are aspects of the songs which fit each of these suggestions.

1. ISAIAH HIMSELF

The individual traits of the portrayal are plain to see, and even the puzzled Ethiopian of Acts 8:34 thought autobiography a possibility. Problems, of course, abound. Did 'Deutero-Isaiah' really think he would die for the sins of his people and live after death to be the executor of the Lord's saving purposes (53:4-10)? Whybray sought to evade at least some of the impossibility here by arguing that the Servant in chapter 53 did not in fact die. His efforts cannot be pronounced successful.

2. A HISTORICAL FIGURE

Jeremiah is a popular candidate for historical identification but though he left a fine legacy, for which we still thank God, was he the sinless Saviour, the light of the Gentiles, the 'arm of the Lord'? A difficulty besets the autobiographical and the historical theories, that in each case the Servant has come and gone without being recognised or making a difference.

3. THE NATION OF ISRAEL

The national theories have in their favour that, following 41:8, the most natural identification of the unnamed Servant of 42:1 is Israel, and also, of course, the Servant is actually called Israel in 49:3. But no one has been able to explain how, in the one case, sinful Israel could bring Israel back to God (49:1-6), or, in the other case, how an 'ideal Israel' (which has never existed corporately) can save anyone.

4. THE MESSIAH

The oldest understanding (compare Acts 8:35) is that Isaiah was consciously portraying the Messiah.

- He allows the possible identification between 41:8 and 42:1 to pass unchallenged in 42:1-4 because his subject there is not who the Servant is, but what he will do: bring divine truth to the Gentile world;

- 42:18-25 raises the question: Can a blind servant bring light to the blind, and an imprisoned servant liberty to prisoners? The Israel which by vocation is the Lord's servant is unfit to do so, being itself politically enslaved and spiritually blind.

- Between 43:1 and 48:22 Isaiah becomes increasingly aware of the sinfulness, spiritual need and rebelliousness of Israel so that by 48:20-21, when the nation is seen leaving Babylon for home, it does so under the banner that there is no peace for the wicked (48:22).

- 49:1-6 rewrites the Servant's job description: his primary task now is to bring Israel back to the Lord and in doing this to be himself the salvation of the world.

- 50:4-9: unlike despondent, unresponsive Jerusalem (49:14–50:3), the Servant is perfect in obedience – even at such cost – and becomes an example for all who would live godly lives (50:10-11). If 42:18-25 distinguished the Servant from the nations, 50:10-11 distinguishes the Servant even from the believing remnant.

- As the perfectly obedient one of 50:4-9, the Servant undertakes a substitutionary role as his people's sin-bearer (53:4-6), voluntarily dies (53:7-9) and lives again to clothe them with his righteousness (53:10-11).

Further reading

R.N. Whybray, *Isaiah 40–66* (Oliphants, 1975)
H.H. Rowley, *The Servant of the Lord* (Lutterworth, 1954)
J.A. Motyer, *The Prophecy of Isaiah* (IVP, 1993)

3. The Anointed Conqueror

Little more need be said here beyond what has been sketched above.

    a. Like the Servant, the Conqueror directs his work to Zion (59:20-21), and this is followed immediately

(60:1-22) by a revelation of Zion-centred worldwide gathering and blessing.

b. He comes as the personal transformer (61:1, 3) and his is the double work of bringing acceptance before God and vengeance from God (61:2).

c. There is a world of wrong requiring just requital, and for this he is dressed in the garments of salvation and vengeance which the Lord himself had undertaken to wear (61:10, compare 59:15b-20).

d. By himself he effects his double task (63:1-6) of vengeance and salvation.

THE MESSIAH: THREE PICTURES, ONE PERSON

Important lines of unity bind these Messianic forecasts together:

1. The Indication of Deity

- The expected King is 'God with us' (7:14), the Warrior God (9:6).
- The *Servant* is the 'arm of the LORD' (53:1 NKJV). This title has been used in the immediate context for Yahweh himself (51:9), and in 53:1 it comes in fulfilment of the promise that the Lord will bare his holy arm (52:10), that is, prepare himself for personal action.
- The *Conqueror* wears the Lord's clothes for the work of vengeance and salvation (59:17-19; 61:10-11), and, like the Lord (59:16), he acknowledges that there is none but himself to act (63:5).

2. The Spirit and the Word

All three Messianic figures are alike endowed with the Spirit and the Word (11:1-4; 42:1; 49:1-3; 50:4; 59:21; 61:1).

3. Links with David

- The King is David's heir (9:7; 11:1).
- The Servant is identified with David (55:3), as the one who will administer David's 'mercies' to the world.

- The Conqueror comes victorious from Edom (63:1) – a standard Davidic motif, for David was the only king to conquer and hold Edom (2 Sam. 8:14; Ps. 60), and Edomite victory became a way of describing the expected David (compare Amos 9:12; Isa. 34; Ezek. 35).

4. Righteousness
All three are alike 'righteous'.

- The *King's* throne (9:7), person (11:1-3) and rule (11:4-5; 32:1) are righteous.
- Regarding the *Servant*, Isaiah 53:11 is particularly important (literally), 'By his knowledge that righteous one, my servant, will provide righteousness for the many.' In other words, what he is in himself he imputes to those whom he redeems (compare 54:17).
- The *Conqueror* brings the inhabitants of New Zion into righteousness (61:3). He wears a robe of righteousness, that is, he is righteous in himself and is equipped to do a work of righteousness. He brings righteousness to light worldwide (61:11).

5. Worldwide-rule Over Israel and the Gentiles
See 11:10-16; 42:1-4; 49:6; 54:1–55:13; 60:1-3; 62:10-11.

JEWELS IN THE CROWN OF ISAIAH'S TEACHING
In the triple crown of the Messiah as King, Servant and Conqueror, Isaiah sets some notable jewels, great truths which run through his book and are part of his abiding message.

1. Monotheism
Like all the prophets, Isaiah worked within the Mosaic tradition, and shared with Amos the idea of executive monotheism. His call narrative equates the Sovereign One (*'a donay*, Lord, 6:1) with Yahweh the omnipotent (LORD of hosts, 6:3)

and 'the King' (6:5). This is the God whose glory fills the earth – that is, he is present in all his glory in every place. He governs the world morally (6:9-10) and historically (6:11-12), and Isaiah's book shows how seriously the prophet took this truth of the divine rule.

Chapters 13–27

The exalted promises about the Davidic king (9:6-7; 11:1-16) might well seem derisory in the context of the tiny enclave actually ruled by the contemporary Davidic kings, but Isaiah does not leave it at that. In the three divisions of chapters 13–27, he takes us progressively from the world of his day (chs. 13–20), into the remoter future (chs. 21–23) and on to the Eschaton itself (chs. 24–27). Each section climaxes in a hope which can be summarised as 'one world, one people, one God' (19:23-25; 23:18; 27:12-13). In other words, the Davidic expectation (e.g. of 9:7) is part of a coherent, thought-out universal – even cosmic – scheme. Isaiah, of course, uses the 'furniture' of his own world to picture what is to come: hence, as the above references show, Assyria, Egypt and Israel are its chief components.

Chapters 28–37

In these chapters it is precisely these nations who were involved in a single historical event, with Assyria the assailant, Judah the target and Egypt the would-be helper. In the hands of the one God, Judah is safe, Egypt is unnecessary, and Assyria is brought to its knees. In other words, chapters 28–37 and especially chapters 36–37 put the rock of history under the structure of eschatology. The prophet records what the Lord has done as an assurance of what he can do, and as a pledge of what he will do.

Chapters 40–48: Prediction and Fulfilment

These chapters bear testimony to Isaiah's monotheism along a different line. True deity is demonstrated by prediction and fulfilment. This is not a sort of conjuring trick, the marvel of the match between what was earlier said and subsequently done. Rather, the point is that sovereign monotheism is revealed in the way the word of God actually controls the flow of history, so that what the Lord announced in advance is what is fulfilled.

Of course, the force of this argument, basic to chapters 40–48, is nullified by the 'Deutero-Isaiah' theory which places the prophet in the middle of the events he supposedly predicts, making him no more than a perceptive political commentator. But Isaiah did not see it so. On the one side there was the living and only God; on the other, dead and spiritually debasing idols (41:21-29; 44:7; 45:21; 46:9-13; etc.).

Isaiah knew well that to the heathen the idol was symbolic of a hidden, spiritual force, but it is indicative of the rigour of his monotheism that he would allow nothing beyond what could be seen, nothing but wood and metal (40:18-20; 44:6-20). There are alternative objects of worship to Yahweh, and people choose them to their own disappointment and destruction, but there are no alternative gods.

2. Holiness

Isaiah's call in chapter 6 centres on the divine holiness. The thrice-holy of 6:3 is a Hebrew idiom expressing what is both superlative and total. In Genesis 14:10, 'full of pits' is 'pits pits', repetition expressing something true of the whole; in 2 Kings 25:15 the purest gold and the purest silver is 'gold gold … silver silver'. Only in Isaiah 6:3 is the idiom of repetition raised to the power of three. The holiness of God is an absolute and total description of the whole divine nature and only a 'super-superlative' can begin to rise to its pure quality.

By itself, as we have seen, the word 'holiness' (qodes) means 'otherness, separatedness'. There is a divine sphere of reality other than the sphere we inhabit, and a divine essence outside our experience. In the case of the God of Israel, this was the sphere of his essential ethical holiness, his moral majesty, at once endangering sin and sinner (Isa. 6:4ff.), but then, remarkably, commanding atonement (6:6-7).

Characteristic of Isaiah
More than any other, Isaiah is the prophet of this holiness. The adjective (qados) is used more frequently of God in Isaiah than in all the Old Testament taken together, and is spread throughout the Isaianic literature. Even if we take into account the adjectival use of the noun (qodes), Isaiah still contains over a third of the total ascriptions of holiness to God. This emphasis is distilled into a title which Isaiah may well have coined himself: 'the Holy One of Israel', which he uses twenty-five times. It occurs only seven times in the remainder of the Old Testament, and, remarkably, never in Isaiah's contemporary, Micah. It is as if Micah thought it too typical of his brother prophet for any other to use it.

Great truths cluster into this title: basically, the transcendentally holy God has brought himself into a close relationship with one people, and has brought them into his fellowship. Without diluting his holiness he claims ownership of them, and, holy though he is, they know his closeness. Obviously the question has to be asked how such a relationship is possible. The answer of the Bible, and, in a signal way, Isaiah's answer, is 'atonement'.

3. Atonement
If chapters 40ff. are denied to Isaiah it remains inexplicable that he never elaborated a doctrine of atonement. At the start of his ministry he saw his people as one with him in sin and condemnation (6:5). Can we believe that he never told them how to be forgiven as he had been?

Isaiah 6
At first sight, the 'live coal' of 6:6 would suggest purification by fire, but this is, in fact, not a biblical idea. In the Old Testament fire stands for the unapproachable holiness of God (Exod. 3:2-5), which both excludes and threatens

(Exod. 19:12, 18-21). This particular ember, however, was glowing with the fire on the altar (Isa. 6:6), the fire of holiness that received, consumed and was satisfied by the substitutionary offerings the Lord prescribed (Lev. 1:7-9; etc.; 17:11). It was thus that sinners were 'accepted' by the holy God (Lev. 1:4; etc.), that is, through the fire of satisfied holiness: the offering has been made and the sinner can enjoy its benefits.

This is well brought out in the words by which the seraph explained the symbol:

> Behold, when this touched your lips,
> Your iniquity went;
> And as for your sin,
> Its ransom price is paid!

Sin and iniquity, respectively actual sins and their inward spring, have been dealt with. The verb in 'your iniquity went' (*sur*) occurs in Leviticus 13:58 of the 'departure' of leprosy. In the same way, the defilement of sin is gone. The second verb – 'its ransom price has been paid' – is *kipper*, to make atonement, to pay the covering price. All this has happened by the will of the Holy One. Seraphs only fly at his command (6:2). When the cloud blotted out the vision of God (6:4), the altar, the means of salvation, was left on view.

Isaiah confessed the sin he knew, and it was to that point of awareness that atonement was applied, but the Lord provided for the sins he alone knows – the detailed list and also the inner corruption of the fallen nature.

Isaiah 53

The great statement of atonement doctrine in 52:13–53:12 elaborates but does not alter the teaching of chapter 6. To the words 'sin' (53:12) and 'iniquity' (53:5), it adds a third word, 'rebellion/transgression' (*pes'a*, 53:5, 6, 11), completing the definition of sin by including its deliberate and culpable wilfulness.

The Servant 'bears' (nas'a, 53:4, 12) and 'carries' (sabal, 53:4, 11) all our sin. The latter, 'to shoulder, to accept a burden', is not used of the sacrifices, but the former, implying 'to take responsibility for' (Lev. 5:1; 10:17), is well exemplified. It receives its classical definition in Leviticus 16:21-22 where the sins of the guilty are 'put on' the innocent and the goat 'bears' upon him all their iniquities.

Substitution

As in Leviticus, so in Isaiah 53, this sin-bearing is substitutionary: the Servant suffers (literally) 'because of/as a consequence of our rebellions ... our iniquities' (53:4); he accepts the stroke due to his people (53:8); he allows himself 'to be numbered with the transgressors' (53:12).

The Servant is the 'guilt-offering' we need (53:10), the 'recompense' offering (Lev. 5–7) which renders satisfaction for both the offence and its consequences.

In fact, the Servant, as Isaiah portrays him, fulfils all the Old Testament conditions qualifying him to be a substitute, four in number:

> a. He is acceptable to the offended God (53:6, 10);
>
> b. He is without stain of our sin (53:9, 11; compare Exod. 12:5);
>
> c. He is identified with us in our condemnation (53:4-6, 10-12);
>
> d. He voluntarily takes our place (53:7-8).

Willingly Accepted

This willingness of the Servant to undertake the substitutionary work is particularly important. It was the one element the animal sacrifices, in their otherwise perfect exemplification of substitution, could not provide, and yet, of course, it is the essential element, for our wills are the central citadel of sin. Isaiah not only saw that, in the ultimate, only a person could substitute for persons, but he also saw why. Only a person can consent to stand in another's place. What was imposed on the unknowing beast was consciously and willingly accepted and embraced by the Servant.

The Servant's Righteousness
Isaiah 53 adds yet another crucial idea to the atoning work of the Servant. He finds us wandering as sheep (53:5-6), but (like the prodigals we are), brings us home as his children ('seed', 53:10), and clothes us with the 'best robe' of his own righteousness. Isaiah 53:11 contains a turn of Hebrew not found elsewhere in the Bible, demanding the translation: 'By his knowledge that righteous one, my Servant, will *provide righteousness for the many*' (compare 54:17).

4. The City of God
Isaiah is very distinctively the Jerusalem prophet, and his whole book reflects his love for his city, sadness over its defection and delight in the glory that is to be. Isaiah talks of:

- The coming Davidic city (1:26-27);
- The ideal world-city (2:2-4, compare ch. 60);
- The cleansed, indwelt city (4:2-6) joyous in salvation (12:1-6);
- The Zion where the Lord reigns in glory (24:23);
- The strong city (26:1-3) in contrast with the destroyed city (24:10);
- The redeemed city (35:10);
- The rebuilt city (44:28);
- The city rising (52:1) in contrast with the falling city (47:1);
- The righteous, beautified city (54:14-17);
- The redeemed city (59:20, compare 1:26-27);
- The city of the Lord's delight (62:1-5, compare 4:2-6);
- The New Jerusalem central to and symbolic of the new heavens and earth (65:17–66:24) – where the

Sabbath is truly kept (66:23), in contrast with the unacceptable Sabbaths of the corrupt city (1:10-20).

Jerusalem thus forms an inclusion for the whole literature,
and its transformation from corruption to glory aptly summarises Isaiah's message. In this way he makes his book a sort
of 'tale of two cities', taking his cue from the Babel incident
in Genesis 11:1-9. Babel was humankind's first recorded attempt to organise life in the interests of a stable and secure
society, on the basis of human technological cleverness, and
without reference to God.

Isaiah sees, on the one hand, the 'Babylon' component
in ongoing human history (chs. 13–14; 21:1-10), expressed
in his own day by the imperial intentions of Babylon (13:1–
14:23) and Assyria (14:24-27), who aimed to bring the
whole earth into one organised community. When he probes
further into the future (chs. 21–23), the Babylon syndrome
is still there (21:1-10), and at the Eschaton this becomes
'the city' of 24:10, the whole world organised as a would-
be 'global village'. But like its Babel origin, this is 'the city
of *tohu*' (compare Jer. 4:23-26), the city where nothing has
meaning any more. Human efforts to produce an organised,
coherent world-society always end in Babel.

But by contrast there is the city to which the world-
remnant comes marching (24:14-16a), where there is
provision for all nations, death is no more and salvation
finally enjoyed (25:1-10a), the strong city (ch. 26).

In 65:17ff., therefore, Isaiah can pass without explanation from 'new heavens and a new earth' (65:17) to the new
Jerusalem (65:18), for they are the same thing: the new creation is a new, secure, organised society by design of God,
the new world is the Lord's mountain (11:9; 65:25).

Further reading

J.A. Motyer, *The Prophecy of Isaiah* (IVP, 1993); *Isaiah*, Tyndale Old Testament Commentary (IVP, 1998)

A. **Harman,** *Isaiah* (Christian Focus, 2005)
I. **Busenitz,** *Joel and Obadiah* (Christian Focus, 2003)
B. **Webb,** *The Message of Isaiah*, The Bible Speaks Today (IVP, 1996)
P. **Hacking,** *Isaiah* (Crossway, 1994)
D. **Thomas**, God Delivers (Isaiah) (Evangelical Press, 1998)
J.N. **Oswalt**, *The Book of Isaiah* (Eerdmans, 2 vols, 1986, 1998)
P.D. **Miscall**, *Isaiah* (Sheffield, 1993)
D. **Prior**, *The Message of Joel, Micah & Habakkuk*, The Bible Speaks Today (IVP, 1998)
B.K. **Waltke**, 'Micah', in D. Baker, T.D. Alexander, and B. Waltke, *Obadiah, Jonah and Micah*, Tyndale Old Testament Commentary (IVP, 1988)
L. **Allen**, *The Books of Joel, Obadiah, Jonah and Micah* (Eerdmans, 1976)
M. **Wilcock**, *Six Minor Prophets* (Crossway, 1997)
S. **Erlandsson**, *The Burden of Babylon* (Lund, 1970)
O.T. **Allis**, *The Unity of Isaiah* (Tyndale, 1951)

THE BOOK OF MICAH

Micah refers four times to 'the remnant' – the Lord's devotees and the objects of his saving mercies: 2:12; 4:7; 5:7-8; 7:18. The book groups itself around these markers:

A. 1:2–2:13. *The Lord of all the earth*. Israel lies under just divine judgment (for instance, 1:3-5; 2:1-3) but will be regathered (2:12-13).

B. 3:1–4:8. *The coming true Zion*. Bad rulers have despoiled the people (3:1-4), prophets have misled them (3:5-7) and overthrow must come (3:8-12), but Jerusalem will yet become a pilgrimage centre for the world (4:1-3), and the remnant will be blessed under their divine king (4:4-8).

C. 4:9–5:15. *The coming purified people and the perfect ruler*. The dominated will become the dominant (4:9-10; 5:7-15); no human plans can foil the Lord's plans (4:11-13; 5:5b-6); the true Ruler is coming (5:1-5a).

D. 6:1–7:20. *The Lord of all the earth*. Israel judged and pardoned. The Lord has a long-standing complaint against his people (5:1-5), but his requirements, though lovely, are humanly impossible (6:6-8. Desolation is well merited (7:1-7), but the undefeated Lord will bring his people to perfect forgiveness (7:8-20).

For a detailed analysis of Micah, see **L.C. Allen**, *The Books of Joel, Obadiah, Jonah and Micah*, New International Commentary on the Old Testament (Eerdmans, 1976).

II

JONAH, NAHUM, HABAKKUK, ZEPHANIAH:
THE NINEVEH FILE

As the capital city of the Assyrian Empire, Nineveh was a name of terror and abhorrence. For two and a half centuries Assyria dominated the Middle East. Its fortunes varied – there were weak kings as well as strong – but the unchanging storyline was pitiless cruelty. The Assyrian might well approach with honeyed words (2 Kings 18:28-32), but the reality was deportation, with the homeland becoming in its turn the destination of alien importees (2 Kings 17:23-24).

RISE OF ASSYRIA

From the accession of Ashurnasipal II (883 BC) until that of Tiglath-Pileser III (745 BC) there was a seesaw of power: prosperity balanced against decline and, more importantly, times of strong central government and times when city and provincial governors proved more than a match for weak emperors. Such a time may account for the reference in Jonah 3:6 to 'the king of Nineveh'. Was he the provincial governor of Nineveh in a time of local ascendancy?

In any event, Tiglath-Pileser changed all that. He achieved unchallenged power and led Assyria to its forty years of imperial greatness. Sporadic rebellions continued, of course, for they were endemic in such a conglomerate of unwilling vassals. By 705 BC, however, when Sennacherib succeeded Sargon, Assyria seemed to be in assured control of all western Palestine.

... AND ASSYRIA'S FALL

But Assyria's period of successful imperialism was comparatively short. Sennacherib's early unbroken success came to an end in Judah, where his arrogance alike against man and God (2 Kings 19:11-13) was more than matched by the ignominy of his downfall (2 Kings 19:35-37). Though it was not evident in the short term, this marked the beginning of the long decay of the empire.

Esarhaddon (681 BC) undertook the conquest of Egypt, achieving notable success, but at the expense of warfare without foreseeable end. He extended the imperial commitment beyond any capacity to sustain it. Egypt could not be controlled, and in Mesopotamia, too, Babylon was always restive. As John Bright notes, this 'massive empire was jerry-built ... held together by sheer force', and 'the unceasing strain of enforcing the docility of subjects scarcely any of whom had anything but hate for her was beginning to tell', so that when Ashurbanipal died in 633, 'The end was near. Assyria's gargantuan structure rocked on its foundations.' Nineveh fell to Babylon in 612 BC.

JONAH AND THE CONCERNED GOD

Four prophets, none of whom can be dated with precision, cluster round the name of Nineveh: Jonah, Nahum, Habakkuk and Zephaniah.

2 Kings 14:25 does no more than place Jonah's ministry earlier than Jeroboam's recovery of the lost lands, some time between 793 and 753 BC. This, as noted above, was also a period when Assyria was weakened by internal power struggles – maybe, therefore, a time when Nineveh was more

likely to be moved by a prophetic voice than might be the case under the more forceful kings. But to place Jonah's mission to Nineveh at such a time, say about 760 BC, takes nothing away from the marvel that an Israelite prophet was called to an understandably abhorrent task, and that he knew his God intended mercies even for Ninevites (4:2-3).

The 'message' of Jonah comes to us as a narrative. Within this Jonah tells something of his personal faith (2:2-9), but of his ministry in Nineveh he only records the text from which he preached (3:4). In Jonah's case, the medium is the message: the shape of the story is also its thrust.

The Second Chance: The Lord and Obedience

On the most direct reading, Jonah's book falls into two parts: Jonah disobeying (1:1–2:10), and Jonah obeying (3:1–4:11). There is much in the structure of the story to favour this simple twofold division. In an unpublished lecture, J.I. Packer pointed out that, seen in this way, Jonah part one matches the command to love the Lord our God – by obedience – and Jonah part two, the command to love our neighbour – by evangelism.

T.D. Alexander balances:

- Jonah at sea (1:1–2:10) with Jonah at Nineveh (3:1–4:11);
- Jonah's disobedience (1:1-3) with his obedience (3:1-3);
- Jonah's conversation with the sailors (1:4-16) with his preaching to the Ninevites (3:4-10);
- Jonah's gratitude for his own deliverance (1:17–2:10) with his ingratitude for the Ninevites' deliverance (4:1-11).

Seen like this, the story pivots on 3:1: 'The word of the LORD came to Jonah a second time'. If the Lord had only been concerned with bringing his word to Nineveh, Jonah would have been left in disobedience, and another would have been sent in his place. But the Lord loves obedience and persevered with Jonah to bring him back, to redirect his course, to make him the obedient man. Hence, the wonder and comfort of the second chance occupies the heartland of the message of Jonah. As with Jacob (Gen. 28:15), the Lord will not leave us until he has done what he has said to us.

The Sovereignty and Comfort of the Lord
A more detailed analysis of the story underlines this centrality of obedience in the divine scheme.

A^1 1:2 Mission to Nineveh
   B^1 1:3-12 Jonah versus the Lord: disobeying
      C^1 1:13-16 Pagans worshipping
         D 1:17–3:4 The recovery of Jonah
          • Jonah's flight arrested (1:17)
          • Jonah's prayer (2:1-9)
          • Jonah's second chance (2:10–3:4)
      C^2 3:5-10 Pagans worshipping
   B^2 4:1-10 Jonah versus the Lord: disagreeing
A^2 4:11 Mercy to Nineveh

While this balanced outline brings before us all the truths intertwined in the message of Jonah, it is the recovery of Jonah from disobedience and alienation from God that occupies the centre ground. This puts the emphasis where it belongs: there is a sovereign God who controls all things, all powers and means are at his disposal, but his awesome, irresistible power is his love at work, with even destructive capacity directed to constructive ends. The heathen sailors put it precisely: 'You, LORD, have done as you pleased' (1:14) – and his 'pleasure' is all-merciful.

The Fish
The greatest threat, the Fish, becomes the vehicle of restoring mercy – and, of course, the Fish is to be taken seriously even though it is no more than a bit-part player in the whole

drama. Much ink has been spilt trying to sidestep elements in Jonah which affirm God's freedom to act in his own world in his own ways. But to class Jonah as fiction on the mere ground that he was swallowed by a great fish (1:17), prayed in that strange location (2:1ff.), met with notable success in his mission to Nineveh (3:4-9), and sheltered under a remarkably swift-growing plant (4:6-10) is to enunciate a principle (the refusal of the unusual and supernatural) destructive of much of Holy Scripture.

The book of Jonah has often been compared with Elijah and Elisha in 1 Kings 17 to 2 Kings 13. In all three cases the prophetic message comes through events more than through recorded words, and there are unusual manifestations: ministering ravens, unfailing larders, fire from heaven, earthquake, wind and fire, whirlwinds and fiery chariots, Jordan divided, purified water-springs, timely she-bears, leprosy healed. D.W.B. Robinson notes a similar narrative in Acts 10 and 11 with angels and visions.

The point at issue is not 'the miraculous'. To use such a category is as misleading as to speak of divine interventions. The Creator God does not intervene like an absentee making occasional visits; and things which would be called miracles were we to do them are natural, logical, run-of-the-mill within his frame of reference. They stand to his reason: 'Everything the Lord wills he does in heaven and earth, in the seas and in all the ocean depths' (Ps. 135:6).

Jonah Was an Historical Figure
The prima facie belief of the author of the book of Jonah is that the narrative is historical. The Lord Jesus Christ himself accepted the veracity of the repentance of the Ninevites (Matt. 12:39-41) and this is the most reasonable view of his references to the Fish.

Within the book of Jonah, the Fish is not a problem but a mercy, a remarkable evidence of divine determination to perfect Jonah in obedience, to rescue him from the frustrations of second-best – and through him to demonstrate a universal mercy, foreshadowing another Galilean who came to call sinners to repentance.

'You who hear prayer, to you all flesh will come' (Ps. 65:2)
There is another way of viewing the structure of Jonah which underlines the book's universalism.

A¹ 1:1-2 Prologue: mission to Nineveh commanded
    B¹ 1:3-16 Jonah's disobedience: the sailors' prayer
    B² 1:17–2:10 Jonah's chastisement: Jonah's prayer
    B³ 3:1-10 Jonah's obedience: Nineveh's prayer
A² 4:1-11 Epilogue: mission to Nineveh explained

The bracketing sections (A¹, ²) need each other. Jonah fled (1:3) not because he misunderstood the Lord's meaning but because he understood it only too well – as 4:2 explains. In other words, within the Old Testament, Jonah does not represent a new truth. The Abrahamic tradition is that Israel is the custodian of the world's spiritual welfare (Gen. 12:2-3; 18:18; 22:18; 26:4; 28:14) and is the context in which the Mosaic revelation of the divine nature (Exod. 34:6-7; Jonah 4:2) was understood. Election is a privilege, but it is much more a responsibility; to be united with the Lord is to join a missionary society. This was Jonah's inherited frame of reference, and he knew it.

But in What Way Does this Universalism Work?
The sailors, helpless before the storm, cried out to their own gods (1:5), but, through Jonah's testimony to the God of heaven and earth (1:9), they came to cry out to the Lord by name (1:14). Immediately (1:15) they were faced with evidence that this God does rule the seas, and they approached him with sacrifices and vows (1:16). This is to say that, returning to land,

they sought the help of a local sanctuary of the Lord, or even made the journey to Jerusalem, learned his ways and responded in the personal commitment a burnt-offering expresses.

Regarding the Ninevites (3:5-9), the divine name (Yahweh, the Lord) is not used. We must presume that Jonah preached to them of 'God', and that they turned with unanimous and costly penitence and reformation to this God, who, on his part, accepted their repentance and remitted the judgment they had deserved (3:10).

Jonah, by contrast, lived within the certainty of revealed truth: the telling phrase 'your holy temple' (2:4, 8) brings with it all he knew of divine holiness and of the provision of the atoning sacrifices. The sailors went this way (1:16), but the Ninevites – like David in Psalm 51 – discovered that it is not the sacrifices as a ritual that bring sinners near to God but the element of compassion in the divine nature (4:2), which on the one hand appointed the sacrifices but which, even in default of sacrifices, welcomes sinners home.

NAHUM AND THE JUDGE OF ALL THE EARTH
The liberal theology which finds Jonah difficult because of remarkable divine actions finds Nahum unacceptable because of his strong emphasis on divine judgment. His book has been described as 'one of the least valuable parts of the Old Testament' with its 'two poems ... which breathe hatred and vengeance'. It does not 'declare God's moral judgment upon Israel or Judah (but) gloats over the fall of Nineveh'. Nahum's God 'wreaks vengeance', which is 'not the teaching of Isaiah 40–55, nor of Jonah, certainly not of the Christian cross'. Nahum 'falls below the standards set by the developed Judaeo-Christian tradition' (C.L. Taylor).

Oh dear! It is not, however, true.

Answering Nahum's Critics
There is no evidence that Nahum 'gloated', nor can the pejorative expression 'wreaks vengeance' be allowed. Like

all the prophets, Nahum expresses a theological case with logical exactitude and personal conviction. As Butterworth says (New Bible Commentary), his is 'a passionate book. The God of the Bible is not cool, remote' but one who sees wrong and puts it right, cares about his world and judges sin with a pure and righteous passion. Or we can say, with R.L. Smith, that Nahum affirms the sovereignty of God over history and the world. He is the good and just champion of the outraged and helpless. Nahum's 'threat against Nineveh does not stem from the personal hatred of the human author ... but from the nature of God, jealous for right, wrathful towards enemies'. Exactly!

And, oddly, even C.L. Taylor himself acknowledges this: that while Nahum only tells a fraction of the truth about God (does any prophet do more? Heb. 1:1), what he affirms is valuable: that those who take the sword perish by the sword; payment will be made. Nineveh suffers what all wickedness must suffer, and 'there is no withstanding the Lord who maintains justice and answers human need'. Indeed, 'current preaching', says Taylor, 'lacks Nahum's concern over entrenched wrong'. Is there anything in all this that is discordant with the 'Judaeo-Christian' tradition or is offensive to the 'Christian cross'?

Nahum and His Times

Nahum is as secretive about himself as any of the prophets. He was from Elkosh, and presumably his audience knew where that was. Likewise they knew at what date he prophesied, but we can only observe that it was after the fall of Thebes (No Amon, 3:8) to the Assyrian Ashurbanipal, 664 BC, and before the fall of Nineveh to the Babylonians, 612 BC.

Within this period the good Josiah reigned in Judah (639–609 BC), but his reformation and revival (2 Kings 22–23) was only an episode within a time of international disruption. Egypt was pressing its imperial claims; Assyria was making its last stand against the rival claims of Babylon, and the Scythians from the far north were rampaging in Palestine, allegedly propping up the Assyrian cause but actually another factor of disruption.

No thoughtful person could live in such days without asking why the world was so, whither it was going and what God was doing.

Looking at Life Through God

Maybe Nahum gives no details about himself because he wishes to concentrate on the one important thing: he had a 'vision' (1:1), a divinely granted perception, a revealed truth to share, recorded in his book, a written word of God about the dreaded Nineveh.

The Lord, Judge and Saviour (1:2-8).

The key to Nahum's book lies in these opening verses. Note how verse 2 (the jealous God taking vengeance on his enemies) is matched by verse 8 (making an end of his enemies), and verse 3a (the patient Lord) is matched by verse 7 (the good and sheltering God, caring for those who trust him).

This, in a nutshell, is Nahum's theology – the foundational Mosaic message of Yahweh who saves his people and judges his enemies. Verses 3b-6, the core of the opening oracle, expresses a truth both parties need to know: this God dominates the whole earth, the very creation itself melts at his presence, and so do its inhabitants (v. 5). None can stand against him (v. 6). The theology of 1:2-7 provides the parameters for the remainder of Nahum's book.

General Application (1:9–2:7)

1. *The world under divine rule:* (1:9-15). The part of the world which is 'against the LORD' is under a 'wicked counsellor' (v. 11) who imposes himself on Judah also (v. 15). He is not named: he stands for the anti-God, self-willed principle that seeks only its own glory and brooks no divine interference. Nahum has bad news for him (v. 14) and good news for Judah (v. 15). This

is the way the world is run: wickedness is rampant until its time comes; the people of God are always cared for and will survive into the coming joy.

2. *A Sovereign God in judgment and mercy* (2:1-7). The Lord's enemies are summoned to man their defences (v. 1), but these defences are as useless as opened gates (vv. 6-7). Judah will be restored in spite of all the enemy has done (v. 2), and the enemy, for all his might (vv. 3-5), will go desolate into captivity (v. 7).

Notice that Nahum names no names apart from Judah. He is laying down the principles on which the world is governed by a sovereign God. Mysteriously, this includes his people being dominated (1:15b; 2:2b), but all will yet be well; restoration will come, and the all-powerful enemy will meet the one who has dug his grave (1:14) and opened his gates (2:6).

Particular Application (2:8–3:18)

1. *Nineveh deserves destruction* (2:8–3:7). Nahum now turns to what has been revealed to him about the times in which he lives. The poem is enclosed between two references to 'fleeing' (2:8; 3:7). The fleeing waters picture the draining away of resources; the fleeing people describe the reality of refugees, desperate for safety, leaving a city without any to care for it. First, neither wealth (2:8-10) nor brute strength (2:11-12) avail because the Lord is against Nineveh (2:13; 3:5); secondly, she will suffer what she made others suffer (3:1-3), because without regard for morality (prostitution) or spirituality (sorceries), she devoted herself to anything and everything which would secure her advantage.

2. *Destruction will come to Nineveh* (3:8-18). Nahum is a skilled poet and his final poem is as good a place as any in his book to observe the dramatic balance of his compositions.

A¹ verses 8-11 A historical parallel. No Amon/Thebes was strong in defences and allies but went captive (vv. 8-10), and so will Nineveh (v. 11)

    B¹ verses 12-13a Illustration: ripe fruit: ease of conquest

        C¹ verse 13b Fire

            D verse 14 Prepare for siege

        C² verse 15a Fire

    B² verses 15b-17 Illustration: locusts: irresistible forces of destruction

A² verses 18-19 A historical fact: the end of Nineveh.

Permanent Principles

Working backwards, then, through Nahum's book:

- We see Nahum addressing his own day (2:8–3:18): rampant wickedness does not have unrestricted tenure. Its time is limited and its time will come.

- But in addressing his day Nahum addresses ours, for he is working on the basis of permanent principles by which the world is governed (1:9–2:7): wickedness cannot ultimately succeed, because it is in essence enmity against the Lord. The Lord's people will always be preserved to enjoy the good news of peace.

- These principles can be accepted as axiomatic because they arise out of revealed theology: the Lord who saves his people and overthrows his enemies and whose power is irresistible (1:2-8).

HABAKKUK AND THE GOD OF PROVIDENCE

The vision of Nahum helps us to live at peace in our troubling world. With him we look out on earth's turbulence through the clarifying spectrum of the character of the Lord: whatever appearances may suggest, the truth is that he remains the same, judging his foes and saving his people. It was and is and ever will be so, as long as earth remains.

That is the wide-lens perspective on history, but, with Habakkuk, we, too, say 'That's all very well, but look at what is actually happening – and, even more, look at what is likely to happen next.' Where is God when it comes to the details? To be sure, he is over all, but is he equally in all? As history sweeps on we can well rest in the assurance that 'God is working his purpose out', but what about Genghis Khan in the remote past, and Pol Pot nearer in time? What about whoever else we may each wish to include in the category of history's monsters? Or, as Habakkuk said: What about Assyria and Babylon?

Habakkuk's Times and Perplexities

The single fact that places Habakkuk in the Assyrian times is that the Chaldeans (1:6), that is, the Babylonians, were coming. When therefore he cries out to the Lord about violence, trouble, plundering, strife and the rest (1:2-3), the disruptions that marked the final decades of Assyrian rule are surely in his mind. When we add that within the kingdom of Judah the reign of the good Josiah was but a twenty-year interlude between the godless reigns of Manasseh and Amon (2 Kings 21, 687–639 BC), and the death throes of the kingdom under Jehoiakim, Jehoiachin and the hapless Zedekiah (2 Kings 23:36–25:26, 609–587 BC), we understand Habakkuk's inclusion of the powerlessness of the law, the absence of justice and of the dominance of wickedness (1:4) among the ills seemingly left without remedy.

Dialogue and Response

Habakkuk's book is presented in three sections:

- A question ('How long, LORD?' 1:2-5) and its answer (1:6-11),
- A second question ('Are you not from everlasting, LORD?' (1:12-17) and its answer (2:1-20),
- And Habakkuk's response (3:1-19).

A Double Problem (1:1-17).

The book flows along in a continuous dialogue. In response to Habakkuk's perplexity that gross misdemeanours go un-punished (1:2-4), the Lord replies that he is about to raise up the Chaldeans (Babylon) as his punitive agent (1:5-11).

Far from answering Habakkuk, however, this creates a worse problem. The Lord has made no secret of the fact that Babylon is an imperialist grab-all (1:6), self-willed and savage (1:7-8), violently taking prisoners, causing ruination (1:9-10), guilty, and making a god of power (1:11). Habakkuk sees that this will indeed settle the Assyrian threat (1:12a), and implement merited judgment (1:12b). Nevertheless, how can a holy God (1:13) use people who flout moral values (1:13b), treat humans as animals (1:14-15) and acknowledge no god but acquisitive power (1:16)?

Wait and Watch (2:1)

In the light of this problem of providence Habakkuk feels himself to be a sentry in a threatened citadel: 'I will stand to my duty, and position myself on the rampart, and keep lookout to see what he will say to me and what I will reply regarding my case' (2:1).

The Lord's Reply (2:2-3)

The Lord's reply invests the vision about to be announced with extreme solemnity:

- It is a vision to be perpetuated ('write!');
- It merits publication ('plain on tablets');
- It is of universal relevance and urgency ('whoever reads must run');
- It is assured of timetabled fulfilment ('appointed time');
- It possesses inherent vitality ('pants for the end') and truthfulness ('not lie');
- Its seeming tardiness demands patient faith ('wait expectantly for it');
- Fulfilment is certain ('will come ... not be late').

The Vision: Habakkuk 2:4-20
This vision is the heart of Habakkuk: the questionings of
1:2-11 and verses 12-17 are answered by it, and the prayer
in 3:1-19 responds to it. It consists of a poem in six balanced
sections, but in summary its thrust is this.

1.The would-be lord and the real Lord:
Sections 1 and 6, verses 4-6a, 18-20. The would-be lord,
marked by pride, moral laxity (v. 4a), self-indulgence, insatiable desire and determination to dominate (v. 5) is contrasted with the person who is right with God and living by
faith (v. 4b). It is the latter who will 'have the last laugh'
(v. 6a), because in contrast to man-made gods (v. 18) who
bring a curse to their makers (v. 19), there is a real Lord who
rules the world in holiness (v. 20).

2. The principle of requital
Sections 2 and 5, verses 6b-8, 15-17. The would-be lord wins
his way by promises giving hostages to fortune (v. 6). But
his pledges will be called in (v. 7), and the plunderer will be
plundered (v. 8). Every humiliation of others for personal
aggrandisement (v. 15) will come home to roost (v. 16). The
Lord will in due course minister his cup (v. 16), and exact
justice will be done (v. 17).

3. False security: sections 3 and 4, verses 9-11, 12-14
Self-achieved gain (v. 9) perishes in the nature of things: it
boomerangs (v. 10). Like a jerry-builder, the would-be lord's
materials are his downfall (v. 11). Blood-guiltiness and iniquity
(v. 12) offer no lasting foundations. All such action must perish.
It is not of the Lord (v. 13) and it violates his world-purpose.

Response (3:1-19)
The broad message of the central poem is that the Lord has
all things in his hands. A purpose of perfect justice will see to
it that wickedness will receive its due reward, and those who
are right with God by faith will enter into that triumph.

The proper response to the promises of God is to pray that they will happen.

- Therefore we find Habakkuk praying that the Lord will again work (3:2, 'renew your deeds') as he did in the recorded past (ch. 2).

- In 3:3-7 (note how the two place names in vv. 3 and 7 form an inclusion) and 3:8-15 (with references to horses and seas as an inclusion) Habakkuk reviews these past deeds of the Lord. He does not follow a storyline but allows his mind to move hither and yon over the great events as the Lord led his people from Egypt to Canaan. For his concern is not with events as such but with the mighty power of the Lord behind them. Therefore (like Psalm 18) we find symbols and motifs of divine action, typical Old Testament ways of describing a theophany – brightness, pestilence, creation in turmoil, rivers and seas obeying his command: the Lord present and acting: earth with all its fabric, 'forces' and peoples totally overwhelmed by this mighty God.

- This is the God who guarantees the vision of a just requital, of a different world and a silenced people. Within it the one who is 'right with God' ('the just', 2:4) has a true God to trust (in contrast with 2:18), and sure ground for patient persistence in faith. With typical Hebrew concreteness (3:16-19), Habakkuk exemplifies how this will work out, not by invoking the great crises of history, but by recalling the smaller hurdles 'ordinary life' requires us to jump: failing crops and herds, that is to say, the economic challenges of living in an uncertain world. Faith trembles before the all-sovereign God to whom all earth's forces and capacities are subservient (3:16), but also 'rests in the day of trouble' (v. 16) and rejoices in the saving

Lord (v. 18) who gives strength (v. 19a) to surmount obstacles (v. 19b).

ZEPHANIAH AND THE GOD OF HOPE

The Old Testament is wonderfully expectant. Just as every next prophet to arise might be the great Prophet (Deut. 18), and every next king the royal Messiah, so every next calamity might be the Day of the Lord. This is Zephaniah's perspective within, say, the last twenty years of Assyrian imperial rule. He has a clear perception of coming disaster for Judah (1:4) and imaginatively traces its progress in the Jerusalem he knows (1:10-13), but what he writes about is the worldwide (1:2-3) onset of the Day of the Lord (1:14b–2:3). He looks round the world as he knows it – west to Philistia (2:4-5), east to Moab (2:8-9), south to Cush (2:12) and north to Assyria (2:13-15) – using his own world map to sketch the universal dimensions within which his vision is working. As Adam Smith says, 'He found his material in the events of his own day', but 'tears himself loose from history' in order to focus on the last day. The three sections of his book make his message plain.

1. The Day of the Lord: CanThere Be Hope? (1:2–2:3)

The darkness of the opening oracles appears to exclude light. The world itself (1:2-3), Judah (1:4-9), Jerusalem (1:10-14a), and then the world again (1:14b-18), are all caught up in a day when wickedness (1:3), false religion (1:4), duplicity (1:5), compromise (1:8) and complacency (1:12) are exposed by divine searching (1:12), and consumed in the Lord's fire (1:7-8, 18). Neither concealment (1:12), fortified strength (1:16) or wealth (1:18) will avail.

And yet ... and yet ...! Why does 2:1-3 call for spiritual repentance and reformation before the Day comes? Is there a hope after all?

2. Disaster Interleaved with Hope (2:4–3:8)

We have already noted that the substance of these verses is a world review in which unsparing disaster falls all round the Lord's people. The Lord's word has gone out against them (2:5). They have been captors of his people (2:7) and have reviled and denigrated them (2:8-10), but the erstwhile captives will take possession (2:7, 9) amid pastoral peace (2:6). And there is more. Philistia, Moab and Ammon fall because of hostility to the Lord's people, and the absolute spirit of self-absorption incarnate in Assyria guarantees a judgment without hope (2:13-15). Nevertheless, when the Lord reveals himself in the destruction of their gods a universal people will come to worship him (2:11). All this, even though neither Judah (3:1-5) nor the nations (2:6-7) merit any offer of hope, or any invitation to 'wait' for the Lord as if hope existed (3:8).

Hope is, in a word, an enigma. This is something we have seen throughout the prophets, for hope does not spring from the logic of our merits but from the logic of the divine nature.

3. Hope consummated (3:8-20)

The opening 'For/Because' of 3:8 says it all. How can Zephaniah say, 'My determination is to pour out my indignation ... because then I will restore ...'? The harmonising of wrath and mercy belongs within the unity of the character of God as the Scriptures reveal him. When the Day comes:

- Babel will be reversed (3:9);
- Sin removed (3:11);
- Jerusalem purged (3:11-13a);
- Eden restored (3:13b);
- The Lord will be King among his people (3:14-17);
- And all the earth will be moved by what the Lord has done (3:16-20).

THE WORLD-THEME OF THE NINEVEH PROPHETS

With Jonah, then, we marvel at the Lord's compassion for the world. With Nahum we ponder the reality and inevitability of divine judgment upon the world. Habakkuk wrestles with the double problem of how a pure God comes to be involved in the morally messy details of world history, and how the believer is to live with persistent faith through those tracts of history when darkness prevails. Zephaniah studies the map of his world, looks through it to the End and enunciates the mystery of world-hope at the heart of world-judgment.

Further reading

J. L MacKay, *Jonah, Micah, Nahum, Habakkuk, and Zephaniah* (Christian Focus, 2008)
L. Allen, *The Books of Joel, Obadiah, Jonah and Micah* (Eerdmans, 1976)
D. Stuart, *Hosea-Jonah* (Word, 1987)
M. Wilcock, *Six Minor Prophets*, Crossway Bible Guides (Crossway, 1997)
O.P. Robertson, *The Books of Nahum, Habakkuk and Zephaniah* (Eerdmans, 1990)
J.A. Motyer, *Zephaniah*, in T. McComisky, Ed., *The Minor Prophets* (Baker, 1998)
Rosemary Nixon, *The Message of Jonah*, The Bible Speaks Today (IVP, 2000)
J.H. Eaton, *Nahum, Habakkuk, Zephaniah*, Torch (SCM, 1961)
P.R. House, *Zephaniah, a Prophetic Drama* (Sheffield, 1988)
J. Ellul, *The Judgment of Jonah* (Eerdmans, 1971)

12

WRESTLING JEREMIAH:
THE RELUCTANT PROPHET

More than any other prophet, Jeremiah experienced the good mingled with bad. He entered his prophetic office in the reforming reign of king Josiah (1:2), but lived to watch the kingdom decay under Jehoiakim (35:1; 25:1) and Jehoiachin (24:1), and saw its ruin under Zedekiah (34:1-2; 40:1). Choosing to remain in Judah rather than go to Babylon (39:1–40:6), he was present when the provincial government of Gedaliah (40:7) was terminated by assassination (41:2), and he who began his career as a reluctant prophet (1:6) ended it as an unwilling exile (43:4-7).

Through Jeremiah's eyes, we, too, see this hopeful dawn and tragic end, but in his person we meet a man beset by a sense of inadequacy, holding on with determined fidelity to a God who frequently baffled him, and acting with a courage always at odds with his personal insecurities. We could well call him the most human of the prophets, the most unlikely prophet, too – and therefore the prophet whose example speaks most movingly to us who are cast in the same mould.

JEREMIAH'S TIMES

639–609 BC. With Assyria in terminal decline, Josiah (2 Kings 22:1–23:30; 2 Chron. 34–35) could virtually act as an independent sovereign, unhindered in his reform and even exerting rule over the former northern kingdom (2 Kings 23:15-19).

- 626 BC. Ashurbanipal, the last effective Assyrian emperor, died but in the same year Nabopolassar (626–605 BC) became King of Babylon. One empire was dying, another rising.

- 664–610 BC. Psammeticus I was reviving Egypt's imperial ambitions, eager to repossess Palestine. Necho (610–595 BC) continued this policy. Throughout Psammeticus' reign, the Scythians from the Black Sea region were raiding even as far south as the Egyptian border and contributing to breakdown and disorder.

- 609 BC. The position of Judah in the crossfire is seen in the death of Josiah (2 Kings 23:29; 2 Chron. 35:20). Necho was aiming to establish his frontier on the Euphrates. It was in Josiah's interests to prolong the existing balance of power between Assyria, Egypt and Babylon because, with the great powers distracted by each other, he had his best chance of sovereign freedom. Politically, the thinking was good; militarily and personally, a disaster. The end of Josiah's reign brought, in principle, the end of Judah.

- 612 BC. Nineveh fell to Nabopolassar, and the Babylonian Empire replaced the Assyrian.

- 605–587 BC. Egypt's overlordship of Judah (2 Kings 23:30-35; 2 Chron. 36:1-4), established by the defeat of Josiah at Megiddo, was short-lived. Babylon defeated Egypt at Carchemish on the Euphrates (605 BC, 2 Kings 24:7), and Judah became Babylon's vassal (2 Kings 24:1). Under the last three kings of Judah doomed rebellions put an end even to puppet sovereignty.

Jehoiakim (609–597 BC) rebelled (2 Kings 24:1), and the new emperor, Nebuchadnezzar (605–562 BC), first used marauders to discipline him (2 Kings 24:2, compare Dan. 1:1-2), but then himself besieged Jerusalem and ended the pathetically brief reign of Jehoiakim's son, Jehoiachin. This was the first captivity (597 BC; 2 Kings 24:8-17; Ezek. 1:2).

Zedekiah (597–587 BC) rebelled, and when Nebuchadnezzar took the city he sacked it and imposed the second captivity (587 BC; 2 Kings 25; 2 Chron. 36).

KINGS, EMPIRES AND EMPERORS

Judah: The good king Josiah began to reign in 639 BC, and in the eighteenth year of his reign he promoted a temple-reformation which resulted in the discovery of the book of the Law and an attempt at national reformation (2 Kings 22–23). Nevertheless, in the divine will, this could be no more than a respite (2 Kings 23:26-27).

The Assyrian Empire was in its death throes and Palestine was a troubled area.

Egypt was governed by the ambitious Pharaohs, Tirhakah (690–664, 2 Kings 19:7-9), Psammeticus I (664–610) and Necho (610–595, 2 Chron. 35:20–36:4; compare 2 Kings 23:29-30). They were anxious to capitalise on Assyria's weakening grasp of Palestine in order to extend their empire.

The Scythians from the Black Sea area were another source of disruption. They pursued no fixed alliances, acting as opportunists, but during this period they appeared to side with Assyria. Probably, like Josiah, it was in their interest to preserve a balance of power between Egypt and Assyria. The net contribution of their Palestine incursions, however, was to increase the unrest and insecurity of the times.

The Babylonian emperors were Nabopolassar (626–605), the victor of Nineveh and the founder of the empire, and Nebuchadnezzar (605–562), the victor of Jerusalem (2 Kings 24–25; 2 Chron.36:11-21).

JEREMIAH'S BOOK

Jeremiah's book is sprinkled with dates.

- His call (1:2) was in 626 BC.
- Thereafter some of his datings are vague, such as 'the days of Josiah' (3:6), but the majority of his dated oracles fall in 608–587 BC.

- Comparing 7:1-2 with 26:1-2 we can date his temple address in 608 BC.
- But 21:1-2 is earlier: 589–588 BC.
- 25:1 belongs to 605 BC.
- 32:1 is in 587 BC.
- 35:1 backtracks to the years beginning 608 BC.
- 27:3 implies an otherwise unrecorded episode prior to Zedekiah's rebellion, and international conference – presumably to co-ordinate the rising – held in Jerusalem, circa 590 BC.

An Anthology?

The point of mentioning these dates is to show that the book is not arranged chronologically, and this sense of an anthology rather than an orderly presentation is enhanced by the varieties of literary genre and the unpredictable way they occur. J. Bright writes of 'the impression ... of extreme disarray ... without any discernible principle of arrangement'.

There are:
- Poetical passages (e.g. 2:2b-3; 5:5-6),
- Biography (chs. 26–29, 34–45),
- Prose discourses (e.g. 7:1-16; 16:1-14; 18:1-12).

There is a notable group called 'the Confessions of Jeremiah' (e.g. 11:18-23; 12:1-4) which are highly personal records of Jeremiah's own spiritual life and his (sometimes stormy) relationship with the Lord. E. Nicholson thinks the 'prose sermons' are akin to Deuteronomy, differing, he holds, in style and theology from the poetry, and probably emanating from a variety of authors, possibly an on-going Jeremianic discipleship-group or a group of Deuteronomic students. In any case they are, in Nicholson's view, evidence of later 'hands' at work, expanding and supplementing Jeremiah's seminal thoughts to make them apply to later situations.

A Test Case (21:1-10)

We can use Jeremiah 21:1-10 to illustrate the problem and to test proposed solutions, especially the suggestion of later writers.

This passage can be dated (21:2) about 588 BC, and it is therefore chronologically surprising in Jeremiah 1–25. So how did it get there?

On the common and realistic view that Jeremiah 1–25 represents the rewritten scroll of Jeremiah 36:32, it could be part of the 'many like words' added by Jeremiah himself. But would he have placed such an addition unsuitably, unthinkingly or haphazardly?

The same objection applies if we follow J.G. McConville in holding that Jeremiah's book represents the prophet's mature reflection and final editing of his oracles. He is unlikely simply to have jumbled passages together.

But even if the final form of the book is due to one or more of the 'later hands' mentioned above, let us suppose that such a 'later hand' came upon a genuine Jeremianic fragment, would he not seek a suitable place for its inclusion?

Order in the Disorder?

It is not permissible to solve problems by assuming that ancient editors were less than devoutly serious and seriously competent in what they did. The books of the prophets as they have come to us give enough evidence of carefully structured composition to make it appropriate to attempt the same exciting and profitable task in Jeremiah.

His book may not turn out to be a 'formal garden' (like Amos), but even in the glorious profusion of Hosea's 'wild garden' the message of the book began to emerge with clarity as we tied back some of the luxuriant growth, and exposed the outline of the prophet's planting. With patience, the same can be found to be true of Jeremiah.

An Outline for Jeremiah's Book

This outline must necessarily be succinct; the key verses are offered as a sort of stepping-stone pathway through the book as we follow the thread of thought.

- *1:1-19: Prologue.* These verses record Jeremiah's appointment (v. 5), enabling (vv. 6-9) and commission (v. 10), followed by an assurance concerning the word entrusted to him (vv. 11-12), and concerning himself as its minister (vv. 13-19). Topically, this is Jeremiah's 'call'; structurally, it is prologue, matched by chapters 45–51 as an epilogue. Both are concerned with the word of the Lord as the ruling factor in the world.
  . Key verses: 1:5, 7:8, 10, 18-19.

- *2:1–6:30: Israel's unfaithfulness.* Faithful to his initial vision of judgment on Jerusalem's wickedness (1:16), Jeremiah sets out to expose Israel's unfaithfulness (2:1–3:5), and the consequent alternatives of repentance (3:6–4:31) or rejection (5:1–6:30).
  . Key verses 2:7-9; 3:12-14; 5:7-11.

- *7:1–13:27: Misunderstood privileges.* But would Israel bow meekly to Jeremiah's charges? It rather seems that, charged with disloyalty, they replied by claiming privilege. Jeremiah counters Israel's false claims regarding the Temple (7:1-20), the sacrifices (7:21–8:3), the law (8:4–9:22); the knowledge of God (9:23–10:25) and the covenant (11:1–13:27).

  Each section ends with a message of doom: privilege does not save; misused privilege is a ground of condemnation (7:16-20; 7:29–8:3; 9:17-22; 10:17-25; 12:7–13:27).
  . Key verses: 7:11-12; 7:21-23; 8:8-9; 9:13; 9:23-24; 11:10.

- *14:1–20:18: Inescapable judgment follows logically.* The argument has three movements:
  1. Not even prayer can now avail (14:1–15:21).
  2. The Lord offers a last chance (16:1–17:27; see 17:19-27).
  3. But the Lord is sovereign (18:1–20:18), and consequently his stated alternatives of repentance (18:5-8) and judgment (18:9-17) still remain.
  . Key verses: 15:1; 17:24-25; 18:11; 19:3-4.

- *21:1–24:10: The failure and triumph of the covenant.* Jeremiah has argued cogently that his people merit judgment and that, if they refuse the sovereign God's way of repentance, they cannot escape. But what, then, about God's promises to his people? Does human disobedience annul God's faithfulness to what he has pledged?

  Thus, there is another aspect of divine sovereignty to be considered: 'Has he said it and shall he not do it?' (Num. 23:19). The Lord is not mocked, but neither is he defeated. In 21:1-10 Jeremiah traces out the coming end of Jerusalem with its grim alternatives (vv. 8-10).

  Following this, with parallel headings (21:11; 23:9), Jeremiah brings the covenant institutions of king and prophet under review. In each case there has been gross failure (21:11–22:30; 23:9-40), but in each case there is also a coming glory (23:1-8; 24:1-10). The covenant has been broken (22:9) but nevertheless the Lord will fulfil the covenant promise (24:7).
  .   Key verses: 21:10; 23:1-2; 23:5; 23:11; 24:5-6.

- *25:1-38: Conclusion: the course and governing principle of history.* In review, Judah (vv. 1-11), Babylon (vv. 12-14) and all the nations (vv. 15-38) are condemned. Two principles are at work: the efficacy of the Lord's word (vv. 8-9, 13-14) and the justice of the Lord's judgment – the 'cup' (vv. 15-29, compare Ps. 75:8; Isa. 51:17, 22-23) pictures the exact measuring out of wrath. Thus Jeremiah who was sent to pull down the nations (1:10, 15) has completed this aspect of his task.
  .   Key verses: 25:11-12, 15, 29.

- *26:1–44:30: The word of consolation.* There is also, however, another side to Jeremiah's ministry: 'To build and to plant' (1:10 NKJV). It is to this that he now turns. The heart of this section is the famous 'Book of Consolation' (30:1–33:26), to which 26:1–29:32 is a preface, establishing Jeremiah's credentials as a prophet of the Lord, and 34:1–44:30 is an epilogue, explaining why hope is deferred.

1. Jeremiah Authenticated (26:1–29:32)

When Amos announced judgment on Israel he felt that, in the light of this unacceptable truth, he had to defend the prophetic office as the voice of the Lord (3:1-8) and also to authenticate his own calling as prophet (7:9-17). With the same logic Jeremiah follows the unrelieved message of judgment (25:1-38) by recording incidents in which his own prophetic status was challenged and vindicated. In this way he affirms the authenticity of the word of judgment, and prepares for the coming message of hope.

In 26:1-16 influential hearers first opposed him but then came to recognise his authenticity (26:16-19); in 27:1–29:32 his opponents are prophets with a contradictory message. The command, 'do not listen to your prophets' (27:9; 29:8 NKJV) is followed in each case by the condemnation of named false prophets (28:1-15; 29:21-32), but Jeremiah's unique status is authenticated by the death of the false prophet Hananiah (28:16-17).

.   Key verses: 26:16-19, 24; 28:15-17.

2. The Book of Consolation: (30:1–33:26)

Commanded to write (30:1-3), Jeremiah predicts both disaster and hope (30:4–31:6), judgment and mercy (30:4-11), retribution and restoration (30:12–31:6) for Israel (31:7-22) and Judah (31:23-26). There will yet be a united people within a new covenant (31:27-40). Jeremiah commits himself to the veracity of these promises by his transaction with Hanamel (32:1-25). He anticipates the fulfilment of the Lord's promises in new covenant life (32:26-44), and traces all to the faithfulness of a prayer-answering God (33:1-26).

.   Key verses: 31:31-34.

3. *Hope Deferred (34:1–44:30)*.

This epilogue touches two topics: the tragedy of Jerusalem under Zedekiah with all its lost opportunities (34:1–39:18), and the subsequent end of Gedaliah's governorship in assassination and emigration. Hope is first deferred by the disobedience of king and people but, secondly, Gedaliah's community was not to be the locus of hope for the future (see 29:1-14), and therefore must be removed so that true hope alone remains.

.   Key verses: 34:15-16; 42:9-12; 43:1-3.

- *45:1–51:64. A prophet to the nations*. This section is an inclusion matching Jeremiah's call as a prophet to the nations (1:10) and thus rounds out the whole book. Jeremiah reviews the map of his world and finds the nations guilty before God (46:10; 47:6-7; 49:8, 13) of pride (48:29; 49:4, 16), oppression of Israel (50:33-34; 51:35) and idolatry (51:15-19). Yet he sees hope for Israel (46:27-28; 50:17-20), and for the nations (48:47; 49:6, 39), and for both together (50:4-5).

    But the structure of these chapters is as important as their content. It is a summation of the thrust of Jeremiah's ministry:

Structure of Jeremiah 45–51

A¹ 45:1-5 Baruch, the scribe of the word of the Lord
  B¹ 46:1-28 Egypt: the Lord's vengeance, the safety of Israel
    C¹ 47:1-7 Philistia
    C² 48:1-47 Moab
    C³ 49:1-6 Ammon
    C⁴ 49:7-22 Edom
    C⁵ 49:23-27 Damascus
    C⁶ 49:28-33 Kedar and Hazor
    C⁷ 49:34-39 Elam
  B² 50:1–51:58 Babylon, the Lord's vengeance, the safety of Israel
A² 51:59-64 Seraiah, the bearer of the word of the Lord

The people of the Lord live in a hostile world. There are the great genocidal enemies (B[1,2]), Egypt, the first, and Babylon, the contemporary; there are also surrounding smaller dangers, near and far (C[1,2]), but, embracing the whole, there are (A[1,2]) individuals entrusted with the word of the Lord. Thus, as he concludes, Jeremiah depicts for the future what he has himself been in his generation – the vehicle of the crucial word of the Lord – and establishes the fundamental shape of world history and the significance of the word of God and its ministers.

- *52:1-34: Postscript.* Events bear witness to the truth of the word of the Lord in Jeremiah: destruction (52:1-30) and hope (52:31-34).

Jeremiah and the Overmastering Word

This, then, is the book of Jeremiah:

- A reasoned exposition of the sins which brought downfall;
- Of the God who cannot be defeated in his purposes whether of holy wrath or sovereign grace;
- Of the powerful word of God enfolding and mastering the world in all its turbulence.

As we have just suggested, the international panorama with which Jeremiah ends his book is no accident, either in its positioning as the 'last word' nor in the way it is presented. In an impressively understated way he outlines a vision of the world unobtrusively held in the embrace of the revealed word of God.

It is in the word and not in its ministers that power resides. What is Baruch but one who copied out what was revealed (Jer. 36)? What is Seraiah but one who carried out what was written? The book of Jeremiah begins with a man who, against all his natural feelings and self-awareness, is mastered by the word, and ends with the whole world gripped by the same word.

Unlike, for example, 2 Kings 2:9 or Micah 2:7, Jeremiah makes no reference to the Spirit of God nor, alone of the 'major' prophets, does he ever use the 'vision' (*hazah*) word-group. On the other hand, of the 359 occurrences of the phrase, 'Thus says the Lord', in the Old Testament, Jeremiah has 157, giving some indication of the strength of his emphasis on the word of the Lord.

'Alas, sovereign Yahweh': the Call of Jeremiah

The call of Jeremiah (1:1-19) is a microcosm of his emphasis on the word of the Lord. Like all the prophets, he does not try to describe or explain the marvel of being addressed by the Lord. He does not tell us if this was an outward voice or an inward perception, only that 'the word of the LORD was to me' (1:4), that is, according to the force of the Hebrew verb 'to be', 'the word of the Lord became a living, present reality'. Of the objective mechanisms of revelation or the subjective process of inspiration he says nothing.

But, when it 'came', the word of the Lord began by revealing Jeremiah to himself (1:4-5). He was a man with a divinely superintended pre-history.

1. He was foreknown by God: 'Before I formed you in the womb', that is, before earthly conception. 'To know' means 'to know all about, to have in mind'; it also means to enjoy 'intimate union with' (as in Gen. 4:1), and to exercise care over (as in Ps. 1:6). The Lord loved, committed himself in care to and knew all about the man who was not yet but was to be. The 'foreknowledge' of God (as in Rom. 8:29) is primarily foreknowledge of what he will himself do.

2. The fact and moment of conception was itself a divine choice: 'I formed you in the womb'.

3. During the period of gestation ('before you came out of the womb') the unborn child was being prepared: 'I sanctified you', that is, set you apart for myself, made you part of my sphere of reality, claimed and possessed you.

4. Jeremiah was a predestined man, planned, conceived, prepared and born for this stated task at this appointed time – not as a matter of human choice but of divine conscription: 'I have appointed you prophet to the nations!'

What the Word Does and Does Not Do: Truth and 'real' Truth

Jeremiah portrays himself (1:6) as a diffident, insecure person, not a buoyant extrovert, but hesitant, conscious of weakness, immaturity and lack of 'gift'. The fact that later he will often be required to be – and will be – forthright, daring, ready to take risks, illustrates the truth of the definition that courage is 'being afraid but going on'. For in response to Jeremiah's confession of immaturity, the Lord does not say, 'No problem, I will change all that', but juxtaposes two Jeremiahs, both real: the frail, immature, unready person of subjective experience and the person of divine vocation. Jeremiah is still one who naturally backs away, but now he lives in tension with the one called by God to go forward: 'Wherever I send you, you must go.' He is the one whose self-estimate is, 'I do not know how to speak', but now he is also under orders to say, 'Whatever I order you.' 'Do not say' (1:7) is balanced by, 'Do not fear' (1:8).

There would be no need for the second command if Jeremiah's nervousness had been eradicated, but it is precisely that same unchanged, timorous self who is sent on the Lord's errands. The crucial question is whether he is prepared to live in the light of the 'real' truth, God's truth, about himself –

that he is a man of the Lord's word – going ('wherever I send you'), speaking ('whatever I command you'), accepting by faith that the Lord is with him in power ('with you am I to deliver'), that he has received the enduement of the word ('my word ... your mouth'), and that on these grounds he is a man of authority (1:10).

Jeremiah's shrinking self-awareness (1:6) remains true, but it is no longer the 'real' truth.

Divine Effectiveness and Human Resolution(1:11-19)

The word of the Lord is given to Jeremiah (1:9) but it remains the Lord's word (1:12), and it is he who pledges himself to its fulfilment. Nevertheless, Jeremiah is no longer a passive recipient (as in 1:9), or a spectator of divine action (as 1:12 might suggest). Rather (1:17) he is called to arms ('Gird your loins'), to action ('rise') and to ministry ('speak'). Faced by terrors ('Do not be shattered'), he must trust that the Lord has made him impregnable ('fortified city', etc.), no matter what ('all the earth') or who ('kings') may come against him. He must also trust that the Lord (1:19) has made him invincible through his own pledged presence.

Responsive Commitment

In 15:16 and 20:9 Jeremiah writes his own comment on all this. In 1:9 the Lord put his word in Jeremiah's mouth, but in 15:16 Jeremiah opens his mouth to feed on the word. The word as an objective gift ('was found') is met by subjective appropriation ('I ate') and delight ('joy').

Yet, at the same time, the entrance of the word brings Jeremiah into the most agonising internal conflict (20:9-10). Faced with the 'defamation of many' (20:10) his inclination is to 'forget about it', but the word of the Lord is a fiery internal force, contesting native reticence, putting him ever in the place of decision: Will he bow to the voice of self-awareness or to the demands of the word of God? The word of God makes him a man perpetually at war with himself.

The False and the True

One of Jeremiah's severest conflicts was provoked not by the existence, as such, of other prophets with an alternative message, but by his personal need to be sure that he was right and not they. This is one of the clearest examples of the distinct individuality of the biblical prophets – for one cannot imagine Isaiah, for example, being worried on this score – and of the fact that inspiration did not change or override temperament.

Jeremiah's Struggles: 23:9-40

The fundamental issue is that of objectivity or subjectivity. The true word originates objectively in the Lord and is communicated to the prophet from outside himself. This objectivity is described in 23:18, 22 as 'standing in the counsel of the LORD'. The true prophet is, as it were, co-opted on to a heavenly council where issues are thrashed out and decisions made (compare 1 Kings 22:19-22). He then becomes the bearer of that decision to the church.

By contrast, the false prophet has no divine vocation or divine word (23:21), but only a dream (23:25, 28a), a message without authority outside the mind of the speaker (23:26). Jeremiah is not, of course, discounting dreams as a possible vehicle of divine revelation: in 31:26 he seems to testify to just such an experience himself. But in 23:25 he is using the dream to typify what is self-derived and self-conditioned – subjective, not objective.

The Voice from Outside

This distinction is vital. Only a voice from outside breaks the closed circle of our own best but merely human thoughts. A prophet, however eloquent, however seemingly helpful, learned or thoughtful, who addresses us out of his own thinking, is simply a variant of talking to ourselves. The 'voice from outside' comes from God and is overheard, says Jeremiah, by one standing in the Lord's counsel.

The Validation of the Word

The distinction between the subjective and objective word is vital, but it does not solve Jeremiah's problem. As we have already noted, the false prophet Zedekiah (1 Kings 22:24) dismissed the alternative message of the true prophet Micaiah with the words, 'By whatever path did Yahweh's Spirit cross from being with me in order to speak to you?' In other words, my inspiration is primary, yours is derivative. If you claim inspiration, I more! Thus, while Jeremiah makes a proper distinction between the divine word and merely human words, he has not yet established a ground for distinguishing true inspiration from claimed inspiration.

There is, however, evidence available which exposes the false claimant.

1. Jeremiah notes that the false prophets have identified themselves with the moral spirit of the age: (23:10-11) 'Adulterers – the land is full of them! ... Indeed prophet and priest alike are profanely immoral.' Nothing more, of course, could be expected of the prophets of Samaria (23:13), for they prophesy by Baal, but 'in the prophets of Jerusalem I have seen something horrible: adulterous living ...!' (23:14a).

2. In 23:14b Jeremiah adds a second evidence: 'They strengthen the hands of evildoers so that no one turns back from his evil.' Immoral themselves, they have no reformatory message or intent. On the contrary, 'they never stop saying to those who spurn me, "Yahweh has spoken: Peace shall be your portion"' (23:17a).

3. Coupled with this, there is a denial of divine judgment: 'And to everyone progressing in the hardness of his heart they say: "No harm will come to you"' (23:17b). Yet it is a primary consequence of standing in the counsel of the Lord that the prophet would 'cause my people to hear my words and bring them

back from their evil way and from the evil of their deeds' (23:22). Jeremiah, then, would certainly have agreed with Paul that 'the knowledge of the truth finds its counterpart in goodness' (Titus 1:1), and with Jude that the truth of our salvation is subverted not only by doctrinal error but by those who 'turn the grace of our God into prurience of thought and life' (Jude 3a-4).

The Lord said as much to Jeremiah himself in 15:19: 'If you turn back (repent) I will bring you back (make your repentance effective): you will take your stand in my very presence (that is, the position of a true servant and prophet, compare 1 Kings 17:1). And if you bring out the valuable from the trashy, you will be as it were my mouth. They for their part may come back to you, but, for your part, you must not return to them.' The true prophet must cultivate an awareness of sin, be disciplined in personal holiness, and live a distinctive, separated life among those to whom he is sent.

Inspiration, Truth, Falsehood and Interpretation
What are the 'valuable' and the 'trashy' of 15:19? Neither by the words he uses nor in any subsequent discussion does Jeremiah tell us. We only know the principle of the thing: that within the mystery of revelation and inspiration the prophet's own discipline, determination, thoughtfulness, and careful selection and rejection play a crucial part.

Yet, when we hear Jeremiah accusing the Lord of deceiving / fooling him (20:7) – and other things also in his 'Confessions' – we need to ask if perhaps these were places where he failed to remove the trashy. And if so, whether there are bits of the book of Jeremiah which may be taken as inspired and others not. And how are we to know?

The problem is wider than Jeremiah. Throughout the Bible, inspiration covers two factors: 'truth of content' and 'accuracy of record'.

- The book of Job includes the slanderous accusations of Satan and the erroneous opinions of Job's friends (42:8) as well as the Yahweh-speeches. The latter are covered by inspiration of truth, but the former by inspiration of record. The insinuations of Satan and the errors of the friends are recorded but not commended, but the accuracy of the record is guaranteed by inspiration. It is part of the ministry of Scripture in Job to alert us to the ways of Satan, and to sharpen our awareness of truth by making us face error.

- In the history books, events are recorded almost wholly without comment, be it, for example, the polygamous lifestyle of the kings or their royal wars. How do we know, therefore, whether we are reading an example or a warning?

- Jeremiah's Confessions, too, are certainly covered by 'inspiration of record', but to what extent is he an example or a warning? Do we say: 'Isn't it marvellous that we can voice our feelings to God without fear or favour?' or do we say, 'There is a line in this matter of frankness which we are warned not to overstep'?

Our only guidance is the immediate context, and, beyond that, the context of the whole of scriptural truth. For example (as we saw) the 'imprecations' in the Psalms belong in an immediate context of covetable spirituality, and a biblical context which includes the denunciatory aspects of our Lord's words. So also in Jeremiah, the essential questions are: Did the Lord ever rebuke him for frankness? In his vexation of spirit did he ever lose reverence in his address to the Lord or turn his back on God?

Can we remind ourselves often enough that while inspiration solves no questions of interpretation, it makes the whole exercise of interpretation worthwhile? Regarding Jeremiah's frankness with God, one will say, 'But I could never speak to the Lord like that!' while another will say,

'It's such a help to me to know that I can stand before God "warts and all", without pretence, and tell it to him exactly as it is.' Nothing in the Bible is there by chance or without purpose and importance. Like everything else in the Lord's world, 'Everything is beautiful in its time.'

THE WRITTEN WORD

It is typical of Jeremiah's focus on the word of the Lord that he gives us our only detailed account of the way the prophets recorded their messages. In 605 BC he was commanded to make a written record of his ministry in the hope that the written word would prove more effective than the spoken word in promoting repentance (36:1-3). There was a touching simplicity about what then happened (35:4);

> Baruch wrote
> From the mouth of Jeremiah
> All the words of the Lord.

The plural 'words' is, of course, most significant: inspiration covers not the general drift or substance of the Lord's message but operates in the conveyance of actual 'words' from the Lord to and through the prophet and on to paper.

When Baruch is subsequently questioned by the Princes' Committee (36:18), his reply has the same succinctness:

> From his mouth he called out to me all these words while
> I was writing them in the book with ink.

Three things come together:

- Objectivity of revelation (the words of the Lord);
- Reality of inspiration (the mouth of Jeremiah);
- Exactness of transmission (Baruch wrote).

This is the imperishable word of the Lord: foes may destroy the writing (36:23) but only to see it rise from the ashes with redoubled force (36:32).

JEREMIAH AND THE FUTURE

In the important section, 21:1–24:10, we listened to Jeremiah insisting that human failure did not impose limits on the faithfulness of God. He would still fulfil his purposes and keep his promises. In particular the Lord would be faithful to David (23:5) and to the great covenant promise (24:7).

The Coming King

Jeremiah refers to David more than to any other single prophet, but his teaching contains no innovations. The 'Branch' imagery (23:5; 33:15) which Jeremiah uses of the coming King occurs in Isaiah 4:2 (compare Isa. 11:1) and is followed in Zechariah 3:8; 6:12. In essence it is a 'family-tree' motif:

- Isaiah's 'branch of the Lord' traces a divine lineage;
- Jeremiah's 'branch belonging to David' points to a human ancestry;
- In Zechariah 'the Branch' is used as a title needing no elaboration, pointing to the Messiah in his kingly-priestly office.

Jeremiah's coming descendant of David is righteous in character (compare Isa. 11:5; 53:11) and rule (Isa. 11:4; 55:4), effecting salvation and security for his people (compare Jer. 30:1-11), and his name is, 'Yahweh (is) our righteousness.' It is attractive to consider that his name ascribes deity to the Messianic King in the manner of Isaiah 9:6, but the use of the same name for Jerusalem in 33:16 suggests that this was not Jeremiah's intention.

In the city the predominant reality is that those who live there find their righteousness in the Lord, that is to say, they are all that the Lord requires them to be – in relation to him, in their own character and conduct, and in their communal life. According to 23:5, this spiritual completeness is secured by the Davidic King. He is himself righteous (23:5a); he exercises righteous rule (23:5b, literally, 'he acts in judgment and righteousness'); and he mediates righteousness to his people (23:6). Isaiah's vision of the Servant of the Lord who 'provides righteousness for the many' (53:11; compare 54:17) springs to mind.

The new covenant

The forecast of a coming covenant is not peculiar to Jeremiah (compare Isa. 54:10; 55:3-5; Ezek. 37:26-28), but he alone uses the significant term 'a new covenant' (31:31-34). He defines it:

- By contrast (31:32);
- By content (31:33);
- By results (31:34a);
- By its ground (31:34b).

Like a bridegroom taking his bride by the hand to lead her to her new home (compare 2:2-3), the Lord led his people out of Egypt (31:31), and they came together into their marriage covenant. The Lord was faithful to all his commitments ('I was a husband to them'), but a flaw emerged on the human side ('they broke my covenant').

Its Necessity

What then is the Lord to do? Notionally, he can either abandon the covenant plan and the people who spoiled it, or reduce the obligations of the covenant to match their poor capabilities. But either of these courses would oblige the Lord to deny himself, to contradict, in the former case, his faithfulness to his pledged word, and in the latter case, his faithfulness to his unchangeable holiness. Rather, in the new covenant, he undertakes to transform his people by giving them an inner nature conformed to his law, a heart designed for obedience (31:33). In Deuteronomy 5:29, as he listens to his people's pledges of loyalty, the Lord cries out, 'Oh that there were such a heart in them that they would fear me and keep all my commandments always!' The new covenant proposes to address exactly this weakness.

Its Character

In consequence (31:34) each individual within the new covenant stands in a marriage union with the Lord: each 'knows the Lord'. This is the significance of 'they shall know me'. As the prophet began his new covenant statement with the sadness of a broken marriage, so he ends it with a perfect marriage – 'knowledge' in its significance of an intimate union of two persons. Within this covenant there can be no gradations of membership whereby one member seeks to lead another into the knowledge of the Lord: it is 'the blessed company of all believing people'.

Its Basis

Finally Jeremiah teaches that the new covenant has been brought into being (31:34 NKJV; 'For I will ...) by a full and final work of forgiveness:

- It is full because it covers both 'iniquity' (awon, the internal warping of human nature whence all sin springs), and 'sin' (hata'at, the specific offences whereby sin expresses itself in thought, word and deed);

- It is final because it blots out even from the divine mind all recollection that we were ever sinners. Jeremiah does not say how this will be done; perhaps he did not know, or perhaps he was quietly relying on the fact that it had already been revealed through Isaiah.

Further reading

J. L MacKay, *Jeremiah* Vol. 1 Chapters 1–20 (Christian Focus, 2004)
— *Jeremiah* Vol. 2 Chapters 21–52 (Christian Focus, 2004)
— *Lamentations* (Christian Focus, 2008)
F.D. Kidner, *The Message of Jeremiah, The Bible Speaks Today* (IVP, 1987)
J. Guest, *Jeremiah, Lamentations* (Word, 1988)
F.B. Huey, *Jeremiah, Lamentations*, The New American Bible Commentary (Broadman, 1993)
J.G.S.S. Thompson, *The Word of the Lord in Jeremiah* (Tyndale, 1959)
J.G. McConville, *Judgment and Promise* (Apollos, 1993)

THE BOOK OF LAMENTATIONS

Origin and Authorship

This well-named book – for it is a sustained dirge over fallen Jerusalem – is anonymous. The traditional ascription to Jeremiah has at least the justification that the author was an eyewitness of Jerusalem's sufferings, and if we are to find an author among known Bible writers, Jeremiah must be the primary candidate. Like the author, Jeremiah was there, he saw it all, and was numbed with shock (Jer. 40:1-5). Lamentations takes us into the realities sketched with historical objectivity in 2 Kings 24–25; 2 Chronicles 36. It is a heartbreaking, wonderful and hopeful book. Its thoughts swirl and spiral, as would be the case for one caught in such a typhoon of sorrows. It is not a book for close analysis.

The Book

Lamentations consists of five poems, matching its chapter divisions. The first four are alphabetical acrostics, that is, in each lament, each section opens with a (usually) consecutive letter of the Hebrew alphabet (twenty-two letters altogether), compare Psalm 119, the outstanding example of this genre. In general, the intention of such a form is to provide, as we might say, an A–Z coverage of the subject. Where the acrostic is incomplete or (as in Lamentations) broken, this, too, is part of the poet's skill, indicating that the subject cannot be fully told but is one that defies human, logical organisation:

- In Lamentations 1:1-22 and 2:1-22 each verse in the Hebrew has three lines and the first line alone carries the alphabetical acrostic letter. However 1:7 and 2:19 have four lines each, as if the poet's emotions boiled over at the thought of the suffering endured, and in 1:16-17; 2:16-17 the order of the alphabet has been reversed.

- In 3:1-66 the poet turns from thinking of the city personified (the city 'as if' a person) to actual people, and his emotional pace quickens. Each of the three lines in each section carries the acrostic letter. It is as if, while we read, we can hear his heart beat in its sorrow and agony. Again, in verses 46-48 and 49-51 the same two letters are reversed, as before. The awful story defies ordered telling.

- 4:1-22 is notably terse by contrast, as if, after the emotional outburst of the third poem, the writer masters his feelings, and in two-line statements, with the first line carrying the acrostic, he tells it how it is, how people actually suffered when Zion fell.

- The fifth poem (5:1-22) is a prayer. The twenty-two-verse formation indicates that prayer is the exact equivalent of the need which the earlier poems have exposed. But now the alphabetical design has been abandoned, for prayer like this is an outpouring before the Lord, driven by urgency.

A. 1:1-22 Suffering Zion, the facts
B. 2:1-22 The anger of the Lord
C. 3:1-66 Individual suffering, resources and responses
D. 4:1-22 People in distress
E. 5:1-22 Flight to prayer

Further reading

J.G. McConville, *Lamentations*, in *New Bible Commentary* (IVP, 1994)
I.W. Provan, *Lamentations*, New Century Bible (Marshall, 1991)
R. Brooks, *Great is Your Faithfulness: Lamentations Simply Explained* (EP, 1989)
J. Guest, *Jeremiah and Lamentations* (Thomas Nelson, 2004)
B. Webb, *Five Festal Garments* (Apollos, 2000)

AN APPROACH TO OBADIAH

The most direct understanding of Obadiah is that he addresses Edomite animosity and opportunism at the time of the fall of Jerusalem to the Babylonians in 586 BC. This was but the culmination of truly ancestral hatred on the part of Edom. The seeds of enmity were sown between Jacob and Esau (Gen. 27:41), and though Esau himself did not sustain animosity (Gen. 33:4ff.), ill feeling remained, to surface in Numbers 20:14ff.

This hatred became the pattern:

- Saul had to go to war with Edom (1 Sam. 14:47).
- David conquered and annexed Edom (2 Sam. 8:14), whereby the conquest of Edom became a Davidic-Messianic motif (Isa. 34; Ezek. 35; Amos 9:11-12).
- Solomon faced Edomite rebellion (1 Kings 11:1ff., 23ff.) as did Jehoram a century later (2 Kings 8:20), and Amaziah fifty years later still (2 Kings 14:7).
- Amos condemns Edom for its age-long festering hatred (1:11), which came to a head in 586 (compare Ps. 137:7; Obad. 10-14).

A¹ 1-4 The Lord's messenger to the nations: Edom is to be brought down
   B¹ 5-9 The mountains of Esau:
      a¹ Illustration: thieves, only selective despoliation (v. 5)
      b¹ Treasures lost (vv. 6-7)
      c¹ Slaughter on the mountains (vv. 8-9)
   C¹ 10-11 Edom's downfall explained (compare v. 10, 'For')

D 12-14 Edom's moral offence exposed: Eight 'should nots'

C^2 15-16 Edom's downfall explained
(compare, v. 15, 'For' – omitted NIV)
B^2 17-18 The mountain of Zion:
  c^2 Salvation on the mountain (v. 17a)
  b^2 Possessions possessed (v. 17b)
  a^2 Illustration: fire and stubble: no remainder (v. 18)
A^2 19-21 The Lord's saviours to Zion

13

EZEKIEL:
TO KNOW THE LORD

The overwhelming vision of God with which Ezekiel opens his book sets the scene for all that will follow. This is a book of the revealed knowledge of God, and everything is turned to that great end. The verb 'to know' comes more than eighty times, mostly with reference to knowing God, and the key phrase, 'and they / you shall know that I am the LORD', occurs more than sixty times, whether it refers to acts of judgment (6:7 NKJV), or to the Lord's faithfulness in keeping his word (6:10), to his renewal of Israel (37:6, 13), or to his self-revelation to the nations (38:23). In and through all the immense variety of his oracles and their wonderfully imaginative presentation, this is Ezekiel's master-theme.

A LOGICAL CHRONOLOGY
In the presentation of his message Ezekiel is the chronologist among the major prophets. Leaving aside for a moment the oracles addressed to the nations (chs. 25–32), the remainder of Ezekiel's book records his messages in time-order. His ministry began in 593 BC (1:1) among the exiles taken to Babylon in Jehoiachin's captivity (2 Kings 24:8-16), and continued

on to the vision recorded in 573 BC (40:1). Ezekiel's oracles to the nations include his last recorded date, 571 BC (29:17), and within these oracles it is out of chronological order. The oracles preceding and following it are dated 587 BC (29:1; 30:20). This shows that Ezekiel was not concerned to preserve chronological precision as such, but that in general he found chronology to offer the most logical presentation of his message.

STRUCTURE
Ezekiel's book is crafted around three visions of God:

The Theophanies

- 1:1-28 The advent of the Lord in Babylon;
- 8:1–11:25 The departure of the Lord from Jerusalem (8:3-4; 10:4, 18-19; 11:22-23);
- 40:1–48:35 The return of the Lord to dwell among his people (43:1-7).

The second and third theophanies are explicitly associated with the first (compare 8:4; 10:20; 43:3). Ezekiel's whole book is focused around this basic vision. The God of revelation (ch. 1), the God of judgment (chs. 8–11) and the God of restoration and consummation are one and the same. It is not an alien thing for the holy God to judge his disobedient people, nor, in doing so, does he depart from determination to bring his blessings and purposes to completion. The enemies who destroyed Jerusalem did not conquer the God of Jerusalem; they were his agents of wrath. The powers who took his people captive cannot inhibit his plan for their glorious future.

Israel and the World
Unlike Jeremiah, who placed his worldview at the end of his book, Ezekiel rather unexpectedly places his international visions (chs. 25–32; 38–39) within the flow of his prophecies.

Yet our sense of the unexpected turns out to be mistaken. The chapters are perfectly in place. From chapter 8 onwards Ezekiel is diagnosing the 'anatomy' of Israel.

- In chapters 8–11 Ezekiel describes the Lord's departure from Jerusalem and the reasons for it.
- In chapters 12–24 the dominant message is one of reasoned divine judgment, lightened by glimmerings of hope (e.g. 14:11; 16:60-63; 20:33-44).
- This message of judgment and glimmering hope is then given a worldwide context by the international review in chapters 25–32, a panoramic outworking of the Abrahamic promise of blessing to those who bless Abraham's seed, and cursing to those who curse (Gen. 12:1-3).

The Fall of Jerusalem

In chapter 33 there comes a chronological and theological turning point: the fall of Jerusalem. Ezekiel had been alerted beforehand (24:25-27) to the fact that this would bring about a change in his ministry (33:21-22), and so indeed it did.

Chapter 33 is in four parts:

- Verses 1-11: A renewal of Ezekiel's commission;
- Verses 12-20: The fairness of the Lord's dealings;
- Verses 21-22: The fall of Jerusalem;
- Verses 23-33: The Lord's case against Judah.

In content, verses 12-20 belong with verses 1-11, and verses 21-22 with verses 23-33. Since Ezekiel's renewed commission and its allied reiteration of the open door of repentance leads into the message of hope for the future which begins in chapter 34, why, we might ask, are verses 21-33 not placed before verses 1-20? For surely it would be neat to round off the message of judgment with the climactic event of the fall

of Jerusalem and then begin a new phase of ministry with its
dominant message of hope.

Certainly it would be neat and logical, but it would
obscure a precious truth. The Lord opens the door of hope
to his people, not after the blow has fallen but before, so
that when they find the darkness closing around them they
have already seen the light of a different future shining. For
Ezekiel's exiles, the fall of the city, as spelled out in 24:25,
meant loss of their 'stronghold ... their joy ... delight ...
glory' and of relatives left in the city. How natural all this is!
Exiles though they were, they had still had a city to return
to, with the expectation of finding again all the joy the city
had formerly brought, as well as the happiness of meeting
members of their families and friends from whom they had
been parted. Now this could never happen. Did they not
need to know beforehand that hope for the future was not
a consolation prize but a preparation? The city was gone but
the Lord was still their God, they could still live in fellowship
with him and find life through repentance.

Hope

Thus Ezekiel's new commission as the Lord's Watchman
leads into the dominant message of hope in chapters 33–37.
As he 'watched' in relation to the judgment of the wicked so
he must 'watch' them home into the coming consummation.

Chapters 38 and 39 relate this undated hope to an international panorama including Israel's restoration (39:21-29).

Ezekiel's book, then, begins to look like this:

A¹ 1:1–7:27. The Lord's advent
Ezekiel the priest (1:1-3)
The vision (1:4-28)
Ezekiel's commissioning (2:1–3:27)
Ezekiel's message in act (4:1–5:17) and word (6:1–7:27)
A² 8:1–11:25. The Lord's departure and its justification
B¹ Ezekiel up to the fall of Jerusalem

'VISIONS OF GOD' (Ezek. 1:1-28)

The 'hand' is the organ which symbolises personal ability and action. The hand of the Lord resting on Ezekiel (1:3) represents the inspiring work of God granting to Ezekiel the capacity to receive divine revelation. What come to him are (1:1): 'visions/sights of God'. It is for this reason that many of the individual items which occupy the prophet's gaze in the following verses are left without interpretation: what is important is the revelation of God in the whole.

1. The Approach (1:4)

Any company approaching across the desert would raise a cloud (Song. 3:6), and Ezekiel's interest may at first have been excited by the possibility of travellers bringing news from home. For just as in Palestine the Mesopotamian powers always came from the north, so also in Babylonia did Palestinian travellers. This cloud, however, turns out to be different, for within it there is 'fire taking hold upon itself, with brightness all round'. The suggestion is of flame leaping out from flame in a continuous stream and creating an intense brilliance. It is, in fact, a 'self-maintaining' fire.

2. Living Creatures (1:5-14)

Ezekiel's first impression of four 'living ones' is that they present human faces (v. 5) but, when they come closer, he sees that each has four faces (v. 6). By this time it seems that they have come up and are towering over him, because his gaze starts with their feet and legs (v. 7), moves to their hands and wings (vv. 8-9), and finally rests on their faces (v. 10).

Thus he learns that they symbolise all creaturely excellence:

- The eagle, the greatest of birds;
- The ox, the greatest of domestic beasts;
- The lion, the greatest of wild beasts;
- And the man, the crown of creation.

Yet though Ezekiel is able to see with this clarity, nothing is standing still: there is ceaseless movement and an all-pervasive impression of fire (chs. 13–14).

3. Wheels Within Wheels (1:15-21)

Whatever the expression 'a wheel in the midst of a wheel' might mean in engineering terms, it is Ezekiel's way of accounting for the capability to move in all directions without any adjustment (v. 17). Living ones and wheels alike are energised and directed by the same Spirit. This implies that their movement is directed by God, and that the eyes which fill the wheels signify divine observation of all things everywhere. But Ezekiel does not offer any interpretation.

4. The Firmament (1:22-25)

The word 'firmament' (*raqia*) means 'something spread out', an 'expanse'. It is under this 'expanse' that the activity takes place: the constant to-ing and fro-ing of the living ones, and the noise of their wings (vv. 23-24). But all this flux of activity is controlled by 'a voice' which 'came from above the firmament' (v. 25), a voice of such authority that a word is sufficient to bring everything to a halt.

5. The Throne and the Enthroned One (1:26-28)

Ezekiel has safeguarded the 'unearthly' realities of his vision by careful use of the words 'appearance' and 'likeness' (e.g. v. 5). Up to verse 25 'appearance' has been used five times and 'likeness' six. In verses 26-28, however, the two words are used twelve times – so sensitively does the prophet approach the divine heart of the 'visions of God'.

- *He is the enthroned God:* 'the likeness of a throne' (v. 26). Beneath the 'expanse' all creation, represented by its created excellencies, is a flux of constant movement and noise. The enthroned God is in total control. The movements can be registered by the human eye but not traced out; it is like lightning (v. 13). But the enthroned God is still in control.

- *He is the holy God, hence his whole being* (v. 27) is suffused with fire – and indeed fire is the dominating impression of the creation over which he presides (vv. 4, 13). Fire is the active force of divine holiness, the unapproachable holiness of Exodus 3:2-5, the deadly holiness of Exodus 19:11-18. Ezekiel will return to this fiery holiness in 10:1-7 but it is interesting that when he describes the fire as 'self-maintaining' he uses a word only otherwise found in Exodus 9:24 (*mithlaqqachath*), where it is the fire of judgmental holiness. For Ezekiel as for Isaiah (6:3) the holy One fills all the earth with his glory.

- *He is the covenant God.* The 'visions of God' began (1:4) in cloud and fire, the typical Exodus-Sinaitic symbols of the presence of God, the God who was moved to action by 'remembering his covenant' (Exod. 2:24) and who, by the blood of the lamb (Exod. 12) and by his constant (Exod. 13:21-22), protective (Exod. 14:19-20) presence and leadership brought his people into a blood-based covenant with himself (Exod. 24:4-8).

Ezekiel's vision ends with an even older covenant symbol, for the brightness round the enthroned God is as 'the bow that is in the cloud in the day of rain', the covenant sign of Noah (Gen. 9:12-17). This aspect of Ezekiel's vision, as much as any other, undergirds the message he will preach. The Sinai covenant had its curses as well as its blessings (Lev. 26; Deut. 28–29), and thus validated both the coming judgment and the ultimate hope which Ezekiel taught. The Noachic covenant, however, with its sign that embraced the whole world in an exquisite circlet of grace, gave ground for Ezekiel's international perspective.

EZEKIEL IN THE LORD'S TRAINING SCHOOL (2:1–3:27)

Ezekiel offers the longest call-narrative of all the prophets. Indeed it would be more correct to say that he entered a planned course of divine tuition (2:1–3:27). It is important to remember that his 'call' begins, not at 2:1 but at 1:4. The first requirement in divine service is to see the glory of God.

For Ezekiel this experience is so overwhelming (1:28b) that he falls on his face. From this position of reverence everything follows.

The Lord's training of Ezekiel (2:1–3:27) falls into seven sections, each addressed to Ezekiel as 'Son of man' (2:1, 3, 8; 3:4, 10, 17, 25 NKJV) and setting him apart as a man to whom the Lord has spoken (2:1, 4, 7; 3:1, 4, 11, 17, 27).

- 2:1-2: *Regenerated*. Ezekiel is the prophet of the Spirit of the Lord. Isaiah's call is centred on atonement (6:7; compare Eph. 1:4); Ezekiel experienced the incoming, indwelling Spirit (compare Eph. 1:13-14). The work of the Holy Spirit here introduces Ezekiel into the fellowship of God. In his unaided humanity he is prostrate before the divine glory; indwelt by the Spirit, he stands as a person before God, enabled to hear what the Lord God will say to him.

- 2:3-7: *Commissioned*. The renewed address to Ezekiel as 'Son of man', that is, 'truly human, simply human', shows that the indwelling Spirit does not cancel or override our human nature but makes us more truly human. The information that Ezekiel is being sent to the 'children of Israel' does not here constitute a precise appointment (compare 3:11), because in

Ezekiel's day Israel was a scattered people in the two main locations of Judah and Mesopotamia. Indeed, the matter is left open by the description (literally) 'nations' (2:3), where the very word, more customarily used of Gentiles, itself has a sinister ring. It suggests both the deterioration of his people and the demanding nature of his task. He is called to a people spiritually degenerate. Persistent rebellion runs through the generations – 2:3: 'they and their fathers'. It is obstinate rebellion (2:3, marad), embittered rebellion (2:3, 'transgressed', pasha', 'rebelled wilfully'). They are 'hard-faced', unwilling to countenance advice, and headstrong, determined on their own way (2:4), presenting a menacing ('briers and thorns', 2:6) and hostile ('scorpions', 2:6) attitude to the word of God. To these the prophet goes with but one weapon in his armoury: 'You shall say to them, Thus the Lord has said' (2:4); 'You shall speak my words to them' (2:7).

• 2:8–3:3: *Equipped.* We have already looked at some of the details in this passage. Now we can note the passage in its proper sequence. The preceding verses (2:3-7) envisage a situation which might well have left Ezekiel puzzled. How can a 'Son of man' say, 'Thus the Lord has said'? How can a mere man 'speak my words'? The plural 'words' is the crux of the matter. How is God's word to be couched in God's 'words'? 2:8–3:3 tells all but explains nothing. There is a mystery and a marvel at work, an actual donation to Ezekiel of a complete, propositional revelation (2:10), which nevertheless (as we have seen) preserves the integrity of his full humanity, in mind, emotions and will. Thus he is equipped to 'speak with/by my words' (a literal translation of 3:4), that is, to use the given words of God as an instrument against the ingrained

stubbornness and wide-ranging wilfulness of those to
whom he goes.

- 3:4-9: *Enabled.* A soldier may possess all the weap-
ons of his warfare, but be personally unable to fight.
There is, therefore, another side to the Lord's work:
resolution, courage and persistence. Ranged against
Ezekiel are the three constant features of unregen-
erate humanity in relation to divine truth: opposition of will (3:7a), a closed mind ('strong of forehead', 2:7b) and an inner nature ('heart') resolutely
disposed ('hard') against God. Did Ezekiel feel any
different when the Lord gave him a face to match
their faces, a forehead to match theirs? Apparently
not, for he still has to be commanded not to be afraid
(hindered by the emotion of fear), nor 'dismayed'
('shattered', immobilised in the face of threat). Like
Jeremiah, Ezekiel's is the obedience of faith, the faith
which recognizes 'I cannot' but which affirms, 'But
he can – so I will.'

- 3:10-15: *Appointed.* Those who are taken into God's
training school are booked for a specific ministry.

Ezekiel 2:3-7 answers the question, 'What is the work?' Ezekiel
2:8–3:3 and 3:4-9 answer the question, 'How can a mere
human do it?'

Now 3:10-15 answers the question, 'Where?'

Thus Ezekiel is first appointed (vv. 10-11), and then introduced into his charge (vv. 12-15). Before either of these,
however, the Lord reminds him of his personal obligation to
the words the Lord has spoken. As in 2:8, Ezekiel is not a mere
'carrier' of the word but must be the first to obey it. The order
of the commands in 3:10 is significant. In the Hebrew, it is
'Receive into your heart ... and hear with your ears.' But surely
the ears must precede the heart, hearing before receiving? By
putting the heart first the Lord demands of Ezekiel a sincere
precommitment to the words of the Lord before any of them

has been actually heard – just as today we make our precommitment to the Holy Scriptures, as if saying: What the Bible is found to teach, I affirm myself bound to believe.

Following this, 'hearing with the ears' underlines the need for clarity of apprehension of what the word both says and means, no vague grasp or garbled understanding but an accurate and articulate mastery of what is revealed.

On this basis, the Spirit of God acts. As the Spirit lifts Ezekiel up he hears a voice (3:12) and a noise (3:13). The voice reminds him who the Lord is: the Lord is sovereign over the whole creation, this is his 'place'. The noise of wings and wheels implies that this glorious God is himself on the move to accompany Ezekiel on his mission.

Thus Ezekiel comes – with a vivid sense of the compulsion, power, majesty and presence of the Lord – and arrives where he was to begin with – at the river Chebar (3:15; 1:1)! Yet it is as though he were coming for the first time, for now he is there as the new man, called, equipped and sent by God. Because of this, Ezekiel sees his old situation in a new light and is 'devastated'. Did they seem just ordinary people when he looked at them through unenlightened eyes? Now he sees them in all their stubbornness, rebellion and hardhearted resistance to the Lord and his word. Yet even so Ezekiel does not rush to minister, but sits quietly through his 'seven days' of priestly consecration (Lev. 8:33).

- 3:16-21: *Responsible*. Ezekiel's commitment to the words with which he is sent (3:10-15) is matched by his commitment to the people to whom he is sent. He will henceforth be held responsible for their spiritual welfare and destiny:

  1. He is reminded that beyond death lies the penalty of sin. To 'die in iniquity / sin' (3:18-20) means to die in that condition with a conscience burdened with sin unrenounced and unforgiven (1 Cor. 15:56), to stand, unready, before God.

2. The holy God brings upon people the due reward of their deeds (3:20). The 'stumbling block' sounds like a deliberate ploy of God to catch people out, but it is not so. In 7:19 the stumbling block is the person's own sin, and in Jeremiah 6:19-21 it is the 'fruit of their thoughts'. The picture is not of a concealed tripwire but of a road block and 'Danger' notice. If people persist on that road a governing moral justice will bring upon them what they deserve and have chosen. The stumbling block is both the divine mercy that would halt them, and the personal decision that drives them to ruin.

3. The same God is the saviour of sinners: it is his will to warn them (3:17; compare 18:32), and the purpose of the warning is to bestow salvation (3:18) and life (3:21).

4. The task of warning is committed to the Watchman. He can never excuse himself. Every individual is his care and he is accountable before God for each. He looks upon people as they seem to the human eye: both the one whose life is ungodly, and the one of apparent righteous conduct (whatever his inner standing before God) who is seen to lapse from the life he once lived (2 Tim. 2:19; James 5:19-20). Ezekiel's task is to turn every sinner from the error of his ways and save every soul from death.

• 3:22-27: *Bound.* At first sight this is a strange, illogical passage. Ezekiel has the awesome responsibility of speaking the word of warning to every individual in the light of eternal issues, but now he is housebound (3:25) and dumb (3:26). Where the human mind sees illogicality, the Lord is teaching a fundamental truth.

Logically, Ezekiel is committed to frenzied activity, but this is not the Lord's way. Ezekiel's first duty is to take responsibility for his own hearing of God's word (3:22-24). In 1:4 the presence of God came to him, but now, as the regenerate man (2:2), Ezekiel must seek the Lord's presence (3:22). When he does, he meets the Lord in all his glory (3:23), the Holy Spirit fills him (3:24) and he learns how to do God's work in God's way. This means seeking God's presence in order to hear God's word, and only speaking when the Lord gives the opening of the mouth (3:27).

METHODS AND MESSAGE (Ezek. 4–7)

The new date at 8:1, coupled with the fact that 8:1–11:25 is a self-contained section, suggests that chapters 4–7 have been deliberately placed here as an adjunct to Ezekiel's call in chapters 1–3.

They suit this position both in the methods they exemplify and the message they express. Chapters 4–5 contain two 'acted oracles' and chapters 6–7 two spoken oracles.

1. Acted Oracles

Ezekiel's frequent use of the acted oracle suggests a man with a vivid imagination to whom the visual approach appealed. There was, of course, more to the use of acted presentations than a simple visual aid. As 2 Kings 13:14-19 shows, the act was linked dynamically with the power of the word. The word of the Lord is never a mere sound in the air or ear, but always an active emissary of the divine will (Isa. 55:10-11; Ps. 147:15). The twofold expression of the word, in speech and act, redoubles its effectiveness.

Ezekiel's acted oracles are always highly complex. Chapter 4:1-17 is typical, involving symbolic numbers that have defied convincing interpretation. Yet, like all the acts, its thrust is unmistakable: the exact apportionment of divine chastisement to human deserving. The symbolism in 5:1-17 traces out the consequences. Siege and sword will account for two-thirds of the Jerusalemites, and even the remaining third, scattered among the nations, will find the Lord's sword following them: an appalling judgment, yet a judgment that encapsulates a seed of hope.

2. Spoken Oracles

The spoken oracles in chapters 6–7 draw out the significance of the acts of chapters 4–5. Broadly, chapter 6 links with 5, with its message of a remnant of hope in the midst of desolation (6:8), and chapter 7 with 4 in matching punishment with deserving – but at the same time taking note of a surviving few (7:16). Both chapters sound Ezekiel's dominant notes: that the Lord is revealed and will be recognized both in judgment and in preservation: 'They shall know that I *am* the LORD.' This repeated refrain divides 6:1-14 into three sections with verse 14 forming a summary:

- Destruction and death (vv. 1-7);
- A self-condemning remnant (vv. 8-10);
- The sure fulfilment of divine threats (vv. 11-13).

The same refrain divides 7:1-27 into three:

- The end for the land (vv. 1-4);
- And its people (vv. 5-9);
- The day of doom leaving no remainder (vv. 10-12a), no recovery (vv. 12b, 13), no resistance (vv. 14-15), a penitent few (vv. 16-19), despoilers (vv. 20-22), land, city and leaders finished (vv. 23-27).

The chapters are thus a true summary of Ezekiel's ministry with its dominant themes of judgment, the glimmering of hope, and the drumbeat refrain, 'They shall know that I *am* the LORD.'

THE DEPARTING GLORY (Ezek. 8-11)

Chapters 8–11 of Ezekiel are as dramatic as any chapters in the prophetic literature. In outline, they are as follows:

A¹ 8:1-3 Ezekiel's journey by the Spirit
  B¹ 8:4-18 Sins that offend the Lord
    C¹ 9:1-11 Judgment and mercy: sinners doomed and spared
      9:8 Ezekiel's first cry and the Lord's reply (9:9-11)
      D 10:1-22 Judgment: the fire of holiness
  B² 11:1-12 Sin that offends the Lord
    C² 11:13-23 Judgment and mercy:
    Sinners doomed and spared
    Ezekiel's second cry (11:13)
    And the Lord's reply (11:14-21)
A² 11:24-25 Ezekiel's return by the Spirit.

The Purpose of the Vision

We are intended, of course, to take Ezekiel's visionary experience exactly as stated. He is resident in Babylon, but he is brought in spirit by the Spirit to Jerusalem and back. The purpose of the experience is to prepare the exiles for the coming fall of Jerusalem by giving them a coherent explanation of it: the Lord's merited withdrawal from and judgment upon a sinful city. The sins that offend (B¹) can be listed:

- Idolatry chosen instead of atonement (the altar, 8:5);
- A secret life of the heart at variance with public profession and duty (8:10-12);
- Alternative sources of prosperity (8:14), Tammuz, the 'fertility' god;
- Their backs turned on the Lord (8:16).

Matching this (B²), the sin that offends is spiritual complacency, denying the possibility of judgment (11:3).

For these things the Lord is progressively alienated (8:4; 9:3; 10:3-4, 19; 11:22-23), and his alienation has its positive demonstration in the outpoured holy fire of divine wrath, the theme of chapter 10.

The Vision

It may at first seem strange that so much of chapter 10 simply repeats details of chapter 1, but it is not strange at all.

It is imperative that Ezekiel should be able to convince his hearers that the downfall of the cherished city is the act of their God, not his defeat by stronger, alien forces, and that there is a nexus between overthrow on the one hand and sin and holiness on the other. Therefore – with typical Ezekiel detail – he labours to affirm that the vision he saw in the destruction of Jerusalem is the vision that came to him by Chebar (10:20). Their God is the God of holy fire, and the fire of destruction comes from the very heart of his nature (10:2, 6-7).

This fire of wrath is committed to the 'man clothed in linen' (10:6) – the agent of mercy (9:2-4) and the agent of wrath are one, for there is no conflict in the attributes of God: in him holiness and mercy, wrath and redemption are at peace with each other. The man who marks those whom mercy spared (9:4) also executes wrath in fire on the unconcerned.

The Remnant
To understand what Ezekiel is teaching here about the spared remnant, we must hold 9:4 (C^1) and 11:15-21 (C^2) together. In contrast to the complacent ones who deny the possibility of judgment (11:1-3), there are those who 'bewail and bemoan themselves over all the abominations' (9:4). They are not spiritually sinless but spiritually concerned, differentiated by their lack of complacency. They feel and lament sin, including their own, and thus are marked out for deliverance.

Hope for the Future
In 11:15ff. Ezekiel learns that the hope for the future resides in the exiles in Babylonia. The destruction of Jerusalem is not the end of the Lord's purposes for his people: the land is lost but not the promises. Indeed, when the Jerusalem sanctuary is no more, the Lord himself will be the 'sanctuary' the people need (11:16). He also pledges regathering (11:17),

reformation (11:18) and regeneration (11:19), leading to obedience (11:20). We simply need to remind ourselves that 'sanctuary' (*miqdas*, 'place of holiness') means the place where the Lord comes to live in person among his people. Exiled in Babylon, Jerusalem in ruins, they have lost the building, but they have not lost the divine presence.

EZEKIEL'S HOPE: NEW KING, NEW PEOPLE (chs. 12–24)

Within the solid core of Ezekiel's ministry in chapters 12–24, chapters 17–20 are of particular importance.

- *Chapter 20:1-44* offers a striking review of the Lord's dealings with his people. At each point he has acted in grace and power, but has recurringly been met with rebellion (vv. 8, 13, 21). Yet, instead of abandoning such obdurate rebels, the Lord 'acted for his name's sake', that is to say, for reasons locked within and true to his own nature (vv. 9, 14, 22). Consequently, there is a future, a new wilderness experience (vv. 34-35), with rebels purged out (v. 38; Deut. 1:35; 2:16), and at last his people will serve him on his holy mountain (v. 40). All this will come about because, from the first to last, the Lord has been motivated by reasons of his own (v. 44).

- *Chapters 17–19*: two allegorical sections (17:1-21; 19:1-14), which together declare the end of David's monarchy as it then was, bracket two passages of hope. In 17:22-24 the return of the monarchy is forecast under the imagery of a shoot taken from Lebanon, and in 18:1-32 all are invited to repent. This matches the picture of those who bemoan and bewail sin in 9:4.

- *Ezekiel 18*, then, does two things:
  1. It opens the door of hope to all who will repent. There is no fatalistic entail in Old Testament religion (18:1-2). Whosoever will may come, whatever the parental background. The entail

can be broken, for all souls are the Lord's (v. 4). The soul that sins shall indeed die (vv. 4, 20), but the Lord, who has no pleasure in such a death, calls his people to repent and live (v. 32).

2. But while hope thus entices sinners into repentance, the requirements of the Lord can never be met, for he demands not just the turning back to him which constitutes one side of repentance, but a consequent, evidential, total righteousness: to 'keep all my statutes and do what is lawful and right' (v. 21). This requires in effect 'getting a new heart and a new spirit' (vv. 30-31). The door of hope is open but the conditions are beyond our capacity.

EZEKIEL'S WORLDVIEW (chs. 25–32)
Like Amos (1:3–3:3), Isaiah (chs. 13–27), and Jeremiah (chs. 46–51) Ezekiel encapsulates his worldview by letting his prophetic gaze dwell on the nations of the world as he knew it. Unlike Amos who allows a review of seven nations to lead dramatically up to his concentration on Israel, Ezekiel, like Isaiah (see 17:1–18:7, 22:1-25), sees his own people as surrounded by a more than menacing world. The centrepiece of his 'map' is 28:24-26 with its focus on Israel's hope: the regathering promised for the undated future.

'Seven', the numeral of completeness, dominates Ezekiel's presentation. He lists seven nations in all, six on the one side of the central panel and one on the other. Yet the two review sections balance each other, with ninety-seven verses in each. In the same way the two major oracles – that on Tyre (26:1–28:19) and on Egypt (29:1–32:32) – are marked off into seven sections each. Thus completeness (sevenfoldness) and balance mark Ezekiel's review, indicating his conviction that he is saying all that needs to be said. The people of the Lord are set within a surrounding and antipathetic world – Ammon to the northeast (25:2); Moab, east

(28:8); Edom, south (25:12); Philistia, southwest (25:15); Tyre, northwest (26:1); and, as ever in this world, there is the looming menace of the superpower, Egypt (29:2). The reason why Ezekiel does not specify Babylon, the power in whose grip he and his people then lay, rather than Egypt, is that, like all the prophets, his world was centred on the promised land, and it was within that perspective that he saw the realities of human history.

The nations of the earth are seen in their individual realities. Thus, for example, Tyre is the economic imperialist, the prototype of the multinational monopolist; Egypt, by contrast, is imperialism incarnate, and its Pharaoh an exemplification of the delusion power injects into the human mind (29:3).

Within his individualised treatment of the nations, Ezekiel dwells on two leading truths:

1. The Lord, as sole world-ruler, governs his world without favouritism yet with a central, consistent concern. If he is against Tyre (26:3), Sidon (28:22) and Egypt (29:3), he is also against Jerusalem (5:8). Indeed the sustained, reiterated exposure, condemnation and sentencing of Jerusalem which preoccupies the major part of Ezekiel's book shows that he would have agreed with Amos (3:2) that to whom much is given all the more will be required. Offences against the Lord's people will not be overlooked (25:6, 8, 12, 15; 26:2, compare 28:24) and for pride (28:2, 6, 9, 17; 29:8) the nations will bear their shame. Yet, at the centre of these worldwide, moral purposes, the nations will also be dominated by divine sovereignty in the interests of securing Israel's future security (28:25-26). The sovereign Yahweh rules the world; he rules with impartial justice; and he rules the world in the interests of his people and in order to fulfil his promises.

2. The whole world is somehow brought within the promise that 'they shall know that I *am* the LORD.' 'The goal of all God's action,' says Christopher Wright, 'is that God should be known and acknowledged among the nations for who he truly is ... Though set very much in the minor key of historical judgment, Ezekiel's insistence that the nations will come to know that Yahweh alone is God fits in with (the) strong biblical affirmation of God's universal intention that the nations should know him to be truly the living God.' In other words, the recognition formula typical of Ezekiel, that 'they shall know that I *am* the LORD', runs as plainly through these chapters as through the rest of his prophecy (25:2, 11, 17; 26:6; 28:22-23, 26; 29:6, 9, 16, 21; 30:19, 25-26; 32:15). The 'minor key' Wright mentions calls attention to the fact that it is much in the context of his judgments upon them that the nations recognise the hand of the Lord. But equally they will be witness of his grace and mercy in restoring Israel, and in this too they will know Yahweh as God.

THE FUTURE RESTORATION (Ezek. 33–39)

Ezekiel, however, is not yet finished. In his new role, as Israel moves into the blessed future (chs. 33–39), he foresees:

1. The return of David. The kingly vision expressed enigmatically in 17:22-24 is openly predicted in chapters 34–35. Typical of Old Testament Messianism, the coming perfect Shepherd of Israel is first the Lord himself (34:11-22) and then 'My servant David' (34:23-31 NKJV).

    The overthrow of Edom (35:1-15) confirms the return of David – for the first David was the only king to conquer and hold Edom, and the subjugation of Edom became a Messianic motif of the reign of the true David-to-come (compare Isa. 33–34; Amos 9:11-12; etc.).

2. Along with the true king, Ezekiel sees the regenerate (36:24-27), restored (36:28-35) and revived people (37:1-14). That which was impossible in the call to true repentance – the new heart (18:30-31) – is now the work of God, still acting for his name's sake (36:22).

Ezekiel's Vision of the Perfect State

In chapters 38–39, Ezekiel, for the second time, as in chapters 25–32, steps aside to remind us that the Lord's plans are worldwide and not just Israel-wide. This is a needful exercise, but at the same time it obscures the way in which 37:26-28, in three verses, establishes the dimensions of the vision the prophet will (typically) elaborate in chapters 40–48.

- *The covenant people* (37:26a, compare the covenant promise in 14:11; the everlasting covenant in 16:60-63). Isaiah (54:10) and Jeremiah (31:31-34) shared Ezekiel's covenant hopes. 'Peace' is fully enjoyed wellbeing and wholeness – in relation to God, society and one's self.

- *The indwelling Lord* (37:26b-28). The sanctuary-concept reaches back to the Tabernacle in the wilderness, expressing the supreme purpose of the Exodus-redemption (Exodus 29:44-46). Interestingly, this passage in Exodus also anticipates Ezekiel's key-phrase: 'they shall know that I *am* the LORD ... who brought them up out of the land of Egypt that I might dwell among them.'

  The 'house of the LORD' was given a new expression by Solomon (1 Kings 8) and by Haggai's builders, but always with the same governing concept: the Lord dwelling among his people. How natural it is, then, for Ezekiel the priest to see the perfect future through this central priestly imagery.

- *The holy people* (37:28). The Tabernacle and the Temples were only secondarily places of atoning sacrifice. The holiness of the divine occupant was their primary reality. But this necessitated making provision whereby the Holy One might dwell among sinners and they might dwell with his holiness. There had to be the 'screening' function of priests and Levites (Lev. 8; Num. 8), and the propitiatory efficacy of the shed blood (Lev. 17:11). Ezekiel looks forward to the day envisaged in chapters 36 and 37 when at last (by divine action) the people among whom he dwells will 'match' the Lord who is in their midst: they will be sanctified.

- *Universal acknowledgement* (37:28). 'The nations will know that I the Lord sanctify Israel.'

The Vision of the New Temple (Ezek. 40–48)

Ezekiel's 'temple-hope' is elaborated with his typical imaginativeness in chapters 40–48. There are, however, three aspects of his vision which indicate that Ezekiel is offering a visual expression of a great idea, not a blueprint for a Temple yet to be built:

1. In this house, the Lord will come in all his glory to dwell (43:7). It is theologically impossible to imagine the Lord dwelling in a place of ongoing animal sacrifice after the one sacrifice for sins for ever has been offered (Heb. 10:12, 18). Such a house has no further place of function. Ezekiel must therefore be using the symbol that comes most naturally to him to express the coming reality of the indwelling God.

2. Once the Lord's people are sanctified (37:28) they have no need for ongoing daily sacrifices to make it possible for them to live in the divine presence. Therefore the sacrifices must also be a symbolic vision of a future time when the holy people will dwell

with their God because they consciously rest on the efficacy of the blood that has been shed.

3. The details Ezekiel gives of the buildings are hardly even a ground plan, and, indeed, contain many an unsolved obscurity. This would not be the case if he were setting out to provide for a future building. He does, however, provide enough to sketch a visionary idea. Furthermore, the measurements of the city (42:15-20) make building it impossible in relation to the land of Canaan as we know it. The land itself is described according to its Mosaic dimension, but 'the measurements of the temple and city are out of all proportion to these' (Fairbairn). There is as much reason for believing the wilderness of 20:35 to be 'real' as to think of Ezekiel's temple in terms of stone and timber. Ezekiel constantly laid the salvation-history of his people under contribution, and it was in the same spirit that he used the temple.

The Meaning of the Vision

What, then, is Ezekiel's vision? Fundamentally, the Lord, alienated by sin, returns to live among his sanctified people (43:1-7). They dwell in ordered array around him, with a screening priesthood, and safeguarding sacrifices, and the presence of the Prince-Mediator (chs. 43–46). The outflowing life of God provides all that his people need (47:1-12) and the Lord's presence gives the city its name, reality and character: 'The LORD is there' (48:35).

J.B. Taylor offers an excellent summary of Ezekiel's temple-message: the perfection of God's plan for his people; the centrality of worship; the abiding presence of the Lord; the outflowing blessings of the 'river of life;' the orderly array of the people in their places and functions.

Fulfilment

Where, then, are we to look for the fulfilment of Ezekiel's priestly, 'temple' hope, especially if the terms in which he expresses it rule out (as they do) the possibility of an actual future building? We can put it like this: just as Isaiah (for example) looked forward to a future Jerusalem (65:19) but intended the Zion to which we have already come (Heb. 12:22), and which is also yet to come (Rev. 21:2), so Ezekiel used terminology natural to himself and appropriate to his time, but foretold the Temple that now is (1 Cor. 3:16; 6:19), which is even now in building (Eph. 2:19-22), and which will yet come in all its glorious reality (Rev. 21:3).

Further reading

J.B. Taylor, *Ezekiel*, Tyndale Old Testament Commentary (IVP, 1969)
R.H. Alexander, in F. Gaebelein, Ed., *The Expositor's Bible Commentary*, 1992
P. Fairbairn, *Ezekiel* (Sovereign Grace, 1960)
C.J.H. Wright, *The Message of Ezekiel*, The Bible Speaks Today (IVP, 2001)
L.E. Cooper, *Exekiel*, The New American Commentary (Broadman, 1994)

14

DANIEL:
GOOD NEWS FROM A DISTANT LAND

I f the Lord's word to Abram (Gen. 12:1) was 'Go out', his word to Daniel was, 'Stay in.' Swept up in Nebuchadnezzar's deportation of captives in 605 BC (2 Kings 24:1-16; Dan. 1:1), Daniel heard the Lord's call, not in a word of command or invitation, but in the harsh outworking of circumstances (compare Eph. 6:5-6).

Daniel's dates run from 605 BC (1:1) to 536 BC (10:1), a span of seventy years. We do not know how old he was in 605 BC, only that he was old enough to show educational promise (1:4). The thoughtful view he takes of his situation (1:8), showing his maturity and his resolute leadership and mature understanding in the crisis of the king's dream (ch. 2), would suggest his early twenties rather than even his late teens. If so, then he must have been eighty-five to ninety years old at the time of his final visions (10:1–12:13), too old to have faced the journey back to Jerusalem: old enough to have the ripe spirituality those chapters evidence, and to evoke the Lord's solicitousness (10:11-19) for an aged servant.

THE ARENA OF TESTIMONY (Dan. 1–6)

Daniel and his friends accepted their appointed place in a pagan society, worked for its qualifications, excelled over its candidates (1:18-21), accepted its rewards (2:48; 3:30; 5:29) and devoted a lifetime to its service (1:21). Any dichotomy we ever allow between 'daily work' and 'Christian work' would not seem to have occurred to them. Being the best they could be for God involved being the best in the place he had put them and in the work (in their case) imposed on them (compare Eph. 6:5).

Graduation

We are told that the success of Daniel and his friends was due to divine gift (1:17). But this blessing – like professional competence in any sphere or day – could not have been enjoyed without cost in study and discipline.

Though no explicit lessons are drawn, the stories in Daniel 1–6 underline this element of professional excellence, and make it plain (Dan. 2; 4; 5) that it was this which opened doors for testimony. It is simplistic and unthinking for anyone in a secular job to say, 'I am here first and foremost to be a Christian, and to make Christ known. Everything else is secondary to that.' This is certainly not the message of the dedicated professionalism evidenced in Daniel and his friends. They did not subordinate their testimony to their career prospects or vice versa; they made their careers the primary arena of their testimony. Would Daniel have had his opportunities to minister the word of God to emperors and kings (chs. 2; 5) had he not established his reputation for professional excellence?

Pressures and Responses

The events recorded in Daniel 1–6 are so true to the sixth century BC that those who claim a second-century date for Daniel could well be asked how a late author was so well-informed about the Babylonia and Persia of four hundred years earlier. But be that as it may, the stories are also a case study of the people of God in an alien world. Daniel and his friends experienced all the weight of a world attempting 'to squeeze them into its mould' (J.B. Phillips, Rom. 12:2):

- New names (1:6-7) to domesticate them into a new social and religious context;
- Education to make them fit in (1:4);
- Jealous and hostile colleagues (3:12; 6:4);
- Pressure to abandon religious distinctiveness in favour of a conformist world-religion (3:4-7);
- Autocratic and unpredictable employers.

Yet, always with great courtesy, they remained uncompromising (e.g. 4:19, 27). In a world matching ours, they exemplified a covetable ideal, balancing due conformity with thoughtful, purposeful nonconformity, plainly in the world and plainly not of it.

Structure of Chapters 1–6
A simple clue is that chapters 1 and 6 provide a framework, focusing respectively on Daniel's refusal of 'the king's delicacies' (1:8) and the king's edict (6:6-10). Within this framework of consistent distinctiveness, chapters 2–5 record the ways in which opportunities arose for bringing the word of God to bear.

A^1 1:21 Distinctiveness of lifestyle
    B^1 2:1-49 The word of God to inform and comfort
    Acknowledgement of the superiority of Daniel's God (2:47)
    B^2 3:1-30 The word of God as non-negotiable.
    Standing for revealed truth.
    The uniqueness of the God of Shadrach (3:29)
    B^3 4:1-37 The word of God in its moral rigour.
    The conversion of Nebuchadnezzar (4:37)

B⁴ 5:1-31 The word of God and the message of judgment.
    Non-repentance and death (5:29-31)
A² 6:1-28 Distinctiveness of spirituality.

The word of God is ministered effectively within the context of a distinctive and consistently spiritual life.

1. *Separation.* The negative distinctiveness displayed in Daniel 1 is far from easy to explain with certainty. Old Testament law does not require vegetarianism, and while suggestions may be made, there is no unequivocal reason why the 'delicacies' (1:8) were refused in favour of vegetables. The word ('pathbag', 1:5, 8) only reappears in 11:26 where it may imply that there is something reprehensible in first eating a king's 'delicacies' and then turning against him. This could, of course, be as broad as a general feeling that hospitality imposes obligation, but this will not cover the situation in 1:8, for if the 'delicacies' were the king's, so were the vegetables.

    Could it be, then, that 'pathbag' involved some actual commitment of loyalty? In this case, Daniel and his friends were drawing back from an unquestioning loyalty to Nebuchadnezzar. Lacocque, however, takes a different view by noting Leviticus 11:37-38, where properly stored grains were insusceptible to 'uncleanness' by contagion. If this is what moved Daniel, then his motive was to preserve a proper purity before God.

    Though all this is only conjecture, the principles involved are thoroughly scriptural: that our ultimate loyalty cannot be given other than to the Lord (compare Rom. 14), and that there are aspects of the life of contemporary society which may very well be innocuous in themselves but which a sensitive conscience could rightly see as contaminants. We are required so to live that, as in Deuteronomy 4:1-8, any onlooker may marvel at the qualitative differences evidenced in a life lived in obedience to the divine law, and that, of course, we avoid the world's contagion (James 1:27; 4:4).

These principles are easier to state than to apply, and there is both room and need for individual discernment. Today, for example, the question of where our first loyalty lies leads one person into pacifism, but leaves another untroubled on that score. For pre- and post-war Christians the principle of contagion was a dominant issue – and, from the highest motives, those who tried to guide us into distinctive living in fact inculcated a reactive holiness: whatever the 'world' favoured, the Christian must eschew. The arts, pastimes and dress became areas of denial. It would be quite wrong to mock, let alone impugn, our caring teachers and their shibboleths, but the fact is that they taught 'separation' as something valid in its own right. The strength of Lacocque's appeal to Leviticus 11:37f. is that it bases Daniel's separateness where it properly belongs, on a clear foundation of obedience to revealed truth.

2. *Spirituality.* The refusal of the king's delicacies in chapter 1 is balanced by the refusal of the royal edict in chapter 6. In neither case was Daniel confrontational. In chapter 1 his approach was marked by courtesy (1:8) and reasonableness (1:11-13). In 6:10 he quietly continued in well-doing (1 Pet. 2:15). The reference to 'early days' indicates well-nigh seventy years of consistency. The crisis was not met either by hostile demonstration or by innovation. Daniel had proved the power of prayer already, and there was no need for anything other than the formed habit of a lifetime.

PRAYER

The formation of a disciplined, sustained, personal spirituality involves of course all these practices which make up a serious mental, emotional and obedient walk with God, but Daniel 6 singles out the life of prayer, and this is typical of Daniel as his book portrays him. In chapter 2, the crisis of the king's dream is met in prayer (2:17-18). In Daniel 9 we meet Daniel busy with the written word of God, discerning from the book of Jeremiah the promise of restoration after seventy years. Immediately he turns to prayer. There are two great truths here:

1. *The Lord's fulfilment of his stated purposes of grace is linked in with the prayers of his people.* For example, the promise of the forerunner (Mal. 3:1; 4:5), with its time settled in the divine calendar (Gal. 4:4), was fulfilled in answer to Zechariah's prayer (Luke 1:13). Daniel recognised that divine promises should excite our prayers, and that the Lord fulfils his purposes by answering the prayers of his people.

Daniel 9:3 sums up the characteristics of true prayer:

*   Concentration ('set my face') upon God in his sovereignty ('Lord', *adonay*);
*   Personal, disciplined commitment (literally, 'to seek prayer', that is, to frequent the place of prayer);
*   Detachment from other concerns ('fasting');
*   The creation of appropriate circumstances ('sackcloth') so that the body works in co-operation with mind and tongue.

2. *Inheriting the promises:* Daniel's prayer shows that those who discern the promises of God, and long for their fulfilment, must be equally concerned that they are themselves fit to enjoy the promises. The prayer falls into three sections, marked off by matching openings and closures:

a. *Verses 4-8* begin and end with the cry, 'O Lord / Sovereign One' (adonay), and the final words, 'We have sinned against you', encapsulate the topic – that confronted by God himself (vv. 4, 7, 8), sinfulness is exposed and must be confessed;

b. *Verses 9-14* stress the revealed law of God. This is the inclusion in verses 9 and 14 and is mentioned in every verse between. The problem, therefore, goes beyond a general sense of sin in the presence of a righteous God (vv. 4-8); it is a matter of conscious, culpable disobedience to revealed divine commands;

c. *Verses 15-19* begin with the Lord making a name for himself by his work of redemption from Egypt (v. 15), and end with an appeal for forgiveness for the people and city called by his name. The God whose person convicts (vv. 4-8), and whose law condemns (vv. 9-14) is the God who himself came down to Egypt (Exod. 3:7f.) to redeem (Exod. 6:6f.). The only way to flee from his wrath is to flee to his forgiveness.

Like all Bible prayers, Daniel's prayer is simply saturated with God as he has revealed himself: to know God is to know how to pray, what to pray about and what prayer will excite a divine response.

3. *The time to say 'No'.* The image-theme links chapter 3 with chapter 2. Nebuchadnezzar was not the man to be content with simply being the 'head of gold' (2:27-38). He intended to dominate the whole thing! Furthermore, the sin of Jeroboam the son of Nebat (1 Kings 12:26-30) was never far below the surface of ruling minds, for religion provides a strong cement for society, and God can be a useful prop for government policies. So the king set out to unify the world around himself by means of a single cult: all must worship the image he has set up (3:1-7).

A Balanced Story
The subtlety with which the story is told is impressive.

- At the beginning 'Nebuchadnezzar sent *word*' (3:2) commanding all to worship the image he had made; at the end 'Nebuchadnezzar spoke' (3:28-30), affirming the uniqueness of the God of the three Judeans.

- The king's arrogant denial that any god could rescue from his power to hurt (3:8-15) is balanced by his acknowledgement that there was such a God (3:19-27), a 'Son of God' who walks through the fire with his servants (3:25), a 'Most High God' (3:26).

- And, central to this story, the three Judeans, first, insisted that the truth of the matter was too plain to need saying (3:16), that the ability of the God of Israel was undoubted, and, in their opinion, would operate on their behalf (3:17). But, second, they acknowledged that his sovereign wisdom in any specific case could not be 'second-guessed'. So they said, 'But if not'. Faith rests loyally, simply and acceptingly upon this God (3:18) to the exclusion of all others. This was their 'Archimedean point', central and non-negotiable. Their words deserve to be carved on every believing mind against the occasion, small or great, when the first commandment is challenged, and faith's loyalty is threatened by compromise.

4. *Revealed truth.* Nebuchadnezzar came to acknowledge the supremacy of Daniel's God (2:47); the resolute 'No' of the three Judeans led the king to testify to the uniqueness of their God. And Daniel's brave challenge to the king's moral turpitude and pride (4:25-27) enabled Nebuchadnezzar to interpret his fearsome experience, and to reach a true personal testimony (4:34-37).

   But the experience of Belshazzar was quite the reverse. In spite of supernatural intervention (5:5-6), and the same faithful ministry of warning which his grandfather had received (5:18-24), there was no softening or heart-response: Belshazzar reacted (5:29) to Daniel's message as though his future had never been called in question – royal rewards were dispensed and Daniel would share in government as a third along with Belshazzar and his absentee father, Nabonidus! Well, Daniel did continue as one of three rulers (6:2), but 'that very night Belshazzar ... was slain' (5:30 NKJV).

God is not mocked. To ask why Nebuchadnezzar came to repentance and Belshazzar did not, even though they received the same ministry, is to ask why Jacob and not Esau, why Peter's repentance (Matt. 26:75) was effective and that of Judas (Matt. 27:3-5) was not. Such things are hidden within the heart of God where wisdom, love, power and justice never fight or fail. Our task is not to probe the divine counsels but to minister divine truth in the context of a distinctive and spiritually habituated life.

THE BOOK OF DANIEL

The book of Daniel, like that of Zechariah, consists of opening narratives – in Daniel, of history, in Zechariah of visionary experiences – followed by predictive meditations. Daniel begins with objective reporting (chs. 1–6) and moves (chs. 7–12) into autobiographical prediction. The two sections belong in one impressive whole, and, in particular, the Daniel who is portrayed in chapters 1–6 is discernibly the man who so movingly records his experiences and feelings in chapters 7–12.

Date and Provenance

A brief paragraph cannot do justice to the complex discussion that surrounds the question of whether we may take the book of Daniel to be, as it claims, an account of sixth century BC experiences, or whether the evidence favours a second-century production. The reasoning behind both positions can be examined in the books mentioned at the end of this chapter.

1. The question ultimately depends on one's attitude to predictive prophecy. Dillard refers to W.S. Turner who insisted that (especially) Daniel 11 must be history dressed up as prediction (vaticinium ex eventu) because it is 'one of the certainties of human nature' that 'human beings are unable accurately to predict the future'. But in the book of Daniel, the limitations of human beings are not the issue: Daniel makes no predictions, but records those brought to him by angels and by 'a man clothed in linen'. And this is no mere debating point, for what is in question is not what humans can do but what God can do.

2. There is also a curious element of psychological conflict. In the second century BC there was much turmoil and suffering in Palestine, and, so writers like Turner suppose, an author wished to bring assurance to his people. Consciously and known to be posing as Daniel, he wrote an account of recently past events in such a way as to make out that God was in sole charge. But:

    a. Such a work would be needless, for the truth of divine sovereignty was a theological commonplace;

    b. How can a recognised fiction help?

    It is (if we may adapt the words of William Tyndale) 'as much use as a tale of Robin Hood'. If the book is to help anyone, such an author would have to succeed in passing it off as a sixth-century prediction – that is, a fraud published with fraudulent intent. Otherwise, if 'everyone' knows what it really is, it can only receive the amused rejoinder, 'So what?'

Problems in Daniel

To accept a sixth-century point of origin honours the testimony of the book itself, and accords with the Old Testament
view of predictive prophecy, but of course it solves no other
problems.

Who was Darius? It still remains, for example, that the
person Daniel calls 'Darius the Mede' (5:31; 9:1; 11:1) has
not yet been discovered by that name elsewhere. Rowley
thought the second-century author was simply historically
bewildered. Others (e.g. Baldwin, Wiseman) have sought
out persuasive, even if not yet proved, reasons to identify
this Darius as Cyrus the Great, the conqueror of Babylon. In
this connection it should be recalled that our knowledge of
ancient history is still far from comprehensive, and even fifty
years ago the figure of Belshazzar in Daniel 5 was derided as
fictional, whereas now he is as secure in the secular record
as in the biblical.

Two Halves of Daniel: Parallels

As in the case of chapters 1–6, so for the whole book, there
is such an intricacy of matching sections, words and ideas
that many different structural outlines have been proposed,
for example by Baldwin, Gooding and Lacocque. The observation on which the following study is based is that Daniel
6 is pivotal, providing an inclusion both with chapter 1 and
with chapter 12.

Themes in Chapter 6

1. Refusal to conform: in the matter of diet (ch. 1), and
   in the matter of personal spirituality (ch. 6).
2. 'The law of the Medes and Persians, which does not
   alter.' This was the principle upon which, first, the
   king was expected to act (6:8), then was manoeuvred
   into reaffirming (6:12), and, finally, by which he
   was trapped (6:15). Yet before the story ends, the

inflexible word of man has been broken – and Daniel
was there to see it happen.

By contrast 12:4-13 tells of a word sealed and sure (12:4),
which will outlast the changes and chances of time and
event, and be found unchanged and true at the end (12:9) –
and Daniel will be there to see that it is so (12:13).

We must now examine Daniel's parallels more closely,
particularly with a view to the meaning of chapters 7–12.

The First Parallel: Setting the Scene (2:1-49; 7:1-28)

With the king's dream (ch. 2) Daniel was given a review of the
whole development of history through to the Eschaton. The
pervasive use of the number four in these chapters, as elsewhere
(e.g. Zech. 1:18-21), points to the 'earthly totality'. Here it is
the sum total of earthly power. We can tick off the four empires
(2:36-40) one by one – Babylon, Persia, Greece and Rome –
and we can recall that it was within the Roman Empire that
the 'stone cut without hands', the Lord Jesus Christ, overcame
the prince of this world (2:44f.; John 12:31).

But when the scene is restated in chapter 7 it is on a hugely larger scale, ultimately defying specific identifications,
demanding a cosmic perspective, taking us up to heaven to
stand before the divine Judge (7:9-10).

The Four Kingdoms

Our first impression of 7:1-7 is of successive kingdoms:

- 7:4: The lion, a kingdom of power, with wings for
  swift expansion but with a semblance of humanity;

- 7:5: The bear, a kingdom insatiable for conquest;

- 7:6: The leopard, with four wings for far-flung expansion, and with four heads suggesting divided counsels;

- 7:7, 9ff.: The beast *sui generis*, with its plentitude
  of power (ten horns), reaching some zenith of self-
  exaltation until the Ancient of Days decides the issue.

While it is impossible, for example, to read the description of the leopard kingdom without thinking of Alexander, with his widespread dominion, and the fourfold division of his empire following his death, yet 7:12 makes it clear that something more is involved than just a simple chronological scheme of four beast-kingdoms. For it says that when the beast par excellence is destroyed the first three still remain, though not as distinct, recognisable powers ('their dominion taken away'). In what sense, then, are they still 'prolonged'? And how are we intended to understand this symbolism of destruction and survival?

World History to the Eschaton
All the prophets saw the Eschaton in terms of the world-map they knew (e.g. Isa. 19:24-25; 27:12-13), and Daniel was no different. Beginning from his own Babylon, he was allowed to probe forward through the Persian, Greek and Roman Empires. In this sense the vision is first of all chronological. But then, as he was taken even further forward, two things become plain:

1. *A principle of divine judgment is operating in history.* The Ancient of Days is on the throne and he gives dominion, not to a beast-king, but to the Son of man. This overthrow of the beast-king will ultimately happen at the Eschaton, but it also happens, as it were in an interim way, whenever human arrogance oversteps the mark. It is this that has led believing minds to look at gross wickedness on earth and say, 'Surely the Coming of the Lord cannot now be delayed.' Every next calamitous uprising of beastly power could be that Day. While history moves towards that day, the Son of man has already been granted dominion, but until that day comes, human rule on earth will continue to manifest the characteristics of the three first beasts whose life was

prolonged. Such rulers rise only to fall, but there will come a time when the real beast-king, whom they palely foreshadowed, will arise – and be destroyed by the coming of the Son of man (Rev. 19:11-21).

2. There is, alongside this, a 'story within the story'. In 7:2 it is a heavenly wind that stirs the waters and awakens the four beasts. The forces of heaven determine the forces of earth. The lion only possesses evidences of humanity by gift (7:4); the bear devours by command (7:5); the leopard is 'given' dominion (7:6); the beast of beasts (7:7) is destroyed out of hand (7:11). God is still on the throne – and not as one reacting to and checking the initiatives of others, but as the executive managing director of all.

    What a mystery this rule of God is! Why does he rouse up beastly rulers? And why does he bring his 'saints' into such straits (7:21, 25) before judgment is given in their favour (7:22, 27)? We do not know. All we know is that, at the end, a huge wickedness will come to rule the earth, bringing untold suffer-ing – 'wearing down the saints' (7:25) – but ever-lasting dominion already belongs to the Son of man (7:13-14) and, with him, to his people (7:27).

The Second Parallel: The Narrowing Focus (chs. 3 and 8)
The words 'kingdoms in collision' summarise the essence of Daniel 3 and 8. Chapter 3 tells of one king's attempt to dic-tate the world's theology and worship, as though it were for him to determine the nature of God. Three men, however, holding to revealed theology, stand against him, and the kingdom of darkness falls before the kingdom of light.

The parallel in chapter 8 elaborates this theme of the clash of ideologies. It will continue to characterise human history, and will reach climactic proportions at the Escha-ton – an actual king arising against the Prince of princes (8:25).

The Kingdoms

Once more, chronology and eschatology dovetail. The two-horned kingdom is interpreted as Media-Persia (8:3-4, 20), and the single horn of the he-goat is Alexander (vv. 5-7, 21), whose broken kingdom became four kingdoms (vv. 8, 22). Of these four, the book of Daniel is going to concern itself only with the Ptolemies of Egypt and the Seleucids of Syria-Palestine. In Daniel's record of his vision and also in Gabriel's interpretation of it, the narrative speeds forward in broad terms (vv. 3-8, 20-22) until it reaches the advent of 'a little horn' (v. 9) and a 'fierce' king (v. 23). It is on these that the focus narrows.

The 'little horn'

In verses 3-8, and 20-22, the foreseen historical facts and the angelic interpretations match each other, but in verses 23-26 the interpretation subtly detaches itself from the vision while remaining true to its main outlines.

The 'little horn' grows up out of the fracture of the notable horn (vv. 8-9), and it has been – surely rightly – seen as a forecast of the advent of Antiochus Epiphanes (175–163 BC) in the line of the Seleucid kings. 'Epiphanes', 'outstanding, magnificent', was his chosen description of himself; his critics preferred 'Epimanes', 'the raving lunatic' – though doubtless not out loud! His history is unfolded in more detail in chapter 11, but here two matters only are forecast:

1. The ambitions and successes of the 'little horn' extend south (to Egypt), east (to Armenia) and include 'the Beautiful Land' (v. 9, compare Ezek. 20:6). His successes are symbolically alluded to in verse 10.

2. Attention is concentrated on how the 'little horn' 'overran Palestine ... sacked Jerusalem amid terrible bloodshed ... abolished the ... morning and evening sacrifices ... (committed) the blasphemy of offering a pig on the altar ... placing a statue of Zeus in the

temple ... human sacrifices ... forbade circumcision ... profaned the Sabbath' (Ferguson) (vv. 11-14). Against the background of this succinct summary of the assault of Antiochus against Jerusalem, Daniel's vision stresses blasphemy against the status of the Lord (v. 11a), the ordinances and house of the Lord (v. 11b), and the Lord's truth (v. 12).

Now, whereas the 'little horn' came in the succession of the four notable horns (vv. 8-9), in the interpretative parallel (vv. 23-25), Gabriel pitches the matter forward into 'the latter time of their kingdom', 'many days *in the future*' (v. 26), when 'transgressors have reached their fullness' (v. 23) – a statement which in context seems to have worldwide reference, and not just the local reference of verse 12:

- Antiochus exalted himself to equal 'the Prince of the host', that is, the Lord as linked with Israel, but the fierce king will actually 'rise against the Prince of Princes' (v. 25).

- It could not have been said of Antiochus that his dominance was 'not by his own power' (v. 24), for it manifestly was.

- Nor was he 'broken without hand' – except in the sense that he did not die on the field of battle. His final attempt to add Egypt to his empire was foiled by Roman intervention (compare 11:29-30). On his way back north he turned on Jerusalem and then withdrew, dying soon after the successful Maccabean counter-offensive.

Patterns of Events Repeated

We may say that there is a recurring pattern in human behaviour and divine response. The central biblical example of the latter is the Egypt-Exodus theme. According to Exodus 3:15, the Exodus-events constituted an eternal revelation of the Divine Name. Consequently, Isaiah can use

Exodus terminology regarding the Lord's deliverances of his people (e.g. Isa. 48:20-22); Moses speaks to Jesus of the 'exodus' to be fulfilled in Jerusalem (Luke 9:31); and the unnumbered multitude around the throne have come out of great tribulation by the blood of the Lamb (Rev. 7:9-17).

In the same way here in Daniel the single incident of Nebuchadnezzar's blasphemy (Dan. 3) projects itself out into the future to become Antiochus Epiphanes (8:9-12), and then looks on to the Eschaton, to the king whose fierce features (8:23) link him back to the enraged countenance of his first exemplar (3:19).

But if the blasphemous principle pervades history until its climactic expression, so does the effortless counteraction of the Lord. Supernatural companionship guarded the Judean three against even the contagion of fire (3:27), and supernatural power ('without hand', 8:25) will bring the fierce king's ultimate blasphemy to an end.

The Third Parallel: Smiting and Healing (Dan. 4 and 9)

In Daniel 7:13-14 the Son of man receives the kingdom in the context both of the destruction of a manifestation of the Beast of beasts (7:11), and of the continuation of beastly powers on earth (7:12). We see more of this ruling 'Son of Man' in the 'Prince of the host' and the 'Prince of princes' (8:11, 25). On each occasion this Messianic figure comes on the scene in the same unheralded way as he came to his three servants in the fire (3:25). And in Daniel 9 he again takes us by surprise as the smitten Prince-Messiah (9:25-26).

The Finished Work of Atonement

The arrival and death of the Son of man are linked (9:24) with a divine purpose, literally, 'to finish rebellion ... seal away sins ... pay the atonement price for iniquity ... bring in everlasting righteousness ... seal away vision and prophecy and ... anoint the Holy of holies'. This wondrous list, with its three negatives followed by three positives, can only be understood by appeal to the wider biblical context:

- The 'rebellion' began with Adam and will be brought to an end in Christ.

- Implicit in this act is the 'sealing away' of sins, so that not even the presence of sin can perturb or distract ever again.

- The ground of all this is 'atonement', the payment of an exact, substitutionary, covering price.

- All the three great words in the sin-vocabulary are involved: the specific 'sins' we have committed, whether of thought, word or deed; the twisted and corrupt nature which is the 'iniquity', from which they sprang; and 'rebellion', the wilful flouting of God's declared will whereby we each become consenting partners with our fallen nature.

- As a result of this full and final atonement, we are clothed with 'everlasting righteousness', the imputed righteousness of Christ (Isa. 53:11; 54:17; Rom. 3:21-22; Phil. 3:9).

- God's purposes, beginning with the protevangelium of Genesis 3:15 and mounting in fullness and intensity as prophet succeeded prophet, will have reached their appointed objective and be 'sealed away' as complete.

- Finally, the atoning work will 'anoint the Holy of holies' as was prefigured in the Mosaic Tabernacle (Lev. 16:15-16). Then the indwelling of the Lord among his people (Exod. 29:42-46, compare 1 Kings 8:12-13, 16, 27) will appear in its final reality (John 2:19-21; Eph. 2:19-22; Rev. 21:3, 22-27).

Could anything be more foolish than to water down this glorious accomplishment to make it fit into the times of Antiochus Epiphanes? Of course, it is only by hindsight that we can link it with the Lord Jesus Christ. But how else, when it comes to that, is Antiochus Epiphanes found in 7:9-12 or later in 11:5-35? In the case of Antiochus, however, we have only a correspondence of prophecy with subsequent history; in finding Jesus and Calvary in 9:25 we are also tracing out a consistent biblical theology of atonement expressed in the nexus between (for example) Exodus 12, Leviticus 17:11, Isaiah 53 and the New Testament.

The 'seventies': A Pattern of Numbers Repeated
Daniel was led by God to see that there is yet another way in which specific divine purposes become recurringly expressed divine principles: the series of 'seventies'.

a. *The first seventy.* Daniel began with Jeremiah's disclosure of a seventy-year captivity (9:2; Jer. 25:12). This drove him to confess his and his people's sin (9:4-19), for he knew – and indeed the example of Nebuchadnezzar in chapter 4 was a case in point – that it is the penitent who enter into blessing. Gabriel's first word to Daniel (v. 23) is that his prayer was accepted and understood. That first period of seventy years can therefore be set aside: the captivity will end as promised.

b. *The second 'seventy'.* 'Seventy' itself turns out to be a divine way of working. Knowing his people as he did, Daniel will have realised (as did Isaiah, e.g. 48:20-22) that a return from captivity did not involve the moral and spiritual transformation which the erstwhile captives needed. There was the deeper captivity of sin, and this would take another 'seventy years' to resolve (9:24).

c. *The origin of the idea of 'seven'.* The whole idea of significant 'sevens' looks back to the regulations in Leviticus 25 about the Jubilee year and its remissions. The reckoning in 'weeks of years' comes from Leviticus 25:8.

d. *The 'seventy weeks'*. The commentaries suggested in the book list reveal the complexities of interpretation that surround these verses, but simplicity suggests that the weeks begin with Cyrus and culminate with the death of Christ and fall of Jerusalem (see boxed feature).

The Abomination
When the Lord Jesus Christ referred to 'the *abomination of desolation*' (Matt. 24:15) he was conflating four Daniel references (8:13; 9:27; 11:31; 12:11). Here is yet another instance where a particular event was destined to recur until its final eschatological expression. Jesus would have been aware that the abomination had been set up by Antiochus Epiphanes, but still he looked forward to its re-expression under the Romans, and indeed (depending on the interpretation of his eschatological discourses) he may have been looking forward also to the eschatological '*abomination*' which is Paul's subject in 2 Thessalonians 2. In any case, in a very basic way this is the subject in Daniel's next and final parallel.

The Fourth Parallel: The Flow of History and the Lord's Victory (Dan. 5 and 10:1–12:3)
The heart of the vision of the future 'noted in the Scripture of Truth' begins in 10:21 and continues to 12:3.

In 11:2-4 the pattern has been set of four kings followed by a fifth in whose time, self-willed and mighty though he will be, there will occur a great shattering of earthly power.

Daniel 11:5-35 follows through this pattern of four kings plus one. It forecasts the history of the Seleucid kings of the north, their culmination in Antiochus Epiphanes, and their constant but ultimately foiled efforts to subdue the Ptolemaic kingdom in the south.

This forecast is so accurate that it is hardly to be wondered at that commentators who adopt a minimalising or dismissive attitude towards predictive prophecy are prone to assert that 11:5ff. can only be an historical record masquerading as prediction. But in the matter of Old Testament prophecy, the Old Testament is a source document. It alone can tell us what Old Testament prophecy is. When, therefore, its definition includes detailed forecasts reaching out over the years, it is open to us to disbelieve; it is not open to us to rewrite the definition. Rather, we should leap to thank God who so prepares his people for trials ahead – giving proof positive that history is indeed his story – and marvel at the word of God in its truthfulness and accuracy.

But as we have already seen, even Antiochus Epiphanes, appallingly dreadful though he proved to be (11:31), was but a trailer for the final anti-god monster to come 'at the time of the end' (11:36-37), without natural reverence (11:37a) or affections (v. 37b), acknowledging no superior (v. 37c), and insofar as he has a god, worshipping naked power (v. 38).

The Meaning of North and South
Interestingly the north-south terminology continues (11:40). Daniel describes the Seleucid kings of Syria and the Ptolemaic kings of Egypt in the post-Alexander period as respectively north and south.

The key to this description is to ask, 'North and south of whom and where?' Bible history always centralises the people of God. The prophets saw all history not only in relation to Israel, but as divinely organised to secure Israel's interests (e.g. Isa. 14:1-2). For much of the monarchical period, Israel lived in an uneasy centre-ground between the imperialists of Mesopotamia (always called the 'northern powers', because their invading armies came into Palestine from the north) and the would-be imperialist, Egypt, to the south. This explains Daniel's terminology: right through to the Eschaton, the Lord's people are caught up in the ebb and flow of worldly super-powers – first Egypt, then Assyria, Babylon, Persia, Greece and Rome in the premier league, but also – and bringing equal physical threat and suffering – with lesser, local powers like the Seleucids and Ptolemies.

To use the north-south terminology in chapter 11 is
to accommodate both an exact correspondence with (for
example) the career of Antiochus Epiphanes, and at the
same time to express the ongoing reality of worldly power
pressuring the Lord's people (compare 7:12).

The Man of Sin

This pressure will reach a fierce climax in the time of the
end (11:40). In 11:36-45 we pass beyond anything that finds
a counterpart in Antiochus Epiphanes and move to the
eschatological personage of whom even Antiochus is but
a pale reflection: the ultimate rebel, the Antichrist, the man
of sin. With such self-absorption (11:36), single-mindedness
(11:37) and power (11:38), he seems irresistible.

This final imperialist, like all his predecessors, stirs up
hatred and meets opposition (11:40) as earthly powers
jockey for postion for the last battle (Ezek. chs. 38–39).
Opposition only exacerbates the dark king (11:44), and the
battle comes to focus round the Lord's people (11:45). Even
though victory is secure in the hands of Michael (12:1),
it will be a time of unparalleled tribulation (12:1) before
resurrection ushers in the eternal state (12:2-3).

Sequence of Thought in Chapters 7–11

It is easy to lose the sense of the whole in the complex details
of Daniel 7–11, yet the sequence is plain enough:

- All through history, with its warring, ambitious powers,
  the Son of man is already on the throne and the victory has been guaranteed to his people (7:13-14, 27);

- He is himself the focus of hatred and opposition as
  both interim kings and the final king exalt themselves
  against the Prince and assault him (8:11, 25);

- At this assault, he falls, as the smitten Prince-Messiah, yet in doing so secures full and final salvation
  (9:24-26);

- Darkness increases and suffering multiplies as the Eschaton draws near. The final Evil manifests himself and triumphs, until the time of the end, bringing the victory of Michael and the eternal glory of Daniel's people (12:1-3).

Unlike the pretentious words of humans (6:8), this is the word of the Lord (12:4).

THE 'SEVENTY WEEKS' (9:25-27)

A. BREAKDOWN
a. The 70-week period is divided into two:
- 69 weeks
- 1 final week

b. Each of these is divided into two:
- 69 weeks = 7 weeks + 62 weeks
- Week 70 is split by a significant event within it, though not necessarily at its midpoint (compare Judg. 16:3; Ps. 102:24 in both of which *hazi hashshebua* is used in an obviously imprecise sense.)

SUGGESTED TIMETABLE AND MEANING
- The 7 weeks run from Cyrus until Nehemiah's rebuilding programme
- The 62 weeks run from Nehemiah until the coming of Jesus
- The final week covers the work of Christ (9:27)
- The 'covenant', literally, 'strongly enacted in the interests of the many', is the new covenant of which Jesus spoke and which he inaugurated by his blood (Luke 22:20), bringing all sacrifice to an end (Heb. 10:12, 18)
- The 'end' (9:26) refers to the destruction of Jerusalem by the Romans in AD 70

Further reading

B. Fyall, *Daniel* (Christian Focus, 2006)
J. Baldwin, *Daniel*, Tyndale Old Testament Commentary (IVP, 1978)
W. Still, *Eight Sermons on the Book of Esther* (Didasko, 1973)
J. Philip, *By the Waters of Babylon* (Didasko, 1972)
S. Olyott, *Dare to Stand Alone* (Evangelical Press, 1995)
S.B. Ferguson, *Daniel*, The Communicator's Commentary (Word, 1988)
H.H. Rowley, *Darius the Mede and the Four World Empires* (Cardiff, 1935)
E.J. Young, *The Prophecy of Daniel* (Eerdmans, 1949)
A. Lacocque, *The Book of Daniel* (SPCK, 1979)

15

THE LOVING WISDOM OF OUR GOD

J esus on the road to Emmaus (Luke 24:13ff.) practised a true biblical psychology – through the head (v. 27) to the heart (v. 32) and so to the feet (v. 33). There is a 'head knowledge' but, in the biblical understanding of things, nothing is truly known until it also kindles the affections, directs the will and changes the course of life. This is what the Old Testament calls wisdom.

SOLOMON

The application of truth to life – often by means of parables or meaningful tales (Judg. 9:7-16; 2 Sam. 14:6-7; etc.) – predated the famed wisdom of Solomon, yet Solomon both exemplifies the essential nature of wisdom, and can be accepted as the founder of Israel's formulated wisdom.

In 1 Kings 3 Solomon asked for wisdom (vv. 9-12), recognising it to be the essential kingly attribute. In the Lord's response (v. 13) we learn that:

1. The gift of wisdom brings with it the gifts and circumstances which will test it. Wisdom is not an

ivory-tower attribute but something Solomon must prove and practise in the realities of life – how to handle wealth and position.

2. The context of wisdom is divinely revealed truth. As Job 28 teaches: humans are clever, but wisdom belongs to God, and begins with reverential obedience.

Solomon's wisdom was wide-ranging (1 Kings 4:29-34), including the arts and sciences, but it especially showed itself in tackling life and its problems (3:16-28; 10:1ff.). All this came to be expressed in Solomon's three thousand proverbs – of which we are privileged to possess the distilled essence (Prov. 1:1; 10:1; 25:1).

What Is Wisdom?

R.B.Y. Scott notes, 'Wisdom in Israel was a way of thinking and speaking ... to propound rules of moral order ... to explore the meaning of life ... (and) to discover a structure of order, meaning and value. (It was) the disciplined intelligence and integrity of men who sought to understand what they had observed and experienced.' This is well said, but it needs one other observation to make it totally true to the Old Testament: as Deuteronomy 4:6 shows, wisdom is grounded upon the law of the Lord and displayed in a life of obedience to him (compare Ps. 111:10; Prov. 1;7; 9:10; 15:33).

PROVERBS: THE WISE LIFE

Its observations of life are so sharp, and its illustrations so apt that there is more sheer fun in reading the book of Proverbs than in any other portion of Scripture. Were interfering busybodies ever put in their place with such absurd accuracy as 26:17? How well 27:14 identifies with one who is not an 'early-morning person'! And the sorely tried spirit which lies behind 17:12 will find an echo with everyone whose acquaintances include a talkative bore.

All of life is reviewed with the same sharpness and accuracy in this deeply practical book. It is frank about the 'own goal' scored by the sexually promiscuous (2:18; 5:3-6; 7:24-27), and sees the adulterous relationship itself – however entrancing it may at first seem – as a visitation of divine wrath (22:14). By contrast, in a refreshingly plain-spoken way, Proverbs affirms the delights of the true marriage (5:18-19), but is too hard-headed to see marriage as a panacea: things can be sadly otherwise, and 19:13; 21:9, 19; 25:24; and 27:15 reflect how, for an ill-matched couple, the bad can become the unbearable.

We could explore Proverbs almost endlessly. Very often it glides over the surface of life without comment, saying and showing 'how things are':

- The exasperations caused by the unreliable (10:26; 25:19; 26:6);
- The influence that money (19:4) and a well-placed gift (21:14) can exercise;
- The harm done by sly innuendo (16:30), even though such a person will not forever get away with it (6:12-15);
- The destructive tongue (11:9; 18:21; 25:23), and the healing tongue (15:1; 16:24; 25:11).

At other times Proverbs probes deeper:

- The accurate psychology of 4:23;
- The exposure of the too-ready solution and the 'quick fix' (18:13; 29:20);
- The sound work-ethic which it commends both positively and negatively (10:4-5; 24:30-34).

But, as we shall now see, there is more to Proverbs than a jumble of observations (however sharp) and precepts (however sound).

The Lord: Wise Creator, Righteous World-Ruler

We can take the temperature of Proverbs by comparing two sayings which lie very close to each other in the book:

> Do not move an ancient boundary stone set up by your
> forefathers (22:28).

In an agricultural economy, land tenure is the basis of social
stability. Boundaries reflect a situation received from a re-
spected past, to be cherished and perpetuated.

In 23:10, the same thought occurs, with a significant addition:

> Do not move an ancient boundary stone or encroach on
> the fields of the fatherless, for their Defender is strong; he
> will take up their case against you.

'Defender' (*go'el*) translates a word used for the next-of-kin,
the one who has the right to intervene, taking all the needs
and troubles of his helpless relative upon himself as if they
were his own. This Old Testament custom is illustrated in
the story of Ruth and Boaz (compare Ruth 3:12-13; 4:3-10),
and the word itself is frequently used of the Lord as the 'Kinsman-Redeemer' of his people, the one who takes on himself
all the debts and disasters of his people and pays the price for
them as though they are his and not theirs (Ps. 19:14; 78:35;
Isa. 49:26; 63:16).

There is more, then, to the saying about a boundary-mark
than first meets the eye. The Lord is involved in it, observes
when the law is breached, identifies with the offended party
and takes action against the offender. This theological basis
of the good life runs right through Proverbs. Its individual
precepts may seem as haphazard and unrelated as the stones
that litter Dartmoor but, like those stones, they are expressions of an underlying bed of solid granite, the wise Creator
and righteous world-Ruler.

The Lord's Wisdom
Following the Dartmoor analogy, just as there the bedrock
makes its presence felt by thrusting upwards in small out-
crops and great formations, so the underlying theology of

Proverbs breaks surface in nearly one hundred verses which refer to 'God' or 'the Lord'.

1. *Wisdom is the Lord's possession.* We need not discuss whether 8:12-31 (especially vv. 22-31) understands wisdom as a divine Person or whether, for vividness, it personifies the idea of wisdom. Either way, the passage prepares for the New Testament revelation of the Lord Jesus (1 Cor. 1:24, 30; Col. 2:3), and its basic claim is clear: that before any creative work was undertaken wisdom resided with the Lord and was uniquely his, an attribute (to say the least) of God in eternity. The same link between the Lord and wisdom is found in 1:29 where hating knowledge is the same as not choosing to fear the Lord.

2. *Wisdom in creation.* The creation itself displays the wisdom of the Lord. This is beautifully worked out in 8:27-31 where wisdom accompanied the Lord in the creation, in ordering heaven and earth, and itself/himself rejoiced in the finished product (v. 31). There is also the direct statement of 3:19-20:

> By wisdom the Lord laid the earth's foundations,
> By understanding he set the heavens in place;
> By his knowledge the deeps were divided,
> And the clouds let drop the dew.

But in Proverbs, as in the rest of the Old Testament, the Creator has a more far-reaching association with his creation than simply that of originator. He is also the wise director of world affairs (21:1); it is he who decides the course of individual life (16:1, 9); and even if in small details that would appear to happen by chance, it is the Lord who settles the issue (16:33).

3. *The wise and the good.* It is this wise Creator who reveals the distinction between good and evil and decides what is the good life.

It is the Creator's glory to keep things to himself should he so decide (25:2). Consequently, wisdom can only be ours if and when he gives it, and knowledge if and when he speaks it (2:6). But he has indeed spoken so that Proverbs is able to say what he hates (6:16-19), and to contrast what he abhors with what he delights in (11:1, 20; 12:22; 15:8; etc.).

Two avenues of life open out before us, and the issues are plain. The Lord observes all life and every thought and action (15:3, 11; 16:2; 20:27), not passively, however, but as One active in rewards and punishments.

- He feeds the righteous and thwarts the wicked (10:3);
- He is a fortress to run to in trouble (10:29; 18:10);
- He destroys the proud, but stands by the helpless (15:25);
- He is far from the wicked but hears the prayer of the righteous (15:29);
- He is purposefully active in everything (16:4), morally alert to avenge (20:22), but also to withhold vengeance where its infliction would prompt sinful reactions in the one who has been wronged (24:17).

Wisdom and True Human Life

It follows from all this – and from the many more references which could be offered under each heading – that the life which conforms to God's wisdom and to his standards of right and wrong is the proper life for humankind on earth, the truly human life. There are three reasons for this:

1. Such a life matches the constitution of the world in which we live (3:19-20);

2. There is a joyful unison between wisdom itself / himself and humankind as created and intended by the Creator (8:31) – so that in living out the life of wisdom we are fulfilling ourselves, being what we were meant to be;

3. Because the life of wisdom is under the active blessing of the Lord, as the verses quoted above show.

THE PURPOSE OF THE BOOK OF PROVERBS

Why, then, is the book of Proverbs in the Bible? Just for this purpose – to reveal, teach and direct us to this life of fulfilment and blessing. Its precepts, whether encouraging or warning, are meant to lead us into the life that matches both our own true nature and the perfect will of God.

See how this is put in Proverbs 1:2-7.

Verse 2

By this book we 'know' (*yada*) what wisdom (*hokmah*) is and we are launched into God's educative programme (*musar*, instruction / discipline); we acquire understanding (*binah*), the ability to see to the heart of things.

Verse 3

This educative programme brings prudence (*sakal*), that is, a true good sense in the management of life: we learn to do what is right (before God), to be just (making right decisions), and to be fair or straightforward.

Verse 4

In ourselves, we are simple (*petha'im*), lacking and needing basic guiding principles of life, open to impulse and influence. But this book can give 'shrewd perceptiveness' ('*ormah*), replacing our natural ignorance with knowledge, rescuing us from floundering through life by giving discretion, and a sense of purpose (*mezimmah*).

Verse 5

Even those who are already to any degree wise need the help given in this book in order to gain fuller learning, a 'grasp' (*leqach*) of the truth; and those who are already discerning can receive fuller guidance, skill (*tachbuloth*) in formulating plans and plotting life's course.

Verse 6
In this way, things that were formerly enigmas and conundrums yield up their secrets.

Verse 7
In everything, the primary factor is the fear of the Lord, for wisdom cannot be separated from its source. Wisdom is, in fact, the Lord revealing himself as a way of life for his people to practise. Because this is so, 1:29 identifies the wise life with the fear of the Lord. Chapter 2:5 shows the other side of the same coin – the pursuit of wisdom leads to the fear of the Lord.

According to 3:7; 8:13; and 16:6, fearing the Lord finds its counterpart in shunning evil; while 10:27; 14:26-27; 19:23; 22:4; and 23:17-18 motivate us to fear the Lord by outlining the blessings that will follow.

Of course, this is not abject fear. It is the reverential fear spoken of in 1 Peter 1:17-19, the sensitive dread of hurting someone who loves us so, reverence for a loving father who cares for his children (4:1; 5:1).

JOB: BUT LIFE IS NOT ALL THAT SIMPLE!

Proverbs is so full of crisp commands, black-and-white situations, and seemingly automatic promises, that it would be easy to miss the fact that it also contains passages like 3:9-12, where the apparently foolproof recipe for prosperity (vv. 9-10) is immediately followed by the recognition that there is another side to life: a darker side of discipline and rebuke (vv. 11-12).

Proverbs recognises this, but does not wrestle with it: that is the province of the book of Job.

Unexplained Suffering

Headlong, the book of Job drops us into life's greatest enigma: personal, unexplained suffering. And from beginning to end Job is never told why he was despoiled of his property, bereaved of his children (1:13-19), deprived of his health and alienated from his wife (2:7-9).

Job's Friends

Job's friends (2:11-13) came to sympathise, and (unfortunately) stay to explain (4:1–25:6). Their explanations, however, are doomed to failure because they insist on an estimate of Job (e.g. 18:5-21) which contradicts the Job that God knows (1:8; 2:3) and the life that Job has lived (31:1-40).

It is important to try to define closely the error of Job's friends, to see what exactly it is that causes God to say, 'You did not speak of me the thing that is right' (42:8). They have a true conception that God's world must be governed by God's justice, which they see as working out in an observable nexus between sin and adversity, virtue and reward. Job would not have disagreed, of course, with their basic premise: that God's world is a closed system of moral exactitude – he says so in his speech in chapter 26, where the fact that he seems to voice the opinions of the friends has led many to think the text is dislocated, and that chapter 26 contains fragments of lost speeches of Bildad and Zophar.

But there is no need to think this. Not only Job and his friends, but the whole Bible affirms the basic truth of justice in God's world. It is exemplified on a grand scale in the Flood (Gen. 6:5–9:17), the judgment on Sodom (Gen. 18:16–19:29) and the slaughter of the Canaanites (Gen. 15:16; Josh. 10:40). In all these instances the Bible is careful to emphasise the judicial enquiry which took place, or the prolonged period of probation granted, so as to secure the absolute moral integrity of the sentence passed.

Psalm 1 gives creedal expression to the same faith. It is not intended as a description of life, but as a philosophy of life, as when we confess belief in 'God the Father Almighty' while the world of human experience calls in question both his fatherliness and his power.

The Error

The friends' error lies in their view that there is an observable nexus between sin and adversity, justice and reward, in their reduction of God to the compass of human understanding. Instead of the attitude of faith, waiting until the holy and just God works his moral purposes out, theirs is an attitude of logic. They are sure that they can trace out the pathways of divine moral providence in rewarding and punishing. In Job's case, he is suffering, therefore he has sinned.

The Problem of Suffering

But even we, who from the start are allowed to know that Job's travail is a deliberately contrived contest between the Lord and Satan, are never told why the Lord initiated it to begin with (1:8). It is all one great puzzle, and the fact is that life is like that. Yet though suffering is the essence of the problem of making sense out of life, it is far from being the heart of the problem.

If there were no almighty and good God, there would be no problem. If everything happened by chance, we would face suffering and say the equivalent of, 'That's the way the cookie crumbles.' Or, if the world were run by human decision and free will, we would face suffering and say, 'It stands to reason that we'd make a mess of things!'

It is only when we bring a good and almighty God into the equation that suffering is felt to be a problem, and, indeed, our intuitive sense that there is a problem of suffering is an inchoate affirmation of the reality of God.

The Lord's speeches from 38:1 onwards probe to the heart of this 'problem'.

- *The wisdom of God:* 38:2–39:30 is a series of questions touching on the wonders of the created world (38:4-38) and of the animal kingdom (38:39–39:30). Of course, not all these questions remain baffling today, but that is not the point. Even where natural sciences can now provide the answers which eluded Job, the result is still, and usually even more, to enhance our appreciation of the wisdom of God. The questions, beginning with the physical (38:2-38), and moving on to the animal world (38:39–39:30), follow the same order as the creation record in Genesis 1. The point is that human wisdom could never match or fathom the comprehensiveness, complexity and detailed interlocking of everything in the wisdom of God.

- *God, perfect in justice: 40:1-2, 6-14.* Job, who has questioned God's justice, is ironically invited to undertake the moral government of the world (vv. 9-14). Of course he cannot! Only God can exercise this perfect justice, involving as it does the power to rebuke (v. 9), the proper dignity of a true ruler (v. 10), a balanced moral judgment exactly applied in individual cases (v. 11), and to do so on a universal scale and in every individual case. The implication is that what Job cannot do, God can. The God with whom Job has presumed to enter into a moral debate is as perfect in justice as he is unsearchable in wisdom.

- *The power of God: 40:15–41:34.* Two absolutely horrendous creatures are now introduced. At first sight there might seem to be something in the opinion of those commentators who view the sea creatures as intrusive, later additions to the book of Job. But first sight can be delusive. It is typical of the spacious way in which Hebrew wisdom expresses itself that the author of Job devotes two long poems to make a single point – and one highly germane to his argument. 'Behemoth' (40:15-24) is the plural of the word *behemah*, widely used for 'beast', 'cattle'. The plural (of amplification) signifies 'the Beast of Beasts', 'the

Great Beast itself'. Alongside comes the awesome, mythical Leviathan (41:1-34), adding the dimension of supernatural power and terror (compare Ps. 74:14; 104:26; Isa. 27:1).

Together, then, the earthly Great Beast and the unearthly Monster, expressing 'totality by means of contrast', typify the sum total of every actual or imagined power. It is to build up this picture of unapproachable, untameable power that the poet heaps detail upon detail, but the heart of the matter is simply this: only the Creator can tame behemoth (40:19). And if none dare stand before the Lord (41:10f.), see, then, how great is the power of God.

- *The problematic Lord: all-wise, all-just, all-powerful.* This is the God of the Bible, the God of Job: all-wise, all-just, all-powerful – all three all together all the time. If only we could deny any one of these three attributes of God the world we live in would become totally logical, without a problem in sight.

Suppose he were wise and just but lacking in power, or wise and powerful but lacking justice, or just and powerful but lacking wisdom! Each supposition provides a bracket into which to put every problematic experience of life, for that would simply be one of those occasions on which either his justice or his wisdom or his power were deficient. We would have the perfect explanation, for we would be able to say: 'Of course, he is all-wise and all-just but unfortunately – as now – he does not always have the power to do what he wants'; or, 'Unfortunately he is not always wise', or, 'not always just'. All life would be logical again!

But if he is indeed the almighty God, then every experience in life must ultimately be down to him, and if everything is at one and the same time an exact expression of what is right, wise and just, if this is so, we can only join Job (40:3-5; 42:1-6) in coming to rest in humble trust on this truly sovereign God in his infallible wisdom, unswerving righteousness and absolute power.

Faith and Resolute Devotion
This call to faith is the major lesson of the book of Job.

The truth is expressed equally beautifully but more briefly in Psalm 23:2-4. Sometimes life is green pastures and quiet waters (v. 2); sometimes it is a valley of the shadow of death (v. 4). The connecting link between these variations is 'paths of righteousness' (v. 3), paths that are right in the Shepherd's sight, that make sense to him. To the sheep, life is a baffling kaleidoscope of fluctuating fortunes, but the Shepherd knows. It is he who decides, directs – and accompanies – and the sheep can rest content.

This is the point Job reaches at the end, but it is not the point at which the book begins. The whole drama starts the moment when the Lord points to his servant (1:8), and is countered by Satan's scornful yet penetrating question, 'Does Job fear God for nothing?' (1:9). That's it! Will Job still be the Lord's man when every advantage arising from faith in God has been removed, and seems to be contradicted?

Would we? Would we celebrate Christmas, marooned alone on a desert island, with goods and family all lost at sea?

Proverbs and Job
The life of wisdom, says Proverbs, can be described, offered as a code and presented as a lifestyle to be followed. Indeed so, says Job, but it is also a life of faith – the faith that trusts in the all-wise, all-sovereign, all-just Lord, the faith that goes all the way in devoted perseverance with him.

ECCLESIASTES: A WORLD THAT REFUSES TO MAKE SENSE
The third great 'wisdom' book in the Bible is Ecclesiastes, and what a problem it presents as soon as we open its pages! What a dark view of life, a seemingly inevitable pessimism!

Here is someone who undertakes to see all life through the spectrum of wisdom (1:13) – and no ordinary wisdom at that (1:16)! He gives himself to a full experience of life: pleasure (2:1), fun (2:2) – but without losing his grip on wisdom (2:3). He goes into property development and estate management (2:4), with a retinue of servants to attend him (2:7), and succeeds in money-making (2:9). And what is his conclusion?

'Everything ('the whole lot') is meaningless, a chasing after the wind; there is no profit under the sun (2:11).

God Makes the Difference

The sort of material sketched above from chapters 1 and 2 of Ecclesiastes could be followed right through the book.

- Work is meaningless (2:17);
- People die like beasts (3:18);
- Mourners are uncomforted (4:1);
- The unborn and the dead are better off than the living (4:2-3);
- Virtue goes unrewarded – even forgotten (4:13-16);
- Wealth does not necessarily bring enjoyment (6:1-2);
- In fact, life is just dreadfully and irretrievably cussed (7:13).

But alongside all this there is another set of truths:

When God comes into life satisfaction and fulfilment come with him (2:24-25). For all its variables, its changes and chances, life is apportioned out by God (3:1-8), and everything, somehow, has its own beauty (3:11). The difficulties of life are divine testings (3:18) and for all that daily life is hard, there is a life with God to be cultivated (5:1). Indeed, life itself, received as a gift of God, is good and proper ('a good which is lovely', 5:18).

It is true that we have no control over the future and must await its onset no matter what it brings (9:1), and nothing can shield us from its barbs (9:2). Yet life itself is a joy (9:9-10), a favour from God. The one thing certain about the future is divine judgment (11:9; 12:14), but, alongside that, God has revealed his way and will to us so that we may live so as to please him (12:11-13).

A Muddle of a Book!

One minute we are deep in pessimism and the game is not worth the candle; another minute life is delightful and fulfilling. One minute we wander and grope in the dark; another minute we have clear directions about living with God and pursuing the good life. One minute we do not know what happens after death – people die as inconsequentially as flies; another minute there is an eternal future and a way of being prepared for it.

But it has to be like that because life is like that – not the life of the unbeliever but of the believer – our life is like that!

The Purpose of Ecclesiastes?

1. Some have suggested that Ecclesiastes is an attempt to see what life would look like without God: the inevitable pessimisms, disappointments and dark ignorances of men and women without divine revelation. And there is, indeed, much in Ecclesiastes which would seem to indicate this, but, no, that is not the point of it.

2. The constant cry of Ecclesiastes is that life is (as the NIV puts it) 'meaningless' (e.g. 1:2; 12:8) or 'vanity' (the rendering in the older versions). The word is not easy to translate by any single English equivalent, but as it is used in Ecclesiastes it means that 'life does not add up'. The ceaseless round of human history (1:4) and of nature (1:5-7) do not seem to be going anywhere: what's the point? People give themselves to pleasure, property, luxury – what does it all add up to? No sooner is life gladdened

by a birth than it is saddened by a death; suffering comes without warning out of a clear blue sky. There is oppression but not comfort, virtue but not reward, work but not fulfilment. Life is like that, a seemingly inconclusive, insoluble muddle. Has it any worth?

Can the believer explain these things any more than the unbeliever? Faced with the biting and blighting sufferings of life – its sicknesses and deaths, its disabled and disappointed people, great ones and loved ones alike dead and gone – can we, any more than the unbeliever, answer the agonised and despairing cry of a tragic race, 'Why, why, why?'

Job and Ecclesiastes: The Problem of Life

Job faced the single problem of suffering. Ecclesiastes is a wider-ranging book. It raises the problem of life itself. And, like Job, it has no explanation of life's problems. It cannot reduce life to a single logical equation in which all problems are solved – but it does have a recipe for living.

A Way Through

Facing life is like standing looking at a great wall, extending endlessly in each direction, blocking off the future. On this wall are written all the problems and groanings of life – and all its lightnesses and joys as well. These are the things that await us, facing us inescapably as we search for a way through the wall. But there is a door. It is labelled, 'God. Revelation. Faith.' It is an invitation to enter the future under God, in the light of his truth, and along the way of trust.

So we enter. We are now in the arena of faith. But conversion involves an about-face, so that we find ourselves still facing the wall. We still face all the groanings, problems and happinesses of life and we still cannot explain them. Now, however, we are coming to them, living among them, bearing their burden and rejoicing in their joys on a different footing – with God rather than without him, living the life of faith in a world that does not add up.

That is precisely where we are, and Ecclesiastes is pre-eminently a tract for our times!

Further reading

N.C. Habel, *The Book of Job* (SCM, 1985)
J.E. Hartley, *The Book of Job* (Eerdmans, 1988)
G. Benfold, *Why Lord? (Job)* (Day One, 1998)
D. Atkinson, *The Message of Job*, The Bible Speaks Today (IVP, 1996)
F.D. Kidner, *Proverbs*, Tyndale Old Testament Commentary (IVP, 1964)
T. Gledhill, *The Message of the Song of Songs*, The Bible Speaks Today (IVP, 1994)
E. Lane, *Proverbs* (Christian Focus, 2007)
R. Mayhue, *Practicing Proverbs* (Christian Focus, 2004)
J.A. Kitchen, *Proverbs* (Christian Focus, 2006)
J.H. Taylor, *Union and Communion (Song of Songs)* (Christian Focus, 1996)
M.A. Eaton, *Ecclesiastes*, Tyndale Old Testament Commentary (IVP, 1983)
D. Tidball, *That's Life* (Ecclesiastes) (IVP, 1989)
S. Olyott, *A Life Worth Living* (Ecclesiastes and Song of Songs) (Evangelical Press, 1992)
D. Thomas, *The Storm Breaks* (Job) Welwyn Commentaries (Evangelical Press, 2003)
H.R. Jones, *Job* (Evangelical Press, 2007)
B. Webb, *Five Festal Garments* (Apollos, 2000)

THE SONG OF SONGS

In a competition for the most beautiful book in the Bible the Song must rise near the top, especially for those who sense the gossamer-like delicacy of its Hebrew. Plainly it is a book about love, as frank as it is delicate and modest in its sexual language and imagery. Beyond that, however, the interpretation falls into two camps.

- *The literalist interpreters* find only a celebration of human love: sexual attraction, marriage and marital unity. Some see the Song as an anthology of love poems (M. Falk, *Love Lyrics from the Bible*, Sheffield, 1986), others seek to trace a love story expressed in the lyrics (T. Gledhill, *The Message of the Song of Songs*, IVP, 1994), each of these views being current expressions of a long line of predecessors.

- *The allegorical interpreters* also have an honourable pedigree for, from ancient times, the Song has been seen as an allegory of divine love: the love of Christ for his people – and before that by Jewish interpreters, of Yahweh and Israel. As represented by the famous 'Annotations' of Thomas Poole this involves snatching as many allegorical suggestions as possible out of each verse in turn without considering if there is any sequence or developing thought. On the other hand, J.H. Taylor, *Union and Communion* (Christian Focus, 1996), pays close attention to the way the Song develops its theme, and matches the allegory accordingly.

- A mediating view is possible, and may be even more biblical than making a stark alternative as above. This is to say that the Song is allegorical *because* it is literal. It is plain that marriage is widely used allegorically in the Bible – the Lord is the husband of his people (Jer. 31:32), apostasy is harlotry (Ezek. 16; 23), the new covenant is a new marriage (Hosea 2:14, 20). The Lord Jesus Christ used marriage imagery (Matt. 9:15; 25:1ff.), and so did Paul (Rom. 7:1ff.; 2 Cor. 2:2; 11:2) and John (Rev. 19:7-9; 21:2, 9). The possibility, therefore, of a book about marriage that is also an allegory of divine love cannot be dismissed, though this still awaits a commentary to try to express it fully.

But behind the allegory of love and marriage as between the Lord and his beloved, there lies the reality of marriage itself as a divine ordinance, governed by divine principles, intended to fulfil divine ideals. And this, of course, is precisely what the Song of Songs does: it is the Bible's supreme treatise on marriage, its intended book of marriage preparation, its inspired marriage guidance. Blessed indeed are those who see it and use it so!

To use again F.D. Kidner's helpful expression, rather than trying to regiment something so lightsome – even elusive – as the Song, see it as a 'wild garden', an English cottage garden where borders and beds are visible but where also plants grow at will, and intertwine. With this proviso, try reading the Song as:

1:1–3:6: Courtship
3:7–5:1: Wedding and honeymoon
5:2–8:14: Marriage

Further reading

G.L. Carr, *The Song of Solomon*, Tyndale Old Testament Commentary (IVP, 1984)
T. Gledhill, *The Message of the Song of Songs*, The Bible Speaks Today (IVP, 1994)
W. Still, *The Song of Solomon* (Didasko, 1971)
G. Burrows, *The Song of Solomon* (Banner of Truth, 1960)
J.H. Taylor, *Union and Communion (Song of Songs)* (Christian Focus, 1996)
B. Webb, *Five Festal Garments* (Apollos, 2000)

16

HAGGAI AND ZECHARIAH:
THE TWO VISIONARIES

The ongoing march of empires brought about a turn of events which the Bible ascribes to the work of the Holy Spirit implementing the promises of God (2 Chron. 36:22-23; Ezra 1:1-4). Even at our distance in time it is easy to stand alongside the Babylonian exiles and to share their wonder at what happened.

THE 'MIRACLE' OF CYRUS
The Assyrians instituted the policy of mass deportation of conquered peoples (compare 2 Kings 18:31-32), and, by the time of Cyrus (539 BC), captives from the former northern kingdom of Israel had been in Mesopotamia for nearly two hundred years, and Judeans had been exiled for between seventy and ninety years. It is not to be wondered at, therefore, that many chose to stay when liberation came. Time and the unstressful conditions seen in Jeremiah 23 had domesticated them.

There were, however, those who kept the Jerusalem-hope alive in their hearts (Dan. 6:10; Ps. 137).

In the seven years after Nebuchadnezzar (605–562 BC), three Babylonian emperors followed before Nabonidus seized the throne in 556. He was an antiquarian rather than the determined ruler Babylon needed for survival, and his devotion to the moon god, Sin, earned him the enmity of the powerful priests of Marduk in Babylon. Presently he even abandoned Babylon to the care of his son, Belshazzar (Dan. 5).

Meantime, Cyrus, vassal king of Anshan (southern Iran), revolted against his Median masters, and by 550 was master of the vast empire of Media (north and north-eastern Mesopotamia). Nothing, it seemed, could stop him. The speed of his onward march made people call him 'beloved of the gods', for surely only supernatural aid could account for it. Babylon fell without a blow being struck, in 539 (Dan. 5).

Isaiah had prepared his people long in advance for the advent of this conqueror (Isa. 41:1-7, 21-29; 43:14-15; 44:24–45:8,13; 46:8-11; 48:14-15), yet, even so, they might well have questioned if it could possibly be that a yet mightier conqueror would reverse the long-standing policy of his predecessors and send the captives home. But he did.

THE RETURN: THE ALTAR AND THE HOUSE

Our knowledge of the return from Babylon in 539 BC and of the following century is confined to the books of Ezra and Nehemiah. Ezra 1–6 is all we know about the fortunes of the comparatively small band who made the first return journey (Ezra 1–2). In Ezra 3 the human side of the drama is lost behind the historian's theological and religious focus. The returnees seem to have made their way back to their old homes (Ezra 3:1). We, of course, would like to know how they fared, what they found, how they tackled the long years of neglect – indeed, how they managed to stay alive! But whatever their initial struggles, whatever the sacrifice, come the seventh month they were, as the Lord's word required (Lev. 23:24-43), in Jerusalem on pilgrimage.

Though the returnees were in fear of surrounding peoples (3:3), the walls of Jerusalem were not their priority; though they must have been chronically poor, they did not grudge expenditure on sacrificial beasts (3:3-5); though they could see the ruins of the Lord's house, it was not their first thought to rebuild it (3:6). They seemed to know that their primary need was to be right with God, and therefore they cleared a space in the rubble and built the Lord's altar (3:2-3). It was five months later (Ezra 3:6-13) that a start was made on the house itself.

REBUILDING THE TEMPLE – ZERUBBABEL

The story of the earliest returnees is recorded in Ezra 4:1-5 and 4:24–6:22. On the imperial side, Cyrus reigned until 530. He was followed by Cambyses (530–522), and Darius 1 (522–486), known, by way of distinguishing him, as Hystaspes. In Jerusalem, Zerubbabel was learning that the work of God is always opposed.

Opposition

We do not know why the existing inhabitants of Palestine were antagonistic to the building work at Jerusalem (Ezra 4:4). But the success of their opposition is understandable. Jerusalem had a bad track record of rebellion (compare 4:15-16), and the far-off rulers of the empire would be sensitive to any suggestion of trouble to come. In any case, the building work stopped until Haggai and Zechariah reactivated it in 520 (Ezra 4:24–5:2).

Starting Again

If political caution made Cyrus embargo the work at the earlier date, very likely the same caution made Darius encourage it when the memorandum of Cyrus was unearthed in Ecbatana (6:1-13). The complicated circumstances of the death of Cambyses and his own accession exacerbated the customary rebellions with which a new emperor was greeted. Darius faced 'a veritable orgy of revolt all over the empire' (J. Bright). By 520 BC, two years into his reign, Darius could well have felt that an inexpensive act of winning some friends was advisable. Thus would the sovereign Lord of all the earth move the hearts of kings and effect the word of his prophets.

HAGGAI: THE PROPHET OF THE HOUSE OF THE LORD AND THE HOUSE OF DAVID

To understand Haggai we must first ask why it was so important to him that the Lord's house should be built at all. Different answers have been suggested to this question:

- Haggai 'took the superstitious view that God had not blessed his people merely because they had not begun to rebuild the temple' (Knight);
- Haggai was a ritualist only concerned with the proper re-establishment of the cultic round (Coggins, Petersen).

Of these views, the first comes nearest the truth, but the charge of superstition is very wide of the mark.

The Indwelling Lord

Exodus 25:8 and 29:44-46 reveal that the Tabernacle expressed the central purpose of the divine redemptive work. It was the Lord's appointed way of securing his indwelling presence at the heart of his people's life, and when the Lord institutes a means of grace, his people neglect it at their peril. It was John Wesley who warned about 'expecting the end without the means, expecting knowledge without searching the Scriptures, expecting spiritual strength without constant prayer'. Haggai would have agreed. He found his people supposing the Lord would be with them all the while that they were neglecting the divinely appointed means of that grace – the house of the Lord.

If the Exodus people had refused to pitch the Lord's tent, or Solomon to build the Temple (1 Kings 8:27, compare 2 Sam. 7:5), it would have been tantamount to saying that it was a matter of indifference to them whether the Lord was living among them or not. Tabernacle and Temple were not primarily places to which the Lord's people went to be with him, but places where he came to be with them.

As a matter of fact, Haggai was not interested in ritual as such. He insisted that it is true people that make ritual true, not the reverse (2:10-14). The people faced problems:

- The ills of a poor gross national product (1:6a);
- Life without personal satisfaction (1:6b);
- Rampant inflation (1:6c);
- Savings that seemed to evaporate (2:16);
- Disastrous results from even their best agricultural procedures (2:17).

They were vitiating their whole life because they were not concerned about having the Lord living among them. They thought they could manage without the indwelling God.

Haggai's Book

If ever 'the medium is the message' it is so in the structure of Haggai's oracles:

A¹ 1:1-11 A pair of oracles on the same date
(1:1, 3): the negative consequences of the unbuilt house
a¹ To Zerubbabel and Joshua: refusal to build the house (1:1-2)
b¹ To the people: the neglected house, cause of bane (1:3-11)
Note: the double call to 'take it to heart' (1:5, 7)

B¹ 1:12-15a The first 'I am with you' (1:13):
The Lord's presence energising present work
B² 1:15b–2:9 The second 'I am with you' (2:4):
The Lord's presence guaranteeing coming glory.

A² 2:10-23 A pair of oracles on the same date
(2:10, 20): the blessed consequences of building the house
b² To the people: the rebuilt house, cause of blessing
(2:10-19)

Note: the double call, 'Take it to heart' (2:15,18)
a² To Zerubbabel: David's restored house (2:20-23)

Haggai's Messianism

The major thrust, then, of Haggai's message is that the Lord's people must give absolute priority to that which, by his promise, secures his presence at the heart of their life. Well-being is conditional on this one essential.

But the structure of Haggai's book reveals a second topic. The book is shaped on the pattern of 2 Samuel 7 where David's purpose to build the Lord a house (2 Sam. 7:1-3) modulates into the Lord's purpose to build David a house (2 Sam. 7:8-11). In precisely the same way, Haggai's call to Zerubbabel to build the Lord's house (1:1-3) becomes the Lord's commitment to Zerubbabel to build David's house (2:20-23).

Commentators have laboured to see the details of 2:21-23 reflected in either contemporary or subsequent events. This has never been satisfactorily done, nor can it be, because it is not intended. Haggai is neither describing nor foreshadowing actual history, but is using eschatological motifs, six symbols for the Day of the Lord:

1. As in Psalm 18:7-15, there is the shaking whereby divine energy brings David to his throne (v. 21).

2. The overturning (*hapak*, using the semi-technical terms for the overthrow of Sodom, compare Deut. 29:23), the Lord's judgment on a sinful world (v. 22a).

3. The Lord's victory in the destruction of opposing kingdoms (v. 22b), the submission of their thrones to his King (Ps. 2).

4. The end of alien threat (v. 22c), their forces 'going down' like Pharaoh's chariots and horses (Exod. 15:1, 4, 5).

5. The self-destructiveness of sin (v. 22d; compare Judg. 7:22; 2 Chron. 20:23-24).

6. The Lord's king comes into his own (v. 23).

God's Promise – The Signet

The solemn eschatological introduction, 'In that day', underlines the wonder of verse 23. How faithful to his promises the Lord is! Zerubbabel, the Davidic heir, was in fact heir to nothing – no throne, crown or realm. The whole Davidic enterprise was lost in the sands of time. But the promises cannot fail. Out of the dry ground (Isa. 53:2) came the glory. As Pusey says, 'God reverses to Zerubbabel the sentence on Jeconiah' (Jer. 22:24).

Whether the 'signet' was worn as a pendant (Gen. 38:18, 25), a ring (Jer. 22:24) or a bracelet (Song. 8:6), it bore the owner's mark; to give it symbolised possessing and enjoying a relationship – as with an engagement or wedding ring today.

Zerubbabel enjoys election ('I will take'), function ('My servant') and closeness (signet). Like the address to an 'ordinary' king of David's line in Psalm 2, reminding him that he is the bearer of the Messianic hope of Israel, so in Zerubbabel that hope is restarted, newly focused, freshly assured and awaiting its perfect consummation.

ZECHARIAH: THE PROPHET OF THE KINGDOM OF THE LORD

The majority of writers on the book of Zechariah dispute its unity, preferring to set chapters 9–14 apart from chapters 1–8, or even also to separate 9–11 from 12–14.

For and Against the Unity of Zechariah

Commentators note that 9:1 and 12:1 have the same introduction as Malachi 1:1, and they interpret this as indicating distinct 'books'. But this is a double-edged argument. It should prompt the question: Why was Malachi kept separate and not made part of the same complex?

The same range of commentators tend to the view that the name 'Malachi' is not a personal name but a title contrived from Malachi 3:1 for an anonymous prophecy. But if so, why not the same treatment for Zechariah 9–11 and 12–14? In fact, the separate existence of a mere fragment like Obadiah indicates that the original conservators of the Scriptures did not practise a 'merging' technique of editing.

The Book of Zechariah

Chapters 1–6 contain vision-based predictions within which the acted oracle of 6:9-15 fits comfortably.

Chapters 7:1–8:23 are a straightforward spoken oracle answering a question about national fasts (7:3), and merging into a prediction of Jerusalem as the pilgrimage centre of the whole earth (8:18-23).

Chapters 9–14 are also predictive oracles, but they have been detached from whatever historical circumstance first gave them birth so that, as they stand, they have become anticipatory meditations of coming glory, coming Messianic reality and the coming Jerusalem.

Literary Distinctives

Why should it be surprising to find such diversity between, as we would say, the covers of one book? If surprise were a ground of literary exclusion, hardly any work of literature inside or outside the Bible would survive intact. Think, for example, of the Christian hymns 'buried' (as Old Testament specialists might say) within the allegorical material of *The Pilgrim's Progress*; or of the delicate prose, the imaginative fancies and the high poetry of *The Lord of the Rings*; or of John Milton writing the stately prose of *Areopagitica*, the classical rhythms of *Paradise Lost*; and the river-in-spate joyousness of *An Ode on the Morning of Christ's Nativity* – not to mention his drama, *Samson Agonistes*, and his Latin, Greek and Italian poetry! Great writers can rarely be confined to one genre, or to one range of vocabulary, or to the woodenness of always using the same word in the same sense.

Uniform Tradition

When arguments for fragmenting the book of Zechariah are weighted against the absence of evidence that the Zecharian literature ever existed in any other form than we have received it, to divide the book raises more questions than it solves. But in any case our task must be to tackle the Zechariah we possess and to see if a message emerges.

Coherence
The visionary chapters 1–6 and the spoken oracles of chapters 7–8 are linked:

- Personally by the name of Zechariah (1:1, 7; 7:1, 8);
- Topically by their shared Temple-Jerusalem focus;
- Structurally by the inclusive references to the words of the former prophets (1:4; 7:12) and to the Lord's promised return in blessing to Jerusalem (1:16-17; 8:3).

Chapters 1–6 and 7–8 are thus linked by the name of Zechariah; but 7–8 and 9–14 are linked by the same style of oracular presentation; and all three sections come to the same conclusion:

- In 6:12-15 the Branch is the Priest-King in his temple and those who come from far have their part in building it;
- In 8:20-23 the Lord of hosts is in Jerusalem and peoples and nations gather to seek his goodwill;
- In 14:16-21 the Lord of hosts is King in Jerusalem and all the nations are equally accepted at the Feast of Tabernacles.

Zechariah is the prophet of the world-kingdom of the Lord.

Zechariah's Picture Book (chs. 1–6)
Among the prophets, Zechariah is the great visionary, in the narrow sense of that word: he saw truth by seeing pictures. As a result, chapters 1–6 are as vivid and compelling as any part of Holy Scripture. There are a number of different ways in which the chapters can be structured, for they are full of interlocking ideas, but a simple arrangement notes that chapters 1 and 7–8

are deliberately balanced, forming a frame, and that chapters 2–6 contain eight pictures in four pairs.

1. *The world under God: obedient people and the new Je-rusalem (1:2-17; 7:1–8:23)*. The initial vision of the four mounted patrols (1:7-11) pictures the Lord's sovereign sway over the whole world – with 'four', as usual, signifying 'on every side', total earthly cover-age. The vision is bracketed on one side by a warn-ing to the Lord's people to distance themselves from disobedience to the Lord's word (1:2-6), and on the other side by the promise that the Lord will yet in-dwell his renewed and prosperous city (1:12-17). These same themes reappear in chapters 7 and 8, where the bracketing idea is transformation, where-by fasts lamenting the past (7:1-6) become feasts celebrating the new acts of God, including making Jerusalem a world-centre (8:18-23).

   Within chapters 7–8 there is another bracket: a warning against refusing the Lord's word (7:7-14; 8:14-17), and at the centre of the presentation, the Lord's purposes for the new Jerusalem (8:1-13).

Thus Zechariah defines the leading ideas of part one of his book:

- Divine promises guaranteeing the future;
- The fundamental importance of obeying the word of the Lord;
- The universal significance of the coming Jerusalem.

We can now trace these themes in the visions.

2. *Obedience and faith (1:18-21; 2:1-13)*.

- Four horns and four craftsmen (1:18-21): this vision pictures the truth that a people set on securing the indwelling of the Lord among them can outface any

threat the world offers. The people of God live surrounded by powers ('four') threatening their dispersal.

Did the vision come to Zechariah as he saw a gang setting
out for their day's work at the Temple-site? The task they
had so long postponed as lacking priority (Hag. 1:2-4) is the
very thing that gives them a power equal ('four') to all the
power of the enemy.

- A man with a measuring line (2:1-13). The call to
  obedient building must rest on faith in the promises
  of God. The man with the measuring line figures the
  mindset that determines the future by limits set by
  the past and the resources of the present. The people
  of God must rather commit themselves believingly to
  the Lord's future, to what he designs for the city: all
  the wall they need is his indwelling (2:4), both as the
  key to victory over opponents (2:8-9), and as magnet
  to the world-ingathering into Zion (2:6-7, 11).

3. *The new people (3:1-10; 4:1-14).* The next two pictures
   focus on priestly atonement and spiritual renewal.

- Clean clothes for Joshua (3:1-5). The reclothing
  of Joshua (3:1-5) looks forward to the coming, true
  High Priest, 'My Servant, the BRANCH', and to the removal of iniquity 'in one day' (3:8-9). As a Messianic
  title, 'the BRANCH' looks back to Isaiah 4:2 and Jeremiah 23:5 and 33:15 and forward to Zechariah 6:12,
  focusing respectively on the Messiah's divine and Davidic ancestry and on his royal priesthood.

  The reference in 3:8 is a perfect bridge between
  the Isaiah and Jeremiah references and the final
  reference in the series in 6:12. As a result of the
  removal of iniquity (3:9) the Lord's people come into
  unbroken peace (3:10).

- The gold lampstand and the two olive trees (4:1-14). The vision of the new clothes deals with the past; the vision of the lampstand looks to the future. Most commentators assume that the olive trees supply oil to the central reservoir which in turn feeds the seven lamps. But as Zechariah rephrases his question in verse 11 to take account of a new feature he has noticed – the 'two olive clusters' – verse 12 should, I believe, be translated: 'What are these two olive clusters that are beside the two gold pipes which empty the golden oil?' In other words, the trees are olive trees not because of the oil they produce but because of the oil they receive. This accords with Jeremiah 11:16 and Revelation 11:4 which interpret the olive trees as the people of God in the world. Zechariah pictures them living in the light of God and nourished with his life.

  So much for the light and the trees, but who are the two 'sons of oil who stand in attendance upon the Sovereign of all the earth' (literal translation of v. 14)? They are important because it is through them that the vital oil of God's Spirit, the efficient cause of their life and prospering (v. 6), is ministered in order to enable the Lord's people to display their true, supernatural nature in the world. In the light of the Branch-imagery in chapter 3, they can only represent the Messiah in his kingly and priestly roles. The priest, central to the vision in 3:1-10, is now joined by the Davidic Zerubbabel (4:6), and in 6:12 they are united in one Messiah.

4. *Purification (5:1-4, 5-11)*

   - The flying scroll and the woman with a basket. In New Testament terms, Zechariah 3 represents the one sacrifice for sins forever, the work of Calvary

(Heb. 10:12), and Zechariah 4 represents Pentecost and the outpoured Holy Spirit. In sequence then, the two visions in chapter 5 depict the purging of the people of God through his law, which exposes and judges sin. God's great objective is that wickedness should disappear from among them altogether (5:9), while at the same time he recognises that in a fallen world, wickedness can still claim residence in its own land (5:10-11). It was in Shinar (5:11) that human self-sufficiency first demonstrated its proud determination to structure a secure world by its own technological cleverness (Gen. 11:1-9), and, in Zechariah's vision, this proud citadel remains yet to be conquered.

5. *Victory at last: the enthroned priest (6:1-8, 9-15)*

- Four chariots. Again we meet with four companies of horses, not now the vigilant patrols of 1:7-11 but war-chariots. Attention is focused on one group only. They have gone north, and return with the message that they 'have given rest to My Spirit in the north country'. The same result, we may assume, has been achieved by the others, but 'the north' is singled out as the stronghold of wickedness (5:11) – for the Mesopotamian powers always invaded Palestine from the north and were therefore called the northerners. Victory in the north is the last battle against entrenched evil and achieves the triumph of the Lord.

- A crown. The victory is depicted not in a vision but in an acted oracle (6:9-15). Pilgrims from Babylon (Shinar/the north) bringing gifts for the Lord's house are to be accepted (6:11), and their gold made into 'crowns', a plural of amplification signifying a 'truly magnificent crown'.

When Joshua the priest is crowned, the kingly and priestly offices are linked in one person. The crowned priest (6:12-13) anticipates the priestly rule of the Branch who 'will be a priest upon his throne, and the counsel of peace shall be between them both', that is, king and priest perfectly at one (v. 13b). For the time will come when the royal Priest, the priestly King, will rule, and from afar people will come to build his Temple (6:15).

The vision is secure in the Lord's promises, but not without the committed obedience of his people (6:15) – a truth which brings Zechariah's picture book full-circle back to the dedicated obedience of the four artisans (1:18ff.).

The Shepherd-King, the Universal Kingdom (chs. 7–14)

As we move from Zechariah 1–8 into 9–14, we have little sense of entering a new terrain for the oracles of chapters 7–8, already comfortable in the context of chapters 1–6, form a transition into the style of chapters 9–14.

The main difference is historical orientation. Time and again in the first six chapters we move easily from the visions to the actuality of the current temple-building in 520 BC. But in chapters 9–14 there are no dates and no sidelong glances at the building work. Even proper names have become detached from specific peoples or locations are now no more than colouring in a universal panorama. We have moved into the 'anticipatory meditations' – units of literature detached from their points of origin and woven into a vision of the Messianic future. Daniel and Zechariah are strikingly parallel in this way. In Daniel vivid historical events (chs. 1–6) blend into predictive oracles (chs. 7–12), just as the truth-bearing visions of Zechariah move on into his anticipatory meditations.

Zechariah's Theme

It remains unaltered throughout: the Lord's people are surrounded, even overwhelmed, by the unbelieving world, and yet are finally dominant, with the world itself drawn to the universal King who reigns in Zion. In other words, the king-ship-theme which Zechariah (compare Hag. 2:20-23) developed in specific relation to the Temple-building in chapters 1–6, and predictively in connection with fasts and feasts in chapters 7 and 8, is now displayed on a worldwide canvas. But whereas in chapters 1–6 the King was linked with the Priest, in chapters 9–14 he is linked with the Shepherd.

Structure
The Jerusalem Bible finds Zechariah 9–14 'a disorderly collection of possibly ancient passages', but this is far from the truth. There is a careful pattern, a clear structure in the individual sections making up that pattern, and many lines of correspondence binding the whole into a unity. As always, the structure displays the theme:

A^1 9:1-17 The universal King in Zion
   B^1 10:1-12 Judah victorious, gathered out of the nations
      C 11:1-17 The true Shepherd rejected
   B^2 12:1–13:9 Judah victorious in Jerusalem against the gathered nations
A^2 14:1-21 The universal King in Zion.

Just as the two bracketing sections (A^{1,2}) proclaim the kingly theme, so the three internal sections (B^{1,2}, C) are united by the shepherd theme: false shepherds under condemnation (10:2-3); the true Shepherd dismissed and replaced and the false shepherds doomed (11:12-15, 16-17); and the Lord's Shepherd smitten (13:7).

Links with the New Testament
The New Testament lends its authoritative voice to the Messianic understanding of this portrait of the King-Shepherd: compare 9:9 with Matthew 21:4-5 and John 12:7; 11:12-13 with Matthew 27:9; 12:10 with John 19:37; 13:7 with Matthew 26:31 and Mark 14:27. But the portrait itself originated in David, the shepherd who became king (1 Sam. 16:11;

2 Sam. 7:8), the king who did not cease to be a shepherd (2 Sam. 5:2; Ps. 78:70-72), and the anticipatory type of the Shepherd-King yet to come (Ezek. 34:23-24, compare Micah 5:2-4).

The Worldwide King of Judah (Zech. 9–10)
Once more the easiest way into Zechariah's opening presentation of his kingly message is to display the structure of the chapters:

A¹ 9:1-8 Lord of the nations: Judah preserved
   B¹ 9:9-19 The victorious King
      C¹ 9:11-13 An invitation: 'return'. Out of the waterless pit
        D 9:14-17 The Lord delivers his flock
      C² 10:1-3b An invitation: 'Ask'. Into showers of rain
   B² 10:3c-5 The victorious people
A² 10:6-12 Lord of the nations: a coming exodus

Such an outline can do no more than offer a basis for further study while making certain main lines of truth plain.

1. The worldwide theme is very plain (9:1-2, 10; 10:10-11).

2. Messianic peace coupled with warlike conquest (9:10, 14; 10:3-5) make a typical pairing (compare Isaiah 11:6-9, 10-16), as do also the balanced thought of the victorious Messiah (9:9) and his victorious people (10:3c-5, compare Dan. 7:13-14, 26-27).

3. In 9:9 the literal translation is that the coming king is 'righteous and saved', that is to say, he has been 'brought safely through' some trial which Zechariah does not specify. In the parallel (10:4-5) his people face and overcome their foes.

4. The victory of the King (9:9-10) is also the victory of the Lord (9:14-16). This, too, is typical of Old Testament Messianic thought, as when, for example,

the Lord himself dons the garments of salvation (Isa. 59:17) but it is his Anointed One who finally wears them (Isa. 61:10).

5. The overall picture is of a world ruled by the Lord in the interests of preserving, delivering and gathering his people.

The worldwide King of the nations (12:1–14:21)
Zechariah's second great message about the worldwide King is in the setting of sixteen 'in that day' affirmations. They fall into two groups, each with its opening prospectus (12:1-2; 14:1-3).

*   The first group has a wide focus, dealing broadly with the whole period of the last days. Jerusalem is the subject of worldwide hostility but has something about it which neutralises every attack (12:2). The incapacity of the attackers (12:3-5) is more than counterbalanced by forces at Jerusalem's disposal (12:6-7) and by surrounding divine protection (12:8). The remaining five affirmations (12:9–13:6) contrast the Lord's intention to destroy the assailants (12:9) with his very different works of grace and purification for his people.

*   The second group is specifically focused on the 'last day', 'the Day of the LORD' (14:1). Then Jerusalem will be under universal attack (14:2), and the victory will at first go to the attackers. But the Lord himself will come (14:3) to make a way of escape for his people (14:4-5), to bring in a new creation (14:6-8), and to establish his universal kingship (14:9) following the last battle (14:10-15). Jerusalem will become the focus of worldwide pilgrimage to the Feast of Tabernacles (14:16), with dire consequences for those who refuse (14:17-19), but for Jerusalem itself an all-embracing holiness (14:20-21a) and a totally pure people (14:21b).

While the overall themes of the preservation of the church through to the End, and of a worldwide people gathering to and accepted in Jerusalem, are plain, certain questions arise.

1. *What Jerusalem does the prophet speak of?* Since it is a city capable both of being assaulted by all nations (14:2) and of receiving 'all the nations' (14:16), the vision runs beyond any geographical city on Zion's hill. It is the 'city without walls' of 2:4 and of the 'Many nations ... joined to the LORD' (2:11 NKJV). Zechariah, like all the prophets, used what he knew to specify what he foresaw. But his promises, like all the territorial and topographical promises of the Old Testament, were lifted up to the truth they always embodied when Jesus said his kingdom was 'not of this world' (John 18:36 NKJV), a kingdom not observable in its coming but 'within' (Luke 17:20-21 NKJV). Zechariah's city is the Zion to which, in Christ, we have already come (Heb. 12:22) and which, at the End, will itself descend from heaven (Rev. 21:2).

2. *Why the Feast of Tabernacles?* Tabernacles came at the end of the year. It was the feast of consummation when all was safely 'gathered in' (Exod. 23:16). This alone would be enough to suggest it to Zechariah as the particular time when the Lord's world-harvest is gathered (compare Isa. 27:12-13).

   Tabernacles, like all Israel's major feasts, was rooted in the Exodus but was different from the others in that it required the people to replicate Exodus conditions, to live again as the Exodus people and to renew their personal experience of divine care in fragile conditions of life (Lev. 23:33-44).

   To keep Tabernacles, then, is to affirm and experience one's own reality as a member of the Exodus people, the redeemed of the Lord, to rejoice in his presence (Deut. 16:13-14), and to rely on and expect his care. Thus Zechariah foresees an Israel without national bounds, the 'Israel of God' (Gal. 6:16).

3. *How are we to understand the judgmental visitations of 14:17-19?* Simply as Zechariah's way of expressing the truth that outside the church there is no salvation. Salvation is for the world but not all the world will be saved. For whatever reason within themselves, their culture and their circumstances, there are those who refuse to come to the Tabernacles and therefore not only exclude themselves from its blessings but bring upon themselves the curses and condemnations reserved for them.

The Smitten Shepherd (ch. 11)

As we noted above, the very structure of chapters 9–14 exposes the centrality of chapter 11, Zechariah's meditation on the true Shepherd. We also saw that this central statement is flanked by the intended smiting both of the false shepherds (10:3a) and of the Lord's Shepherd (13:7-9).

Chapter 11 is a balanced statement. It opens with a poem about the wail of the shepherds in a time of judgment (11:1-3) and ends with another poem (11:17) of woe against worthless shepherds. The intermediate verses picture the rise and rejection of the true Shepherd (11:4-13), the consequent dissolution of the flock (11:14), and the replacement of the true Shepherd by the false (11:15-16).

Zechariah does not tell us how he arrived at this understanding, nor does he always stop to make the details as clear to us as doubtless they were to him. It is at least worth asking whether we have here a summary of seven acted oracles, playlets through which the prophet sought to catch public attention:

- *Verses 4-7*: The Lord's Shepherd is called as an antidote to mercenary owners and pitiless shepherds, and because the flock need tender care in a time of judgment;

- *Verse 8a:* The Lord's Shepherd takes prompt action to insist that he alone was the shepherd of the flock, and will share his office with no others;
- *Verses 8b-9:* Such a disaffection arises between Shepherd and sheep that he determines to leave them to their own way;
- *Verses 10-11:* For them this means the end of the covenant, the termination of the 'beauty' of their relationship with the Lord, but those who are the Shepherd's primary care ('the downtrodden of the flock', v. 7) understand;
- *Verses 12-13:* The Shepherd is dismissed with ignominy;
- *Verse 14:* The flock as then constituted is dissolved;
- *Verses 15-16:* Finally, the true is replaced by the false.

The Good Shepherd
We who, by hindsight, view Zechariah's words through the spectrum of the Good Shepherd can but marvel at his perception and understanding. The same is true of his final reference to the smiting of the Shepherd (13:7ff.). Nothing can make this poem anything but unexpected, as, indeed, is the case in every shepherd reference in these chapters, whether we think of the flock-reference in 9:16 or the shepherd drama itself in chapter 11.

In the same way, there is the enigmatic piercing of 'me' and 'him' in 12:10, the unexplained identity in rejection and suffering between the Lord and his Messiah, followed by the opening of the fountain for uncleanness.

Throughout, we find glimpses, hints and clues rather than a plain exposition of this theme. It is one of those places where the Old Testament remains obscure (as in, for example, Isa. 53:9, and many other Messianic allusions) until its fulfilment in the Good Shepherd who laid down his life for the sheep.

The Remnant

The poem of the smitten Shepherd brings the first series of 'in that day' affirmations to a conclusion. The whole series spotlights aspects of the last days but the poem intervenes to lay a cardinal emphasis on one single feature. Within the last days this will happen: a Shepherd belonging to and dear to the Lord will be struck down by his command (13:7a). Out of the ensuing chaos (12:7b-8) a remnant will be preserved and, under divine care (13:9a), will be refined in the crucible of suffering. These are the people enjoying the Lord's fellowship (13:9b) and the fulfilment of his covenant promise (13:9c).

Further reading

J.A. Motyer, *Haggai*, in T. McComisky, Ed., *The Minor Prophets* (Baker, 1998)
D.R. Jones, *Haggai, Zechariah, Malachi*, Torch (SCM, 1962)
J.L. Mackay, *Haggai, Zechariah, Malachi* (Christian Focus, 1994)
J. Baldwin, *Haggai, Zechariah, Malachi*, Tyndale Old Testament Commentary (IVP, 1972)
D.L. Petersen, *Haggai & Zechariah 1–8* (SCM, 1984)
R.J. Coggins, *Haggai, Zechariah, Malachi* (Sheffield, 1987)

17

Ezra and Nehemiah:
The Two Administrators

T he Lord's ways are rich in their variety, and so are the means he uses to achieve his ends. We have seen the key roles played in the returned community by two prophets and visionaries, calling and encouraging their people to an obedient faith and administering to them a rich cordial of hope. Ezra and Nehemiah were very different men with different gifts, aims and achievements, but equally important to the welfare of the people of God.

Descended from Aaron himself, Ezra was a priest by inheritance and a student by gift and temperament, 'a ready scribe in the Law of Moses' (Ezra 7:6). Nehemiah was a high-ranking civil servant, 'cupbearer to the king' (Neh. 1:11), and, as such, a person of trust, position and influence. Sixty years after the ministry of Haggai and Zechariah these two brought their individual gifts and differing functions to Jerusalem and set the Lord's people on course for the centuries of waiting still to come before the advent of the Messiah.

PRIORITIES
The balancing ideas of the word of God and prayer sum up the spiritual priorities of Ezra and Nehemiah.

- Ezra was skilled and comfortable in the place of prayer (Ezra 9:3-15), but his great devotion was to God's word.

- Nehemiah put the word of God at the centre of the life of his new city (Neh. 8:1–9:3), and loved to hear preaching (6:7), but his book portrays him first and foremost as a man of prayer (1:4-11; 2:4; 4:4-5, 9; 5:19; 6:9, 14; 13:14, 22, 29, 31).

And, of course, neither man was in Jerusalem by his own volition but by the prompting of God (Ezra 8:22; Neh. 2:12). In this wonderful pair, therefore, we see, first of all, that the word of God and prayer are, by the will of God, the reconstituting and renewing factors in the life of the church.

Ezra, the Man of God's Word

Unlike the prophets who for the most part are secretive about themselves, we have colourful portraits of Ezra and Nehemiah. Ezra 7 amounts to a character study of the person whom the Lord blesses and uses.

God's Word and God's Hand

The historian seems to go out of his way to forge a link between Ezra and the word of the Lord (7:6, 10-12, 21, 23, 25-26). An almost equal number of verses refer to the fact that 'the hand of the LORD' was with Ezra (7:6, 9, 28; 8:18, 22, 31). The 'hand' is the organ of personal intervention in action: the Lord himself was with Ezra, implementing by his direct action whatever he willed his servant to do. The implication is clear: Ezra, the man of the word of God, is the man of the power and blessing of God.

In 7:6 the two elements lie side by side: the Lord's law – his 'teaching' – and the Lord's hand. The link is explicit in 7:9-10. The prospering of Ezra's journey (compare 8:31) is traced to 'the good hand of God', and the 'good hand' is explained by the fact that 'Ezra had set his heart to seek the

Law of the LORD'. The Lord's blessing is consequent upon character, the setting of the heart, and character is formed by the object upon which the heart is set, the Lord's teaching.

God's Law

What 'law' was this?

1. It was no 'mere' oral tradition but a written document, not simply in Ezra's mind but in his hand (7:25).

2. Its origin was in the transcendent God – the 'God of heaven' (7:12, 21) – even to its words (7:11), and it expressed the mind of God, his 'wisdom' (7:25).

3. It was practical in its intent, embodying 'statutes' (*hoq*, the unchangeable directives of God), and 'judgments' (*mispat*, the authoritative decisions of the divine Judge for doctrine as well as for practice).

4. It was a gift from the Lord to his people (7:6), bequeathed, indeed, through Moses (7:6), but the human transmission did not vitiate its divine origin and content.

Ezra, however, was no innovator. King Artaxerxes confidently expected the people in Judah to recognise and accept what Ezra carried in his hand. Novelty or the unexpected would have created obstacles, but the king did not foresee any problems arising, nor did they. Some people withheld obedience but no one questioned what Ezra brought or what he was sent to do. We can therefore identify Ezra's law with that which was already recognised and in principle obeyed in Judah (Ezra 3:2, 4). F.D. Kidner reviews all the proposed identifications current among Old Testament specialists, reflecting varieties of views regarding the origin, growth and editing of the Pentateuch, and sensibly concludes that there is no serious obstacle in the way of accepting what all agree was the view of the author of the book of Ezra, that this was the law book which had existed in Israel since the days of Moses.

In summary:

- Ezra was a man of fixed purpose: his heart was 'set' on the law;

- The law was his constant preoccupation: to 'seek' means 'to be diligent in coming to some place or thing' (e.g. Deut. 12:5; 2 Chron. 32:31; 1 Kings 22:5). The 'heart', understood here as the 'mindset', was followed by the mind itself, concentrated and diligent;

- Ezra sought a true knowledge of God's word. Like the Old Testament itself, Ezra would not have called 'knowledge' anything that did not move from the head to the heart and onto the will in that order. Hence we read that he sought the law of the Lord in order 'to do it'. For the same reason the Lord's 'law' or 'teaching' is also called his 'wisdom' (7:25; compare Job 28:28; Ezek. 33:31);

- Ezra was not an innovator but an enforcer. He brought the law to where the law was known, 'to teach in Israel' (7:10), for he acted on the principle that the greatest need of the people of God always is to come to a clearer understanding and a fuller obedience to the word their God had spoken. In this Ezra, priest though he was, perfectly upheld the prophetic tradition.

THE BOOK OF EZRA

1:1–6:22: THE FORTUNES OF THE RETURNED COMMUNITY
Returning in 539 BC under Zerubbabel and Joshua (1:1–2:70), they gather in the seventh month to set up the Lord's altar, and lay the foundations of the Lord's house (3:1-13). Opposition comes from outside (4:1-14) which succeeds in halting the work (4:24). Opposition continues from 539–520 BC (4:4-24). Under the ministry of Haggai and Zechariah (5:1) the work resumes and a further hostile appeal to the emperor fails (5:2–6:13). The house is finished (6:14-22).

7:1–10:44: THE MINISTRY OF EZRA
In 458 BC Ezra receives royal direction to come to Jerusalem to teach the law of the Lord (7:1–8:36). He discovers that the community has not preserved its distinctiveness. Ezra addresses the problem of mixed marriages by penitential prayer (9:1-15) and resolute actions (10:1-14).

NEHEMIAH, THE MAN OF PRAYER

Nehemiah comes before us as a man at the top of his profession, but we know nothing of his background or of the stages of his rise to position and influence. On the principle that the Bible only tells us what we need to know, we may assume that Nehemiah grew up in Babylon with the exiled people, but was imbued with the spirit of Psalm 137:1-6. He knew himself to be an alien, and his heart was engaged with a city he may well never yet have seen. When, therefore, his brother Hanani brought news of Jerusalem, he listened avidly. Cut to the heart by its content (Neh. 1:2-3), he reacted at once in fasting and prayer (1:4).

Nehemiah's memoirs reveal him as a vigorous, active man, gifted in organisation, administration and leadership, unhesitating (e.g. 13:25) in action. Yet on hearing about Jerusalem's plight, he did nothing but pray: he 'sat down' as one planning no other course; and the 'certain days' of 1:4 became five months of prayer, as the dates in 1:1 and 2:1 indicate. If we take the recorded prayer of 1:5-11 as intentionally typical of the terms of Nehemiah's praying, then each day we hear him repeat the 'this day' of 1:11, a plea filled with urgent expectation and yet equally with quiet patience, awaiting the Lord's chosen time.

Prevailing Prayer (1:5-11)

Over the months Nehemiah's prayer took shape:

A^1 verses 5-6a Lord, you are great: hear prayer
    B^1 verses 6b-7 Our unfaithfulness
    B^2 verses 8-10 The Lord's faithfulness
A^2 verse 11 Lord, you are sovereign: grant mercy

The Revelation of God

Like all Bible prayers, Nehemiah's begins by telling God about God, dwelling on the divine nature. Only so do our problems come into perspective. Only when we remind ourselves freshly about him can we pray with due reverence, proper seriousness, correct self-awareness and knowledgeable faith.

'The God of heaven' is a typical Nehemiah-emphasis (1:4-5; 2:4, 20, compare the references to 'heaven' throughout the prayer in 9:6 ff.). The plural 'God' (*elohim*) points to one who possesses the fullness of his resources and of his executive power over earth. Suitably, when in terror before the king (2:4), or faced with the opposition of Sanballat (2:19-20), 'The God of heaven' springs to Nehemiah's mind. The title, says Kidner, 'reflects the character of God – not only for its encouraging aspect of staunchness and love, but ... for the majesty which puts man, whether friend or foe, in his place'.

In prayer, Nehemiah's mind is saturated with God:

- His greatness, faithfulness and moral demand (1:5);
- His welcome to prayer (1:6);
- His strictness or faithfulness to his own holy nature (1:7-8);
- His conditional offer of hope (1:9);
- His work of redemption (1:10);
- His power of sway over the mighty ones of the earth (1:11).

In no part of his prayer does Nehemiah fail to focus his thoughts back on to the Lord.

Sin and Repentance

Alongside the wonder of God, Nehemiah's prayer gives prominence to sin and penitence. He sees the Lord's ear open 'while I confess'. His confession is comprehensive, bringing together 'the children of Israel', 'we', and 'I'. Sin is national, corporate and personal, and must be confessed within those categories. But compared with that comprehensiveness only one actual sin is specified – the cardinal sin of the Lord's people (compare Amos 2:4) – to possess the Lord's revealed word and to disobey it (1:7): this is the explanation of all their tragedy (1:8), and also the way back into blessing (1:9).

Redemption
The conclusion of Nehemiah's prayer (1:10-11) touches two very significant points:

1. We have a constant standing-ground before the Lord on the basis of which we can pray with confidence: we are those whom he 'redeemed'. The verb here is *padah*: he found and paid the ransom price for us.

2. We come before him as those personally devoted to him – the positive side of our penitence – 'delighting in his name', that is, in all that he has revealed about himself. Just as our cardinal sin is to reject revelation, so our hallmark of reality is to delight in it.

The Mind of Prayer

The references given above show how readily Nehemiah prayed, not only about but within situations of stress. It seemed that his mind turned to prayer naturally, intuitively, spontaneously.

The first instance of this is typical (2:4). For five months Nehemiah had been praying 'this day' (1:11), and, no doubt, had been wondering when and how the opportunity to speak to the king would arise. It came about in the most terrifying way. The New International Version of the Bible reflects the most common understanding of 2:1: 'I had not been sad in his presence before'. But the Hebrew neither contains nor suggests the keyword 'before', and the literal rendering is rather more dramatic: 'Now I was not grim-faced in his presence.' To Nehemiah, it was just as any other day, with the same obligatory carefulness not to offend his Majesty. But something of his inner turmoil was, it would seem, unconsciously beginning to show – but by the will of God!

The king noticed and became suspicious: 'On what ground are you grim-faced? You are not sick. This is nothing but ill-intent in the heart.' 'Grim' and 'ill-intent' are the same versatile Hebrew word-group, ra', 'evil'. As cupbearer to the king, Nehemiah was excellently placed to be frontman in a coup. Even a suspicion of this could provoke the death penalty. No wonder, therefore, Nehemiah was 'very much afraid'. But in this extremity he remembered 'the God of heaven', and the heart which the king saw as the secret place of conspiracy became the secret place of prayer.

NEHEMIAH'S MEMOIRS

1:1–2:16: CATCHING A VISION
When news of Jerusalem's plight reaches Nehemiah (1:1-3), he turns his grief into prayer (1:4-11).

Prayer is answered, and he is given leave to go to build the city wall (2:1-6). He asks for and gets supplies at royal expense (2:7-8) but rouses hostility among provincial rulers (2:9-10). He acquaints himself with the facts (2:11-16).

2:17–6:19: BUILDING THE WALL
Nehemiah shares his vision (2:17-18) and begins to assemble his team. Offers of help from outside are refused (2:19-20) and the team goes to work (3:1-32). External opposition mounts but the work progresses (4:1-23). Internal divisions are soothed by Nehemiah's leadership and example (5:1-19). Nehemiah himself is subject to death threats (6:1-14) but the wall is finished (6:15), though there are still disloyal elements (6:16-19).

7:1–13:31: CREATING A COMMUNITY
Only those with a birthright can live in the city (7:1-73). The word of God is central to the city's life (8:1–9:3). Recognition of sinfulness (9:4-37) leads to a covenant before God (9:38–10:27) with specific stipulations (10:28-39). The citizens gather and the wall is dedicated

(11:1–12:47). Further reading of Scripture leads to further regulations (13:1-3). Returning after an absence, Nehemiah finds all his reforms have been undone and acts for their restoration (13:4-31).

EZRA AND NEHEMIAH: THE SHARED VISION

1. The Separated People

Both Ezra and Nehemiah involved themselves in the question of mixed marriages. Ezra (Ezra 9 and 10) did his best to clear up a messy situation, and seems to have succeeded, but over twenty years later it reared its head again to trouble Nehemiah (Neh. 13) – even though marital purity had been a cardinal element in his great covenant (Neh. 10:30).

This aspect of the work of the two great men is often called their 'exclusivism'. Some even go so far as to contrast it (to its disadvantage) with the worldview, say, of Isaiah 40–55. Within the two books this 'exclusivism', exemplified in the marriage controversies, also appears in the insistence of the returned community – at its inception (Ezra 4:1-6) and then sixty years on in the time of Nehemiah (Neh. 2:18-20) – that the building work, whether of house or wall, could not be shared: 'You have nothing to do with us' (Ezra 4:3); 'You have no portion (personal stake), right (legal claim), or memorial (ancestral connection) in Jerusalem' (Neh. 2:20). These were strong words, and played their part in creating tensions between the community and the surrounding peoples.

Not Exclusivism but Distinctiveness
It must, however, be seriously questioned whether the Judeans' attitude is correctly described as exclusivism. Throughout the Old Testament the Lord required his people to be distinctive.

- The basis of their distinctiveness was the holy nature of their God whom they were to resemble (Lev. 19:2).

- The mode of their distinctiveness was obedience to the Lord's revealed law, giving them a different lifestyle (Deut. 14:1 ff.).

- The purpose of their distinctiveness was that they should be a magnet to the nations (Deut. 4:5-8; Isa. 2:2-4).

Distinctiveness inevitably made the people separate, but not inevitably exclusivistic. The Passover regulation for the reception of non-Israelites (Exod. 12:48-50), and the requirement that the extended household be circumcised (Gen. 17:13, 27) – bringing even foreigners within covenant privileges and protections – indicates an open attitude to non-Israelites. Where distinctiveness involved exclusion it was for specific periods and given reasons – even if some of those reasons are not as plain to us as when originally given (Deut. 23:1-6, compare Neh. 13:1-3).

It is plain unwillingness to see the issues involved that chooses to call distinctiveness 'exclusivism', and then proceeds to define 'exclusivism' in elitist, illiberal terms, and to condemn it out of hand. Robinson Crusoe was a true liberal when he made his goat enclosure unrestrictively spacious – only to discover that, as a result, the goats inside were as wild and uncontrollable as those outside! It was incumbent on Ezra and Nehemiah to define and secure the community of the church. Otherwise there would be no demonstration of the magnetic life of the Lord's people, no secure conservator of revealed truth and nothing worth the world's while to join.

2. The Community of the Word of God

Ezra:
We would love to know more of the background of Ezra's personal vision 'to teach in Israel statutes and judgments' (Ezra 7:10): how did it develop in his mind and become a call of God? What negotiations with King Artaxerxes ensued before the king authorised Ezra's mission to Jerusalem? But we are not told – except that all was under 'the good hand of God'. Ezra's task was to:

- Lead a 'second return' (7:13);
- Establish the rule of the law of God in Judah and Jerusalem (7:14);
- Bring gifts to the house of God;
- Organise sacrifices (7:15-23);
- Exempt Temple staff from tax (7:24);
- Establish a judiciary, instructed in the law, to implement the law of God throughout the land (7:25-26).

We are told little else about Ezra except that he based his enterprise on prayer and fasting (Ezra 8), and when the problem of mixed marriages with the heathen was brought to his attention (Ezra 9:1-2), he flew to contrite prayer (9:3-15), accompanied by others who 'trembled at the words of the God of Israel' (9:4). He found the community as a whole ready to follow the lead of 'those who tremble at the commandment of our God' and to order their lives 'according to the law' (10:3 NKJV).

Although we happen to know that Nehemiah found mixed marriages a problem that recurred, this episode indicates the success Ezra had in bringing the law of the Lord to his people and putting them under the rule of that law.

Nehemiah

In Nehemiah 6:15 we read the moving words, 'So the wall was finished'. Consequently, Nehemiah's work must now take another direction. He had built a new city; it remained to create a new community; who was to be excluded (7:1-3), who included (7:4ff.) and how was life to be ordered (8:1–12:26)?

1. This was to be a community composed of those who had a birthright (7:5), not as a matter of claim or supposition (7:61-65) but of proved reality. This corresponds to the fact that the Zion to which

Christians have already come (Heb. 12:23) is 'the church of the firstborn who are enrolled in heaven'.

2. This community of true-born citizens gathered around 'the book of the Law of Moses, which the LORD had commanded Israel' (7:6–8:1). If we are moved by the simple words announcing the completion of the walls, surely we are equally moved by the apparently automatic focus of the people on Ezra when the book was to be read and taught. It is as if everybody said, 'Who else?'

Ezra With Nehemiah

Ezra makes his first appearance in Nehemiah's work at this point, and some see it as a problem that the two leaders should have overlapped all through the period of wall-building without any reference to Ezra. This, indeed, is one of the arguments for the view that in fact Ezra followed Nehemiah. There are, however, two factors to be taken into account:

1. The way the Bible writes history. It does not set out to tell us all we would like to know but only what we need to know. It therefore encapsulates the work of Ezra in one incident: he came to teach the Lord's statutes in Israel and to order the community according to them. This is what he did in the specific instance of the mixed marriages. He acted and he succeeded; he saw a problem and he settled it scripturally. We must not read Ezra 10 by hindsight from Nehemiah 13 and conclude that since the problem re-emerged Ezra failed. Rather, we should affirm his success in that it did not need to be readdressed for another quarter of a century, and then, apparently, in a much more limited form.

2. Compared with Nehemiah's high-profile governorship, Ezra's was essentially a backroom task: he was a scholar and a teacher, training and appointing

others to be the front men. There is no reason why he should appear in the wall-building story. It is not that he had faded into obscurity or was under any sort of cloud – he could surely even have been one of the priest builders of Nehemiah 3:1 – but simply that it was not his scene. When, however, the word of God was to be set at the centre of the life of the people of God in their new city, who better to play the prominent part than the man whose life-work it had been to achieve this?

SO WHO CAME FIRST, EZRA OR NEHEMIAH?

Nehemiah's dates are usually considered to be certain. He lived in the reign of Artaxerxes I (464–423 BC) and therefore came to Jerusalem in 445–444 (Neh. 1:1). The biblical narrative would lead us to assume that Ezra and Nehemiah both served Artaxerxes I, and that Ezra arrived in Jerusalem in 458–7 and Nehemiah in 445–444. Some consider, however, that there are problems best solved by dating Ezra within the reign of Artaxerxes II (404–359), whereby he did not arrive in Jerusalem until 398–397 (Ezra 7:1, 7).

In the books mentioned below, Rowley argues for the late date for Ezra; Kidner, Wright and Williamson hold to the biblical order; Anderson offers a summary without committing himself.

Two background points must be noted:

1.   There is no manuscript (that is, no objective) evidence for any order of events other than that in the Bible.

2.   Rowley acknowledges that the text as it stands 'precludes' dating Ezra after Nehemiah and needs slight adjustment to accommodate a revised chronology.

WHY CHANGE THE BIBLICAL ORDER?

What are the problems?

1.   If Ezra was already in Jerusalem when Nehemiah arrived, we would expect some mention of him before Nehemiah 8:1. We have noted above that there are good reasons why Ezra should not be mentioned, but, in fact, this objection merely means that had the objector written the Bible he would have written it differently!

2. Nehemiah came to build the walls and Ezra refers with joy to an existing wall (9:9). It seems simple, therefore, to assume Ezra to refer to Nehemiah's wall. The matter is, however, rather more complicated.

   a. Ezra speaks of a gader, not the word used of a city wall but of a fence along a path (Num. 22:24), a thorn-hedge (Hosea 2:6) or vineyard hedge (Ps. 80:12).

   b. If we understand Ezra to be referring to a wall round Jerusalem, he also says it is round Judah. It is much more likely that he is using the word metaphorically: the Lord has given his people a sure, protected enclave in Judah and Jerusalem.

   c. But suppose Ezra does mean the city wall, albeit using an unexpected word. To a degree, the previously recorded history has prepared us for this. In Ezra 4 we find that the history of opposition to building has been carried beyond the time of the first returnees (4:1-5, 538–520) into the time of Ahasuerus (4:6, Xerxes I, 486–465 BC) and on into the reign of Artaxerxes I (4:7-23, 464–423 BC). Note how the period of Xerxes is passed over, suggesting that what is important is the time of Artaxerxes I. In other words, the continuing story of opposition is intended to prepare us for the later history of Ezra-Nehemiah.

Artaxerxes' reply (4:17-22) indicates that the city was, in fact, being rebuilt. Ezra 9:9 could then be a reference to this building work, and Nehemiah's grief came because he heard about the destruction implied in Ezra 4:23. It is a persuasive scenario.

3. Ezra's Jerusalem was thronged with people (10:1) but Nehemiah's city sparsely populated (7:4). There is no substance to this objection. Ezra 10 speaks of a 'large congregation' of 'everyone who trembled at the words of God' (9:4), gathered 'from Israel' (10:1) while Nehemiah refers to registered residents in a new city.

4. The most complex argument for the priority of Nehemiah concerns the names of the high priests at the relevant times. Ezra's high priest was Jehohanan (10:6), supposed to be grandson of Eliashib, Nehemiah's high priest (3:1). The Elephantine Papyri record a Johanan as high priest in 410 BC. This, of course, would show conclusively that Ezra followed Nehemiah, were it proved to be true. But:

   a. Ezra 10:6 does not say that Jehohanan was high priest, merely that (for whatever reason) he had an office in the Temple buildings.

b. Both Ezra 10:6 and Nehemiah 12:23 make Johanan Eliashib's son, not his grandson.

c. In order to establish that 'son' here means 'grandson', it is urged that in Nehemiah 12:11 Jonathan, the actual grandson of Eliashib, is a scribal error for Johanan. There is no evidence for this. To make the emendation assumes the truth of the point at issue.

Further reading

H.H. Rowley, *Men of God*, chapter 7, 'Nehemiah's Mission and its background' (Nelson, 1963)
J.S. Wright, *The Date of Ezra's Coming to Jerusalem* (Tyndale, 1947)

THE LORD'S PEOPLE, THE LORD'S WORD

Nehemiah's memoirs bring a significant sequence together: the people with the birthright gather round the word of God:

- To hear and understand (8:1-8);
- To rejoice in possessing revealed truth (8:12);
- To obey what they read (8:13-17);
- To persevere in reading (8:18);
- To be led by the word of God into penitence (9:1-2);
- Worship (9:3);
- Prayer (9:4-37);
- Committed obedience (9:38–12:26).

This is the picture the historian of Ezra-Nehemiah evidently desires to leave with us. Two things sharpen the outlines of the picture.

1. The obedience-covenant (9:38) contained specific commitments: the people's basic determination was to obey God's word (10:29). Within that broad ideal some matters were underlined: marriage (10:30), the Sabbath (10:31) and the seventh year (10:31); also the burnt offerings and first-fruits (10:34-39).

2. But among these, we read, 'We imposed a commandment on ourselves' for the upkeep of the Temple

(10:32). Note the clear distinction between what is a scriptural and what is a man-made ordinance. Much Pentateuchal study today assumes that laws were made over the passing centuries and, in order to give them authority, were ascribed to Moses. But according to Nehemiah 10:32 this was not so: a man-made ordinance was specifically recognised as such and differentiated from the divinely authorised law. The people of God are aware of what gives them legitimacy and distinctiveness: they possess, recognise and revere what God has spoken.

Neglect of God's Law

After an absence of twelve years (Neh. 13:6) Nehemiah returned to find that the stipulations of his covenant had fallen into disuse (13:7-31). He did not react by assuming that changing times need changed rules, that truth is a living, developing thing, and that the church lives courageously at the cutting edge of theological research and innovation. Far from it: with his characteristic vigour (13:8, 17, 25) he set about restoring the scriptural status quo, for the characteristic of the people of God is to conserve, to be good stewards, to continue throughout this earthly life as the people of God gathered round the word of God.

Would that, when the Messiah came, he found the people of God as Ezra and Nehemiah sought to leave them, the people of the Book!

Further reading

C. J. Barber, *Dynamics of Effective Leadership: Learning from Nehemiah* (Christian Focus, 2004)
D. Tidball, *Esther: A True First Lady* (Christian Focus, 2001)
B. Davis and A. Luter, *Ruth and Esther* (Christian Focus, 2003)
F.D. Kidner, *Ezra and Nehemiah*, Tyndale Old Testament Commentary (IVP, 1979)
R. Brown, *The Message of Nehemiah*, The Bible Speaks Today (IVP, 1998)
J.I. Packer, *A Passion for Faithfulness* (Nehemiah) (Hodder, 1995)
H.G.M. Williamson, *Ezra, Nehemiah* (Word, 1985)
J.S. Wright, *The Date of Ezra's Coming to Jerusalem* (Tyndale, 1947)
J.G. Baldwin, *Esther*, Tyndale Old Testament Commentary (IVP, 1984)

THE BOOK OF ESTHER

The Persian emperor whom the Bible calls Ahasuerus (Esther 1:1) was otherwise called Xerxes, 485–465 BC. The book of Esther is a brilliantly told record of an episode, taking place for the most part within the domestic life of the palace.

THE STORY OF ESTHER

The King's Party: Vashti's Revolt 1:1–2:18

Faced by a wifely revolt, Ahasuerus divorces Vashti, and a beauty contest is organised to provide him with a queen. Esther, a Judean, wins the contest – though, for a reason undeclared, her nationality is kept secret.

Incidentally 2:19-23

Mordecai, Esther's adoptive father, becomes aware of a conspiracy against Ahasuerus. His information leads to the execution of the conspirators, and the matter is written down in the court chronicles.

The Ascendancy of Haman 3:1-15

While all toady to the new royal favourite, Mordecai refuses to bow. Probably the background to this antipathy is historical. The family of Kish (2:5-6) had no reason to rejoice in the family of Agag (3:1; 1 Sam. 15:9, 20). Haman determines on requital and secures an edict to exterminate all Judeans.

What Will Esther Do? 4:1-17

Esther learns about the edict for the first time. Even though she has kept her nationality quiet, Mordecai knows that she is in just as much danger as any Judean. Is it for this crisis that she has been favourably placed in the palace? But without the king's summons, Esther can only approach him at the risk of death.

Softly, Softly, Catchee Monkey 5:1-14

Esther takes her life in her hands, but, thanks to her outstanding beauty, she is welcomed by the king. She knows not to blurt out the whole story there and then, but invites the king and Haman to a party. Still playing her cards close, Esther refuses an opportunity to make her request to the king, contenting herself with inviting him and Haman to a second feast. Haman's glee is uncontrollable. He builds a gallows seventy-five feet high for Mordecai.

Incidentally 6:1-14

The king tries to solve sleeplessness by having the court chronicles read out to him. He learns of his debt to Mordecai – and discovers that no reward has ever been paid. At this exact moment Haman arrives in the palace to seek Mordecai's execution. He is immediately asked what reward would suitably mark the king's favour, and, with himself in mind, he suggests a town parade with the favoured one dressed in royal robes and mounted on the royal horse – and finds himself acting as Mordecai's page around the city square!

Esther's Second Feast 7:1-10
Esther's party lasts into a second day and the right moment comes for Esther to spring her trap. Haman is exposed as the adversary of the Judeans – and therefore, of course, of the besotted king's wife! So Haman is hanged on the gallows he has prepared for Mordecai.

Mordecai's Finest Hour 8:1–9:17
Marvellously, Mordecai is now where Haman used to be. But from this point onwards the book takes a tragic turn. Given the opportunity to write a new edict, cancelling the first, Mordecai turns it into an opportunity for revenge, giving the Judeans permission to slaughter their enemies. Five hundred die in the capital alone, but, as if this were not enough, Esther herself requests a second day's slaughter: three hundred die in Shushan and seventy-five thousand in the provinces.

The Feast of Purim 9:18–10:3
Haman has cast lots (*pur.* 3:7) to discover the most propitious day to slaughter the Judeans, but, since it is all reversed, the same day becomes an annual festival of rejoicing.

GOD'S PROVIDENCE
The book of Esther is a literary masterpiece, but it is also a tract on the wonderful providence of God. God is not referred to, but his secret working is evident on every page – even in the beauty contest, the king's sleeplessness and the arrogant arrival of Haman at such an unearthly hour. The tragedy is that the sheer, protective goodness of God should meet with such a shoddy response from his people, whereby a providence of grace became a reign of terror.

<u>Further Reading:</u>

B. Webb, *Five Festal Garments* (Apollos, 2000)

18

MALACHI AND JOEL: HOPING TO THE END

Malachi and Joel make a striking pair with whom to end our Old Testament safari. Though it is true that all the prophets have their arrows on the string, pointing to the New Testament, Malachi and Joel dovetail most remarkably in their anticipation of what is to come. With the kindly assistance of hindsight, we note that Malachi foretold the forerunner of the Messiah and the Lord's own sudden coming to his Temple (3:1; 4:5), and Joel foretold Pentecost and the great, foundational outpouring of the Holy Spirit (2:28-32). Through their eyes we see the expectation still vigorous as the old covenant holds its breath in excited anticipation of the new.

MALACHI

The view that 'Malachi' – 'my messenger' – is a contrived title taken from Malachi 3:1 and applied to an anonymous prophet has gained ground among the commentators, but without solid reason.

1. Malachi, they urge, is a name not known elsewhere – but, for that matter, neither is Habakkuk or Jonah.

2. The similarity of Malachi 1:1 to Zechariah 9:1 and 12:1 is noted, and the conclusion drawn that since they are distinct, anonymous prophecies so also is 'Malachi'. But it is by no means a foregone conclusion that the Zechariah sections are separate prophetic 'books'; indeed, as we noted, it can be respectably argued that they constitute a well-integrated whole with Zechariah 1–8. In any case, Zechariah 9–11 and 12–14 were not provided with pre-fabricated authors, so why should Malachi?

MALACHI'S QUESTIONS AND RESPONSES
• 1:2-5
• 1:6–2:12
• 2:13-16
• 2:17–3:6
• 3:7-12
• 3:13–4:6

Malachi's Book

Malachi, then, can be accepted as the individual so named by his parents, and, as for his book, he makes life easy for the Bible-reader by planning round six questions (1:2, 6-7; 2:14, 17; 3:7-8, 13).

Why Malachi did this, and where he got his questions, we do not, of course, know, but it sounds like an edited version of the give-and-take of open-air preaching. Imagine, then, Malachi, returning home from some local Speakers' Corner. His wife asks how he has fared, and when he replies, 'Oh, I'd no sooner started than the hecklers started, too', she says, 'Your answers are always so good. Why don't you collect them into a book?' Was it out of some such background that Malachi gathered and arranged the questions people were asking, and used them as the vehicle of his message?

Malachi and the Covenant Tradition

What is plain is that Malachi was a covenant-traditionalist.

Failure and Restoration

Malachi's second, third and fourth questions and responses contain explicit references to 'covenant' (2:5-8, 10; 3:1). We will look at these first before proceeding to note the pervasive thinking in the remainder of the book.

1. The priesthood has not protected the purity of the sacrifices as a means of grace. The crucial regulation that 'your lamb must be perfect' (Exod. 12:5) has been flouted (1:8, 13-14), forfeiting the Lord's favour (1:9) and dishonouring his dignity (1:14). Along with this lowering of the Lord's standards, the priesthood has also fallen short in its function as guardian and teacher of divine truth (2:5-9), adjusting what the Lord had revealed to make it pleasing to human whim (2:9).

2. When he turns to the people (2:10-13), Malachi notes their compromised loyalty. Whether by descent from Abraham (Gen. 17:7) or through the decisive historical event of the Exodus (Exod. 4:21-22), they were the Lord's family, and his covenant commitment to them as their Redeemer (Exod. 20:2) was intended to have been met responsively by their covenanted commitment to him (Exod. 20:3). But it is not so (2:11) – no matter how much they continue to bring their sacrifices as normal (2:12).

   Furthermore, at the point envisaged in the seventh commandment (Exod. 20:14), where human covenanting should take the divine as its model, they have tragically failed (2:14).

3. The covenant reference in Malachi's fourth question (3:1) marks a change: the Lord is going to take action to reverse and remedy the covenant failures of his people. He will himself come as 'the Messenger of the covenant' with a view to a pure priesthood (2:2-3) and a purged people (2:4-6).

Covenant Love and Covenant People

Malachi's questions and responses one, five and six do not use the word 'covenant' as such, but resound with covenant terminology.

Question one concerns the Lord's love in choosing his people (1:2) and looks back to Deuteronomy 7:7-8 and Genesis 25:21-23.

Question five (3:8-12) depends on the covenant principle that obedience to the Lord is the key factor in avoiding the curses of the covenant and enjoying its blessings (compare Lev. 26:3-45; Deut. 27–29; 30:15-20).

Question six, with its reference to Moses on Horeb (4:4), continues the covenant theme and leads it to its eschatological climax.

Malachi's Covenant Theme

There is, then, a clear movement in Malachi: questions one to three (1:2–2:16) focus on the corruption of the covenant both in its provision of grace and in its call for obedience, while questions four to six (2:17–4:6) announce the restoration of the covenant by divine action.

In this sequence, Malachi teaches that deterioration sets in when the Lord's love is doubted (1:2-5). This results in:

- Casualness in respect of divine ordinances of grace (1:6–2:9);
- Compromised loyalty (2:10-12);
- Abandonment of divine standards in personal relationships (2:13-16);
- The Lord's remedial action is personal: he comes himself (3:1);
- To bring about pure priesthood (3:2-3);
- To purge away sin (3:3-6);
- To bring his people into blessing through obedience (3:7-12);

- To bring his people into the eschatological victory
  (4:2-3,) for which he has preserved them (3:17).

MALACHI'S WORLDVIEW
Malachi 1:11, 14

The universal scope of these verses has given rise to a variety of interpretation (see the commentaries mentioned below). There is no main
verb in either verse – Hebrew does not express the present tense of the
verb 'to be' and frequently omits the verb altogether.

PRESENT-TENSE VERBS?

Those who insist on a present tense provide a variety of interpretations: that Malachi held that all worship, wherever and from whoever,
was acceptable to the Lord and all sacrifices, no matter to whom or to
what actually offered, are in fact offered to the Lord and welcomed by
him; or that the reference is to the dispersed Israelite communities or
to foreign converts within them.

LOOKING AT THE CONTEXT

1. If verse 11 *must* be understood as present tense, then so must
   verse 14, and it is manifestly untrue that, in Malachi's day,
   the Lord's 'name' – that is, the Lord as he had revealed himself through Moses (Exod. 3:15) – was feared among Gentiles
   (v. 14). On the other hand, to understand a future tense allows the two verses to parallel each other.

2. 'Verbless clauses are usually not explicit as to tense' (Stuart): it
   is the context which 'bears the burden of establishing the tense'.
   a. In every other way Malachi was an orthodox, non-in-
   novative prophet, and the unbroken prophetic tradition is
   opposed to syncretistic universalism. It is impossible to see
   Malachi as breaking new ground, without comment, on such
   a fundamental issue.
   b. Malachi 2:10-12 teaches the polluting influence of pagans
   on Israel. Specifically, 2:11 calls mixed marriages an 'abomination' (*to'ebah*), loathsome to the Lord. They 'profaned'
   (*chalal*) the Lord's holiness, and foreign wives are devotees of
   'an alien god'.
   c. Malachi looks forward to the purifying of the sons of Levi to offer
   'an offering in righteousness' (3:3 NKJV). How then can the heathen,
   without any purification, offer what the Lord will find acceptable?

LOOKING TO THE FUTURE

To understand both verses as looking forward to the gathering of a worldwide people:

    a. Contextualises Malachi among the prophets;
    b. Is true to the rest of Malachi's thought;
    c. Is fully in accord with Hebrew usage.

Further reading

D. Stuart, **Malachi**, *The Minor Prophets*, Vol. 3 (Baker, 1998)
P.A. Verhoef, *Haggai, Zechariah, Malachi* (Eerdmans, 1986)
J.G. Baldwin, *Haggai, Zechariah, Malachi* (IVP, 1972)

The Structure of Malachi

Within this broad presentation of covenant truth, there is a more detailed structure in Malachi. The fact that the second and fifth questions are double questions prompts a search for and discovery of other significant comparisons.

1. *Divine love, past, present, continuing and eschatological.* The first question (1:2-5) doubts the Lord's love for his people; the sixth (3:13–4:6) doubts his providential dealings with them, his proper apportionment of life's rewards and punishments.

- In vocabulary, these two questions share references to 'wickedness' (*risha'a*, 1:4; 3:15; 4:1).

- They share the invitation to watch for future developments (1:5; 3:18; 4:1).

- They have the same pattern of presentation: the question (1:2a; 3:13-15), an invitation to patient trust (1:2b-3a; 3:16-18) and ultimate assurance (1:4-5; 3:18–4:6).

- They offer balancing truths. In 1:2-5, while the distinction between Jacob and Esau lies hidden in the mind of God, divine action will yet show the reality of divine election. In 3:13–4:6 distinction between people is seen in the contrast between arrogance and reverence (3:15-16); between the mind locked by logic into human experience (3:14-15) and the mind dwelling on God (3:16); between self-seeking service looking for reward (3:14) and the loving service of sons (3:17).

- At the Eschaton, the Lord will affirm the absoluteness of these moral and spiritual distinctions (3:18; 4:1-3). 'I have loved Jacob' (1:2) is paralleled by 'they shall be mine' (3:17): the remote past confirmed by the undated future.

- The visible desolation of Edom (1:3) anticipates the ultimate downfall of the wicked (4:1, 3).

- The Lord presiding in sovereign providence (literally, 'over the territory of Israel' 1:5) is an interim guarantee of the Lord's ultimate preservation of his sons (3:17), and his healing of all their ills by the Sun of Righteousness (4:2).

The 'call', then, of these sections is for the patience and perseverance of faith. Faith rests on revelation, the revelation of the mind of God in his choice of his children. The love which prompted that choice (1:2; Eph. 1:4-5) may seem to be called in question by the experiences through which the Lord's chosen ones have to pass (1:2), but at any given moment evidences of the Lord's faithfulness predominate (1:3), and in time the truth of this will be beyond doubt (1:4-5; 4:2-3).

2. *Covenant obedience and covenant blessing.* There are numerous verbal and other links between the second (1:6–2:12) and fifth (3:7-12) questions:

- The curse (2:2; 3:9);
- Food on the Lord's table (1:12; 3:10);
- Doors shut and windows opened (1:10; 3:10);
- Rebuke (2:3; 3:11), universality (1:11, 14; 3:12) and the Lord's pleasure (1:10; 3:12).

- The main link, however, is topical: by the misuse of the
  Lord's ordinances blessing becomes cursing (2:2), but
  by their proper use cursing becomes blessing (3:9-10).

Within these correspondences, in question two the point at
issue is what the Lord requires in the sacrifices he has appointed as a means of grace. The Old Testament principle
of substitutionary sacrifice laid it down as essential that the
substitute must be without the stain of our sin (Exod. 12:5;
Isa. 53:9, compare 6:5), but because they lack proper respect
(1:7-8, 12-14), the priests have flouted this requirement. This
lack of reverence expected of them (2:7) has led to a drift
away from revealed truth (2:6-7) for both priests and people
(2:8), whereby both violate the Lord's covenant (2:8, 10).

In *question five*, priests and people are called to return to the
Lord along the road by which they have departed from him.
The ordinances of the Lord call for specific acts of obedience
such as the tithe. Those who have drifted from the Lord's
word in disobedience must therefore commit themselves
in responsive obedience, and so enter into blessing (3:10),
sound economy (3:11) and world-influence (3:12).

In summary, then, within the Lord's covenant there is
primarily the outreaching of grace – the provision of the
means of being right with God. In response there is the life
of obedience. Together these constitute the recipe for spiritual health, divine blessing and worldwide acclaim.

3. *The centrality of moral seriousness.* The word 'centrality' is important. Not only do the third and fourth
   questions lie at the mid-point of Malachi's ordered
   presentation but also they move from the present
   (2:13-16) into the future (2:17–3:6), from what his
   people are doing now to what the Lord will do then.
   One concern holds the centre-ground of the book
   and prevails from our 'now' to the Lord's 'then'. The
   third question focuses on sin ignored and the fourth

on sin purged, and the movement of thought is from the offering the Lord does not regard (2:13) to the offering he finds pleasant (3:4).

• In his practical way, Malachi addresses actual issues. In *question three* the sin chosen to illustrate the people's lack of moral seriousness is marital deceit and easy divorce. Marital promises are given their highest value when marriage is seen as a covenant (2:14). When the Lord pledged (covenanted) his word it was with the inflexible determination to keep it. When we pledge our word in the matrimonial covenant we take upon ourselves the dignity and obligation of this covenant role. Malachi, however, saw a very different scene before him. The 'weeping' of 2:13 may be that of cheated wives (2:15). The errant husband may cover his ears, but the Lord's ears are wide open. Or it may be the 'weeping' of the deceiver, using every device to gain hearing before God. Either way, Malachi is depicting people coming to God and expecting to receive from God, even though they are morally and spiritually careless, complacently seeking benefit while ignoring sin and guilt.

• *The fourth question* (2:17) follows on from the third. People who have (as they see it) devoted every effort to plead for blessing and yet have come away empty-handed now choose to look in the wrong direction: not inwardly, to see in themselves reasons for the failure of their religion, but outwardly, to the plentiful evidence of moral iniquity in the world around. Instead of understanding that it is they whose moral values are questionable, they turn to accuse the Lord.

But just as Malachi teaches that the Lord's love will receive eschatological vindication (questions one and six), so he looks to coming divine intervention to establish the absolute morality of the Lord's providential standards. Priests and people alike have violated his covenant (2:8, 10) and, in marriage, a place where his covenanting and ours most plainly coincide (2:14), promises have been broken with complacency.

When the Lord, then, comes personally (3:1) as the Angel of the covenant, what hope have we (3:2)? By the strange divine logic which we have already observed elsewhere, we have every hope – for the fire of his holiness (3:2) will not destroy but purge priests (3:3) and people (3:5) alike. The means of grace (3:3) and the avenues of obedience (3:4) will be what the Lord delights in.

Malachi 3:6 opens with 'For' (omitted, NIV). It explains the unexpected. How can the Angel of the covenant be so gracious to covenant-breakers? Why are we not consumed? Because the Lord does not change. The God of all grace cannot cease to be himself.

THE DAY OF THE LORD

HEAVENLY PORTENTS

As early as Amos (5:18) the 'Day of the LORD' was already firmly established in Israel's expectation. Amos did not have to explain his reference but was able without further ado to attack popular misapprehensions that the coming Day would inevitably be one of triumph for Israel, devoid of the Lord's moral judgment.

A DAY OF DARKNESS

Amos expected a day of darkness, and Joel would concur. Joel does not, however, explain what he means by the darkened sun and moon which will herald the day. Most likely these are to be taken literally. Light was God's first gift to his creation (Gen. 1:3), and the creational ordinances of day and night were governed by sun and moon (Gen. 1:14-18). There could hardly be a more dramatic and fear-inducing sign that creation was winding down to its end than the withdrawal of light and the obliteration of the distinction between day and night.

JUSTICE AND MERCY

Furthermore, it would be consonant with the blending of mercy and justice in the divine nature that he, who could with unimpeachable justice destroy every sinner without warning, should rather give notice of judgment to come by an unmistakable portent as wide as creation itself.

EARTHLY PORTENTS

Leading up to the darkening of the sun and moon before the Day of the Lord, there are the earthly portents of 'blood and fire and columns of smoke'. The Lord Jesus Christ spoke of the period before his second coming as marked by war (Mark 13:7), and this gives colour to the interpretation which sees the same meaning here: blood – the loss of human life; fire and smoke – the destruction of property.

EXODUS SIGNS

Possibly so, but it seems more fundamentally biblical and certainly more satisfying to recall that at the Exodus there was the blood of the Passover (Exod. 12), the fire of holiness (Exod. 3:2-5; 19:18) and the pillar of cloud of the divine presence (Exod. 13:21-22). Throughout the whole course of history leading up to the Eschaton, the 'portents' – the realities which mark the times – will be the atoning grace, the unabated holiness and the constant presence of the Lord with his redeemed. In other words, the church, the locus of these realities, is meant to be the harbinger of the end.

JOEL: THE PROPHET OF PENTECOST

To move from Malachi to Joel is to exchange the prosaic for the rhapsodic. Malachi with his patient, practical mind fields the questions hurled at him, and even when he takes up the eschatological theme it is with a sober facing of moral realities. Joel does not, of course, lack this grounding in reality and factuality, but his mind is plainly more excitable and on his lips the identical message takes flight. The down-to-earth is clothed in the dramatic.

The Pentecost Poem (2:28-32)

Joel (as secretive about himself as is customary among the prophets) is best known for his 'Pentecost' prediction and we can start our study there because, as we shall see, it is the hub of his book.

The poem itself is in three stanzas:

1. *The Lord's worldwide people (2:28-29).* This first stanza has a bracket or inclusion to mark it off: the outpoured Spirit (28a, 29). In this vision, however, Joel was not

innovating. He shared it, for example, with Isaiah (32:15; 44:3), Ezekiel (39:29) and Zechariah (12:10).

2. *The course of history (2:30-31)*. The second stanza of the Pentecost poem lifts our gaze forward to the 'Day of the Lord', and sees it as heralded by 'portents on earth' of 'blood and fire and columns of smoke', and immediately preceded by 'portents in heaven' – the darkened sun and the blood-red moon.

3. *The open door of the gospel call (2:32)*. The third stanza of Joel's Pentecost poem is bracketed by the inclusion 'whoever calls ... the Lord calls', and this is its theme.

Up to the onset of the Day of the Lord, salvation is by appeal. For individuals (v. 32) aware of their need to be 'saved' and to find some way of deliverance, it is a matter of personal decision. The Lord has revealed his name and nature, and upon that Lord each may call.

At the deeper level of ultimate reality, however, it is the Lord who calls, for, on the one hand, 'Whoever comes to me I will not cast out', but on the other hand, 'No one can come except the Father draw him' (John 6:37, 44). The Father's gift to the Son of the whole company of the redeemed, settled in eternity (Eph. 1:4), a gift accomplished at Calvary (Eph. 1:7), experienced in the act of faith (Eph. 1:13), and sealed in the handing to the Son of the Lamb's book of life (Rev. 5:1-10) will be consummated around the throne of God and of the Lamb (Rev. 7:9-17).

In verse 32, Joel doubles the place name, 'Zion ... Jerusalem' (compare Isa. 30:19) for emphasis. There is no salvation outside the city where God chose to set his name (Deut. 12:11; 1 Kings 8:27), or apart from the saving mercies guaranteed through the atoning sacrifices offered there. This is the Zion that now is, where God the Judge is satisfied to have around him the spirits of the just made perfect, and where the blood of Jesus in all its perfection assures the eternal blessings of the new covenant (Heb. 12:22-24).

The Progress of Joel's Thought

We must now study the way Joel groups his teaching round this central Pentecost poem.

The Locusts

It is much debated whether Joel's locust plague (1:4) and its consequences (1:5-12) were real, or whether he was simply using the locusts as a figure of the destructive invasion described in 2:1-11. Not a great deal hangs on this question either way. We need to remember that expectation was deeply engrained in the prophets' psyche: every next king might be the promised king, every next prophet the prophet like Moses and every next calamity a presaging of the Day of the Lord. To Joel, then, this locust plague of unprecedented proportions (1:2), ruining the fruit of the earth (1:7, 10-11), and coupled, apparently, with a drought (1:16-18) which destroyed even the seed in the ground, could not but suggest that 'the Day of the LORD is near ... come as destruction from the Almighty' (1:15).

As he pondered this, his thought extended itself to that other constant in 'day of the LORD' imagery – the invasion of the nations (compare Ezek. 38 and 39). If he is to prepare his people for the Day, he must teach them how to deal with the locust-tragedy (1:5-12, 13-20), and help them to hear the trumpet which warns of the approaching danger (2:1).

1. *Penitence and prayer (1:2–2:17).* Joel 1:2-20 and 2:1-17 are parallel to each other, and constitute a lesson in how to deal with life-threats – even the most destructive of them – and, of course, how to be ready for the Day of the Lord. In each section the threat (1:2-5; 2:1-11) leads into a call to lamentation and repentance (1:5-12; 2:12-14), and this is followed by communal crying out to God (1:13-19; 2:15-17).

We need to be aware of the extent to which we have lost the Bible's sense of the immediacy of the hand of God in all of life's experiences. The modern Western mind is Greek and scientific, that is to say, focused on process, fixated on cause and effect, and the 'chain' of events. The benefit of this is that it has opened up to us more and more of the marvels of the world we live in, the intricacy and depth of the wisdom which has integrated into one all the forces and factors in the cosmos. In the Bible this awareness would have led to worship (Ps. 104; 139:13-17), but for moderns it rather leads to seeing the world as a self-contained, impersonal, closed system of interlocking causes and effects. Why do we need God when we can work the system?

The question 'Why?', even on Christian lips, so often means, 'Why doesn't God run the system better?' or, possibly, suggests that Satan craftily slipped in while the Almighty wasn't looking – as if the Lord were no better than Baal, the god who might not be there when you want him (1 Kings 18:27).

To restore balance and perspective, we need to stand alongside Joel, see through his eyes and match our thoughts to his. With him we live in a world where there are no accidents, where the sovereign God manages, controls and directs all things, and is faithful, so that he will not allow us to be tried beyond our strength (1 Cor. 10:13). Faith, of course, accepts what can be known about second causes but insists on dealing directly with the First Cause, believingly accepting all life as directly from his hands, and, as our foremost reaction to life's adversities, running to him who sent them – with sorrow and penitence as Joel teaches.

The double trumpet of Joel 2:1, 15 dramatises this truth. The first is the trumpet of warning: the enemy is coming; the second is the silver trumpet of prayer, summoning the Lord to our aid (Num. 10:8-10).

THE SPIRIT OF GOD IN THE OLD TESTAMENT
The Old Testament offers a rich revelation of the Spirit of the Lord:

- The Lord's agent in creation (Gen. 1:2; Ps. 33:6; 104:30; Isa. 40:7);

- Coming to 'rest' upon Israel's elders (Num. 11:25-29);

- 'Clothing himself' with those whom he purposes to use (Judg. 6:34);

- Actively present to empower (Num. 24:2; Judg. 3:10; 11:29 – where the translation 'came' represents the Hebrew verb 'to be', that is, 'became an active reality');

- Endowing the line of Messianic figures (Num. 11:17; 27:18; 1 Sam. 16:13; Isa. 11:2; 42:1; 61:1);

- The Spirit as the inspirer of prophecy (Num. 11:25-29; 1 Sam. 10:6-10; 1 Kings 22:22-23; Neh. 9:30; Ezek. 13:3; Zech. 7:12; 13:2).

- His title 'the Spirit of God' proclaims him as divine. He possesses the divine attributes of holiness (Isa. 63:10), goodness (Neh. 9:20) and wisdom (Dan. 4:8); where he is present, God is present (Ps. 139:7), and he is vexed by sin just as is the Lord himself (Isa. 63:10). 'The Spirit,' says G.A.F. Knight, 'receives the personality and the very character of God himself.'

Joel's teaching is comfortable within this context. The notion of 'outpouring' points to an origin of the gift in the Lord himself (John 15:26), and to the abundance that is its characteristic (John 7:37-39). In Isaiah 32:15ff. the picture of the creation transformed by the outpouring suggests the element of universality as does Joel's 'all flesh', looking forward to the worldwide 'Israel of God'.

2. *The faithful, restoring God (2:18-27).* As we continue to trace the sequence of Joel's thought, we note that 2:18-27 begins with the simple conjunction, 'and'.

Joel has been dwelling on the realities of the coming Day of the Lord and on the need to handle the dark days of life with acceptance, sorrow and penitence. Now he teaches that our penitence has an automatic consequence – an 'and', the eager intervention of the Lord on our behalf and his pity for us (2:18).

The poem has an extended chiastic plan:

A¹ verse 18 The Lord and his people: his zeal and pity
 B¹ verse 19 Provision and satisfaction: material
  C¹ verse 20 Locusts, removed
   D¹ verses 21-22 Fruitfulness
    E verse 23 Joy in the bountiful Lord
   D² verse 24 Fruitfulness
  C² verse 25 Locusts, restoration
 B² verse 26 Provision and satisfaction: spiritual
A² verse 27 The Lord and his people: his indwelling

Chapter 2:18-27 follows exactly from 1:2–2:17. The prophet envisaged a dire threat in the natural realm (1:2-12) and in the historical / human realm (2:1-11). When these are met with lamentation, prayer and penitence the Lord is found sufficient for the human threat (2:18-20) and for the natural threat (2:25-27), bringing his praying people into a fresh abundance and spiritual joy (2:21-24).

But 2:18-27 also leads on into the Pentecost poem. It is not enough that the environment and circumstances should be renewed. There is need also for new people, people renewed by the Lord's Spirit for prophetic commitment to the Lord's revealed word.

3. *World judgment and world rescue* (3:1-21). The universal emphasis in the Pentecost poem provides the main link with Joel's subsequent oracles in which he majors on a worldview, and on world judgment as a component of the Day of the Lord (3:2, 4, 11-12).

- The universal darkness of 2:31 reappears in 3:15, but, on the other hand, the 'rescue' available in Zion (2:32) now includes the rescue of the created world itself, restored to newness and abundance (3:18), indicating the removal and end of the curse.

- The poem was Jerusalem-centred (2:32) and this emphasis features in three ways in chapter 3:

    a. The Day of the Lord will bring restoration for Judah and Jerusalem (3:1, 18, 20);

    b. The nations will be judged for their misdeeds against the Lord and his Jerusalem-people (3:2-6, 19);

    c. Jerusalem is the locus of salvation (3:16-17) and of eternal security (3:20-21).

• It is as the God who dwells in Zion (3:16-17, 21) that the Lord acts in judgment and mercy on his Day, that is, the Day of the Lord, notwithstanding its unique reality, is not based on any new revelation of God. It does not arise out of some unknown or unrevealed facet of his character, but out of the revelation granted to Moses, and affirmed by the prophets.

• Most particularly, it should be noticed that 3:1 begins with 'for'. The whole chapter is an explanation of what is meant by the promised salvation and deliverance of 2:32. Deliverance and salvation from what? The due rewards of our own misdeeds and the dire reality of divine judgment on sin when the Day of the Lord finally does come.

Questions About Places
Questions must be raised about the topographical and national references in this chapter.

    a. There is no known place called 'the Valley of Jehoshaphat' (3:2, 12). Literally, 'the Valley of "Yahweh Judges"', it points not to a location but to an event. It is also 'the Valley of Decision' (3:14) or 'of Decisiveness', the place where issues are settled once and for all.

    b. Does this also apply to 'the wady of Shittim/Acacias' (3:18)? There is no known 'wady of Shittim' but Shittim, of course, is well known as a place name – the place where Israel fell foul of the wiles of Balaam (Num. 25:1), the place from which Joshua sent spies into Jericho (Josh. 2:1). So, while the reference is not plainly topographical, neither is it unmindful of the background of Shittim in Israel's history. As Joshua made the place of moral defeat into the place from which he launched his victories, so the Day of the Lord will herald the modulation of the sad song of his people's defeats into the glad song of final inheritance.

'Shittim', as a word, however, means 'acacias', a shrub notable, say the commentators, for growing in dry habitats. If this sense lies to the fore, the picture is of barrenness transformed as the dry river beds suddenly brim with the Lord's overflowing water of life.

c. Joel selects Tyre, Sidon, Philistia (3:4), Edom and Egypt (3:19) as specific enemies to be overthrown when the day comes. Historically, all these nations suffered overthrow – in some cases, terminal, and in that sense the prophecy has received interim fulfilments. But Joel is looking forward to the last day, and we may understand him to see in these nations abiding illustrations of divine condemnation: of the commercial cupidity of Tyre, Sidon and Philistia, so well exposed by Amos (1:6-8, 9-10); of the ceaseless, bitter hostility of Edom (Amos 1:11-12); the genocidal intent of Egypt (Exod. 1:22), the first great enemy and the only one actually to plan the extermination of the Lord's people.

Structure of 3:1-21
Joel's final chapter is bracketed by two sections of restoration (vv. 1-3, 18-21), within which there are three sections dealing mainly with the judgmental aspects of the Day of the Lord (3:4-8, 9-13, 14-17):

A^1 verses 1-3 Restoration (v. 1) and reasoned judgment (vv. 2-3)
    B^1 verses 4-8 Exact judgment: as they did so shall it be done
    B^2 verses 9-13 Irresistible judgment: massed international strength versus the Lord's sickle

B³ verses 14-17 Decisive judgment and divine refuge
A² verses 18-21 Restoration (v. 18), reasoned judgment (v. 19), eternal security (vv. 20-21).

THE CENTRALITY OF THE PENTECOST POEM	
1:2 – 2:17	3:1-17
• The day at hand	• The day at hand
Focus on the Lord's people 2:28-32	Focus on the World
The Pentecost Poem	
2:18-27	3:18-21
• The Lord's people restored	• The world renewed
• The Lord in the midst	• The Lord in Zion

The Lord, Unwearied, Undefeated
One theme is common to the Pentecost poem and to the three sections of Joel.

As the people of God live through what seems to be the imminent coming of his day – the locusts of chapter 1, the enemy nations of chapter 2 – the Lord whose just anger is evident in these chastisements nevertheless remains on their side. In order to escape him, they must simply flee to him – and find that he is ready to restore all that they so justly lost (2:20, 25). He is still in the midst of his people and their eternal security has not been imperilled (2:27).

In the same way, when the day finally comes, the Lord whom that day reveals in inescapable, irresistible, fully merited wrath is found to be the one in whom his people find 'refuge' and 'fortress' (3:16). They think that he is coming to pour out wrath finally and fully, but discover that he has come to renew creation (3:18), to give his people a secure inheritance (3:20), to acquit them and to come to live among them (3:21).

But this indwelling is not only an objective presence (as in the Tabernacle in the wilderness). It is the presence of the Lord, by his Spirit in the heart, renewing and transforming.

ONE MESSAGE

In their fascinatingly different ways Malachi and Joel are fundamentally at one. For Malachi also is open-eyed to the sins of his people and the inevitable judgment of God. Yet just as Joel shows the significance of penitence, so does Malachi (3:7), adding in his down-to-earth way the practical outworking of this in obedience (3:10). But even more significantly, Malachi matches Joel in his awareness that, wonderfully, the fire of the Lord's coming will be the dross-consuming fire of the crucible, and the Lord's devotion to his people is ever unchanging (3:2-6).

In all this, Malachi and Joel provide a deeply satisfying summary of what the Old Testament is all about – whether we look through the eyes of Moses, search the experience of the kings or hear the words of the prophets. In one way or another, from the call of Abraham to the expectations of Malachi, the unaltered divine promise resounds, and the divine commitment remains as resolute at the end as it was the outset: 'You will be my people and I will be your God.'(Jer. 11:4; 30:22; Ezek. 36:28b)

Has he said it and will he not do it?

Further reading

J.G. Baldwin, *Haggai, Zechariah, Malachi* (IVP, 1972)
R.J. Coggins, *Haggai, Zechariah, Malachi* (Sheffield, 1987)
D.R. Jones, *Haggai, Zechariah, Malachi*, Torch (SCM, 1962)
J. Gailey, *Micah to Malachi* (SCM, 1962)
M. Goldsmith, *Habakkuk and Joel* (Marshalls, 1982)
R.T. Kendall, *Between the Times: Malachi* (Christian Focus, 2003)
J.L. Mackay, *Haggai, Zechariah, Malachi* (Christian Focus, 1994)
M. Wilcock, *Six Minor Prophets*, Crossway Bible Guides (Crossway, 1997)
J. Benton, *Losing Touch with the Living God* (Malachi) (Evangelical Press, 1985)

Scripture Index

Subject Index

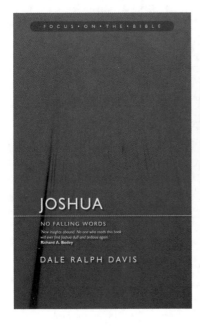

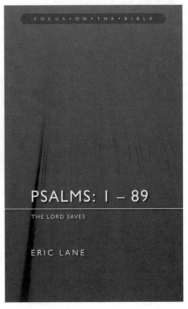

Focus on the Bible Commentary Series

Christian Focus Publications
publishes books for all ages

Our mission statement –

STAYING FAITHFUL
In dependence upon God we seek to impact the world through literature faithful to His infallible Word, the Bible. Our aim is to ensure that the LORD Jesus Christ is presented as the only hope to obtain forgiveness of sin, live a useful life and look forward to heaven with Him.

REACHING OUT
Christ's last command requires us to reach out to our world with His gospel. We seek to help fulfil that by publishing books that point people towards Jesus and help them develop a Christ-like maturity. We aim to equip all levels of readers for life, work, ministry and mission.

Books in our adult range are published in three imprints.

Christian Focus contains popular works including biographies, commentaries, basic doctrine and Christian living. Our children's books are also published in this imprint.

Mentor focuses on books written at a level suitable for Bible College and seminary students, pastors, and other serious readers. The imprint includes commentaries, doctrinal studies, examination of current issues and church history.

Christian Heritage contains classic writings from the past.

Christian Focus Publications Ltd,
Geanies House, Fearn, Ross-shire,
IV20 1TW, Scotland, United Kingdom
www.christianfocus.com